THE
BOMBER
BOYS

THE BOMBER BOYS

• HEROES WHO FLEW THE B-17S IN WORLD WAR II •

Travis L. Ayres

NAL
CALIBER

NAL Caliber
Published by New American Library, a division of
Penguin Group (USA) Inc., 375 Hudson Street,
New York, New York 10014, USA
Penguin Group (Canada), 90 Eglinton Avenue East, Suite 700, Toronto,
Ontario M4P 2Y3, Canada (a division of Pearson Penguin Canada Inc.)
Penguin Books Ltd., 80 Strand, London WC2R 0RL, England
Penguin Ireland, 25 St. Stephen's Green, Dublin 2,
Ireland (a division of Penguin Books Ltd.)
Penguin Group (Australia), 250 Camberwell Road, Camberwell, Victoria 3124,
Australia (a division of Pearson Australia Group Pty. Ltd.)
Penguin Books India Pvt. Ltd., 11 Community Centre, Panchsheel Park,
New Delhi - 110 017, India
Penguin Group (NZ), 67 Apollo Drive, Rosedale, North Shore 0632,
New Zealand (a division of Pearson New Zealand Ltd.)
Penguin Books (South Africa) (Pty.) Ltd., 24 Sturdee Avenue,
Rosebank, Johannesburg 2196, South Africa

Penguin Books Ltd., Registered Offices:
80 Strand, London WC2R 0RL, England

Published by NAL Caliber, an imprint of New American Library, a division of Penguin Group (USA) Inc. Previously
published in an AuthorHouse edition.

First NAL Caliber Printing, October 2009

Set in Sabon
Designed by Alissa Amell

Printed in the United States of America

PUBLISHER'S NOTE
While the author has made every effort to provide accurate telephone numbers and Internet addresses at the time of
publication, neither the publisher nor the author assumes any responsibility for errors, or for changes that occur after
publication. Further, publisher does not have any control over and does not assume any responsibility for author or
third-party Web sites or their content.

Dedicated to all the boys who flew the Forts

Acknowledgments

At first reluctant to talk about their experiences and even more reluctant to have the word *hero* applied to them, Anthony Teta, Peter Scott (Seniawsky), Art Frechette, George Ahern and Bob Valliere offered their time, their memories and their patience to the author. Without the contribution of any of these five men, *The Bomber Boys* would be an incomplete work. I have thanked them many times during this project, and I thank them again.

John Conners was an early inspiration for this book, and his wife, Helen, was gracious and helpful. Former B-17 airmen Charles Armstrong, Jerry Chart, John Cuffman, Philip Duke, William "Jack" Ferguson, Charles Lyon, Frank Pogorzelski, Paul Spodar and Michael Swana were as open and cooperative as the original five Bomber Boys. Most of them I only met by telephone—a situation I deeply regret.

Tom Ayres was the most talented writer I have ever personally known. He was also my writing coach, my brother and my best friend. His feedback and encouragement during this project was very helpful and greatly appreciated.

Jim Donovan is a great agent. Every author should have an editor as easy to work with as Brent Howard at NAL Caliber.

Special thanks to my wife, Elizabeth, and my daughters, Alissa and Tina. Each of them inspires me in their own way.

• Contents •

• Introduction •

In 1996 my wife and I were renting a house on a small horse ranch in Connecticut's Totoket Valley. Our landlord was an outgoing and energetic gentleman named Anthony Teta. His friends called him Tony.

Tony was twenty-five years older than myself, but we soon discovered we shared many common interests and we became quick friends. Because of Tony's youthful appearance and seemingly boundless energy, I never even thought of him as being part of the World War II generation. He certainly never approached the subject.

One afternoon as we drank iced tea on his patio, I happened to mention a television program I had seen about the Eighth Air Force and its operations during the Second World War. I was surprised when Tony said:

"Yeah, I was in the Eighth."

"You were? What did you do?"

"I was a navigator on a B-17 with the 305th Bomb Group," Tony replied casually.

"How many missions did you fly?" I asked, sensing a story.

"Thirty-five missions." He said it in the same even tone with which he might have asked, "Do you want more tea?"

I asked more questions, but Tony changed the subject, saying, "It was a long time ago. I don't remember many specifics."

Out of respect for my new friend, I let the matter drop, but over the next few weeks it kept running through my head—thirty-five missions. There had to be some interesting stories in Anthony Teta's World War II days.

The idea of a book on the men of the U.S. Army Air Force was not yet part of my thinking. I was already too busy writing a book about my great-grandfather, who had been a Confederate soldier at the battles of Shiloh and Stones River.

Still, I immediately felt a connection between my Civil War ancestor and the former World War II airman. For the past two years I had worked tirelessly trying to uncover every small scrap of information available about the old Confederate. Now, here, living right next door, was a living example of the kind of men who had helped win America's other great war.

Later, Tony introduced his friend John Conners to me with the comment, "John was also in the 305th."

"You two served together?" I asked.

"No, I was there a year or so before Tony," Conners said. My interest had just doubled.

"You know, I would love to sit down with you both and talk about your experiences," I said.

"We're going to a meeting of Army Air Force veterans in Cheshire this Tuesday. You're welcome to come along," Tony offered.

"We can talk a little on the drive there," John seconded the invitation. I gladly accepted. In fact, I would accompany the two 305th veterans to many of the monthly meetings of the Army Air Force Roundtable of Connecticut, in Cheshire, and occasional meetings of Connecticut's Eighth Air Force Historical Society, in Hamden, during the coming months. Soon, I was on a first-name basis with several other former B-17 airmen. As these men began to realize my interest in their past was sincere, most of them began to open up—sharing a story here and there.

I liked it best when I could sit with two or three of the

veterans at once. On those occasions, I would simply listen as the airmen became lost in their own conversations about the war. Sometimes, for a second or two as I watched Tony Teta describing a particularly vivid incident, I could almost catch a glimpse of the nineteen-year-old navigation officer he had been during World War II.

For a history buff like me, it was heaven. It reminded me of what the great Civil War historian, Bruce Catton, had once written about his boyhood. As a youngster, Catton had sat listening as the old Union veterans of his hometown had told their war stories. Those early encounters had remained precious to Catton decades later, even after he had written his Pulitzer Prize–winning Civil War classic, *A Stillness at Appomattox*.

As I listened to the former B-17 airmen, I had no illusions of becoming another Bruce Catton, but I did know the makings of a good book when I heard them. I also knew I should arrange real interviews with the veterans, and I fully intended to do so, when time allowed.

A couple of years went by. My Civil War book was finished. I still visited with my airmen friends, but other projects kept popping up. Then one day in 1998 the phone rang. It was Tony Teta. He told me that John Conners had died.

The passing of John Conners was a cold reminder to me that if the wartime experiences of these former air combat veterans were going to be documented, someone had better get started. Like Catton's old Civil War vets, the Bomber Boys would be gone too soon.

As much as I knew I would enjoy conducting the interviews, I also knew the process would be time-consuming. Surely I would have to interview perhaps twenty veteran airmen to find five compelling stories to fill a book. To my surprise, my first five interviews provided the remarkable stories that make up *The Bomber Boys*. Granted, I sought out two of the five, when other veterans told me, "You have to talk to Peter Scott and Art Frechette." Their stories are truly unique.

All five of my subjects (and the late John Conners) knew each other at least casually through their involvement with one or both of the aforementioned air-veteran organizations. Three of the Bomber Boys are close friends. None of them knew each other during the war. Like many American World War II combat veterans, they are modest men. For most of their postwar years they kept their memories of the missions over enemy territory to themselves, or tried to forget those missions altogether. Friends, coworkers and even wives (sometimes especially wives) received only scant information if they asked about the war. Often the wives were grateful to be excluded from this part of their husbands' lives. When a woman watches her spouse entangled in a violent nightmare flashback, she quickly concludes she would rather not know the details of the dream. So these men put the war years behind them and became productive, hardworking citizens, good fathers and then grandfathers.

In their late sixties or early seventies, as careers came to an end, the former airmen found themselves drawn to their own kind. Anthony Teta first met John Conners in a restaurant where they discovered their 305th connection. The Cheshire Round-table and the Eighth Air Force Historical Society were comfortable fraternities where the Bomber Boys could share the company of others who had "been there." This is not to say they went to the meetings to talk about their own experiences. To my knowledge, of the five, only Art Frechette was ever a featured speaker at any of these gatherings (prior to my interviews with them), and his wartime experiences were so incredible he could hardly have avoided the limelight.

Tony Teta, Art Frechette, George Ahern and Bob Valliere were regulars at the meetings but seemed content to listen to others tell their stories. Peter Scott was the most reserved of all. Long after

I had convinced the other four to allow me to interview them, Peter remained reluctant. Finally he just said, "No."

Somehow, I sensed that Peter really wanted and needed to tell his story but he just was not sure about me. In a last-ditch effort, I made a promise: "Peter, if you let me include your story in the book—I'll do my very best to get it right." There was a long pause, and then he said, "Okay, let's do it."

I interviewed Peter in his home on four occasions. After the final session, he walked me to my car and shared a secret with me.

"I tried for years to forget about all of this stuff. It was pretty rough for the first year or two after I got back. Now, lately I've been having those nightmares again." Then as he apparently saw the guilty expression on my face, he smiled and added, "Well, maybe this will finally give me some closure."

Peter was the last of my airmen to be interviewed. With the completion of the interviews, I knew I had five interesting and deserving stories to tell. In truth there was a sixth story I would have liked to include. John Conners was gone, and I had not known him long enough to gather very many details about his time with the 305th Bomb Group. His widow, Helen, kindly granted my request to interview her and provided much information about his life. However, like the other air vets, John had told his wife little about his life as a B-17 gunner. Finally I was forced to conclude there simply was not enough available information to write John's story at the present time.

Although John Conners's story is not part of this book, his memory and spirit are. He was an inspiration for the project from the beginning, and in my mind he will always be the sixth Bomber Boy.

Teta, Scott, Frechette, Ahern and Valliere all lived within forty miles of each other when I was writing their stories. Conners's home was also in this same small area. It was here in this little section of Connecticut that I stumbled across two B-17 airmen who led me to the other Bomber Boys. As much as I respect and admire the character and accomplishments of these six remarkable men, I am not inclined to think the Connecticut River Valley has a monopoly on this vanishing breed of American. Go to Texas, Illinois or Utah, ask the right questions, do a little digging, and I suspect you will discover aging air veterans who once manned the Flying Fortresses, Liberators, Marauders and Mitchells. If you do, urge them to write or record their wartime experiences.

I wrote *The Bomber Boys* to document the war experiences of five men, and during two years of research, I located numerous other airmen who were crewmates of the original five. Unless you yourself are an air-combat veteran of World War II, you and I can never really know what it felt like to be one of them, when they were just eighteen to twenty years old and facing death on every mission—but with their own words I have tried to put the reader in their shoes. It is an honor to tell their stories.

—Travis L. Ayres

THE
BOMBER
BOYS

• Prologue •

At the end of the only parachute jump of his life, Peter Seniawsky landed hard in a German farmer's field. He was not even sure he had actually jumped from his crippled B-17 bomber. He only remembered waking up in midair and pulling the ripcord. As he gathered his parachute to his chest, his eyes scanned the surrounding area for a place to hide from the enemy soldiers that he knew would already be searching for him and the rest of his crew.

A small gully close by seemed to be his only immediate option. He scrambled over the edge of the gully and tumbled into a shallow stream. After pushing his parachute under the water and placing several stones on top of it, Peter climbed back up the stream bank to chance a look. He spotted someone immediately—a farmer armed with a shotgun.

The man was walking in Peter's direction. The young airman had never before thought of having to kill someone. It was almost a certainty that the bombs his B-17 crew had dropped on German cities had killed people. But the targets had been military and industrial sites, and the dead were unseen and abstract. This was different. Peter could clearly see the farmer's face as he walked across his own field.

Peter knew he could not hesitate. He had heard the stories of how German civilians sometimes shot downed Allied airmen before the German soldiers could reach them. If the farmer kept walking in his direction Peter would have little choice but to kill him. He reached down to his side for his .45 automatic pistol. It was not there. No pistol and no holster. Peter silently cursed himself for his thoughtlessness in leaving his sidearm on his bunk that morning. *What now?*

The man continued walking in Peter's direction, finally stopping no more than fifty feet away. A noise had caused him to stop—the sound of a small machine gun. It was just a short burst, but when Peter looked to the east, he spotted four German soldiers emerging from the woods. They were close to a hundred yards away and they began yelling to the farmer in German. He responded, waving his arms and yelling back to them. Of course, Peter could not understand any of it, but he was certain his whereabouts were the main subject of the conversation. If any of them reached the edge of the gully and looked down the streambed, they could not help but spot him.

In a seemingly hopeless situation, Peter looked around again for even the slightest opportunity for escape. *Escape*. That was too grand a word for what he was trying to do. He was somewhere deep in Germany. Where, he did not know. How many miles to the French border to the west? He did not know. Which way *was* west? He did not know. Even if he could miraculously reach France, what then? The entire country was occupied by Germans and French collaborators.

He had no weapon and only a candy bar for food. He did not speak German or French and was dressed in an American aviator's uniform. Escape *was* too grand a word. Peter Seniawsky was trying to survive—to evade capture, whether it be for a day, an hour or just five more minutes.

He spotted a lone tree on the other side of the stream. If he could reach that tree without being seen and if the farmer and soldiers did not search past the stream . . . if he was really lucky. He eased down the bank, crossed the stream, climbed the other bank and began slowly crawling toward the tree. Although he could not know it at the time, Peter was beginning one of the most amazing escape adventures of World War II.

Every American bomber airman of the European Theater during the Second World War shared one thing with Peter Seniawsky— the desire to survive against very long odds. For most of these Bomber Boys (the majority only in their late teens or early twenties), the will to survive ranked a close second to doing their job. Once their bombs were dropped over the day's target, survival was priority one. They flew to the target for Uncle Sam and flew back to base for themselves. There were many ways to die—flak, Luftwaffe fighters, midair collision, weather, engine failure.

Tens of thousands did not survive. Many who did survive wondered *how*, as they landed at their air bases in Flying Fortresses riddled with flak holes or missing what everyone assumed were essential parts of an aircraft. The ones who came home were the first to say the real heroes were the ones who did not. But to the survivors belong the sometimes painful memories that must be stirred if the true stories are to be told.

• The Lucky Bastards Club •

ANTHONY TETA
Navigator

305TH BOMB GROUP

366TH BOMB SQUADRON

Tony Teta tossed his canvas duffel bag to the ground and climbed out of the back of the mud-caked army truck that had carried him on the final leg of his long journey. What he saw, as he got his first look at his new home, did not impress him. Chelveston was no more dismal than the dozens of other American air bases sprinkled across the English countryside surrounding London, but it was dismal enough. Except for a small tower building, most of the base structures were simple sheet metal huts, some rectangular and some resembling barrels lying on their sides, seemingly half buried in the earth. In the distance, B-17 bombers belonging to the 305th Bomb Group were parked around the perimeter of three intersecting runways.

Tony pulled up the zipper of his leather jacket. The December air was cold and damp.

"Lieutenant, don't forget your briefcase."

It took Tony a few seconds to realize the enlisted man was talking to him. The rank and silver wings on his jacket were still new enough that Tony found himself amazed he was actually an

officer and a B-17 navigator—after all, he was only nineteen
years old.

"Thanks," Tony said, taking the case that contained his navigation charts and instruments. The other members of his crew
wandered off to find their barracks, the enlisted men heading in
one direction, the pilot and copilot going in another. Someone
pointed Tony in the direction of the Navigators Barracks.

Walking through the doorway, Tony noticed little difference
in the inside temperature and the winter chill outside. He dropped
his bag and gently placed the navigator's case on the rough plank
floor. A row of over/under bunks lined each wall of the hut. In
the center of the room, a few veteran airmen were warming
themselves in front of a blackened metal stove. A box of coal
nearby was nearly empty. Tony guessed correctly that the one
little stove could never adequately heat the entire room.

When no one seemed to notice his arrival, the new navigator
walked over to the group at the stove.

He introduced himself with his usual friendliness. "Hi, I'm
Tony Teta." A couple of the men nodded acknowledgment, but
nobody spoke. Tony ended the uncomfortable silence:

"Well, can you tell me which bunk is mine?"

With an expression that was neither a smile nor a frown, one
of the airmen stopped warming his hands and turned to point
to an empty bunk.

"You can take that one, if you want."

Tony was about to thank him when the man motioned to
another bunk.

"Or you can have that bunk there . . . and there's two more
over there. Take any of them that's empty. None of those guys
are coming back."

The new navigator looked around the room. He counted
eleven empty bunks. The 305th had, in the past few weeks, made
raids on Schweinfurt, Cologne, Hanover and Berlin, four of

Germany's toughest targets. The bomb group had lost eleven of its aircraft, almost a full squadron, and nearly one hundred of its airmen had been killed or were missing. Eleven of the casualties were navigators.

Somehow the room seemed even colder to Tony now. He mumbled, "Thank you," picked up his gear and stored it next to the closest available bunk. It had been a cramped and slow voyage across the Atlantic, followed by a long and bruising ride in the troop truck from Scotland to Chelveston. He was dead tired. When he lay down in his bunk and finally rested his head on the pillow, Tony should have felt relief. All he felt was alone.

It was more than fate that had brought Lieutenant Anthony Teta to the cold and lonely barracks of Chelveston, England. It was a desire to fly that had been inside him for as long as he could remember. As he lay in his bunk, he recalled a warm summer day in 1935.

He was barely nine years old that summer, but he told everyone he was ten. The sand felt hot and comforting beneath his bare feet as he ran at full speed along the little road that led to the Hamden, Connecticut, airfield. Most of his friends were choosing up sides for a pickup game of baseball about then, and on most Sundays Tony would have been there too. He was a small kid, with a small strike zone. He drew a lot of walks, but he could also hit. And he was fast—a good base runner, especially in the late innings when the other boys were getting tired. Tony never seemed to get tired. His constant energy amazed everyone who knew him, including his mother and father.

On this Sunday, Tony would miss the baseball game without the slightest regret. Somewhere far overhead he could hear the sound of an airplane engine, and it heightened his anticipation. This was one of those rare Sundays in Hamden when the barnstorming biplanes came to town. Tony had seen them once before. There were two planes, one bright red and the other yellow. His dad had even paid to take a ride in one of them. Tony had been simultaneously proud and jealous of his old man.

Finally Tony reached the edge of the airfield and slowed his pace to a fast walk, once he realized he was on time for the show. A large crowd of people of all ages was scattered along the edges of the field, which was perhaps a thousand feet long and a hundred feet across. Climbing into the bed of a nearby pickup truck, Tony got a good view.

In the center of the field someone had made a circle with lime chalk. The circle was no more than twelve feet in diameter. Raising a hand to his forehead to shade his eyes, Tony searched the cloudless sky for the plane. There it was—just a yellow speck against the sun's glare.

The boy felt an unusual lightness in his stomach. "Butterflies," his mom had called it. The yellow bi-wing airplane was lost in the sun for a few seconds, but the changing sound of its engine told Tony it was beginning its dive.

He could see it free-falling like a roller coaster that has just passed a crest in the track.

In a few more seconds the yellow plane was in a hard dive at a forty-five-degree angle, the engine roaring. Nervous laughter escaped from some in the crowd, while the majority watched in awed silence. Everyone waited anxiously for the pilot to begin pulling out of the dive, but still the yellow plane plummeted toward the airfield. A few in the audience began to look around for possible exit routes. Tony smiled and remembered what his dad had told him. The pilot was giving them "their money's worth."

The pilot held the little biplane in the dive so long that even Tony began to wonder if he was too low. At last the plane began to pull out. From the sound of its engine, it was clearly straining.

Some parents tried to cover their children's eyes when it seemed there was going to be a deadly crash, but the plane's path flattened out and it became a yellow streak as it passed just a hundred feet above the field.

Tony could see the pilot clearly as the plane passed overhead, and he watched with fascination as a white object fell from beneath the aircraft. It was, Tony would find out later, a ten-pound sack of Pillsbury's Best Flour. The bag tumbled only twice before it smashed into the ground and exploded into a curling white cloud. When the flour dust finally settled, Tony saw that the pilot had scored a perfect hit inside the target circle.

From that day, Tony's imagination became fixed on airplanes and flying. Much of his chore money was converted into model airplane kits, which, once constructed, were hung with string from the rafters of his attic hideout. His model planes shared the attic with Tony's other hobby, homing pigeons.

The pigeons were both entertaining and frustrating for young Tony. Purchased from an older neighborhood kid, the birds flew right back to their original residence when they were first released. Tony had to buy them back more than once before the pigeons finally adjusted to their new digs.

Pigeons were only part of Tony's childhood menagerie, which on occasion included a fox and a troublesome snake. Actually it was young Tony who caused the trouble when he released the harmless serpent on a crowded school bus. The bus driver, who had to stop and evacuate dozens of hysterical children, was not amused.

Tony meant no harm—he just loved animals, and he loved to have a good time. As a teenager, he worked at a local stable and earned enough money to purchase a horse. The animal had previously been owned by a traveling circus, and Tony discovered that his new horse was extremely well trained, not only for riding but for doing tricks. Soon Tony was entertaining the neighborhood, racing up the street on the back of his circus horse, stopping now and then to allow the spirited animal to do a spin or rear up on its hind legs.

Even with schoolwork, his part-time job and his pets, Tony still had plenty of energy to devote to his interest in aviation. By the time he was in high school, he was writing letters to a Missouri flying college for course information and reading any available books or articles about flying. When American bombers began flying missions into German territory in 1943, Tony was only seventeen years old, but he was already certain what branch of the service he would volunteer for, when he came of age.

His parents knew their son would have to go to war, but they were less than enthusiastic about Tony's preference for the Air Corps. A letter from a young relative helped to change their minds. Tony had a cousin who was already experiencing the trials of life in the infantry. His letter advised Tony: "Go into the Navy or the Air Corps. Anywhere but the Infantry."

Tony made sure his mother read the soldier's words. "At least in the Navy or Air Corps, you'll be sleeping in a bed at night." The Tetas relented, and at the age of seventeen and a half Tony signed up to join the Army and volunteered for Air Corps service. He turned eighteen in May of 1943, and it was official. Tony, just a month shy of high school graduation, was on his way to basic training.

After basic, it was off to Maxwell Air Base in Alabama, where three weeks of testing would determine if he was qualified to fly. The IQ marks were extremely high. Failure at Maxwell spelled the end to many a young serviceman's dream of flying for the Army Air Corps. Test applicants were rated for qualification as pilots, navigators or bombardiers. Tony scored high and qualified for all three positions. Flooded with a wave of young patriots wanting to be pilots, the Air Corps found itself with more qualified candidates than airplanes. The officer in charge was impressed with young Teta's math scores and recommended, "You should consider going into navigation. It is a tough school, but I'm sure you would not wash out."

"Will I get to fly?" Tony asked.

The officer smiled and replied, "You'll fly plenty."

Tony signed up. Soon he was on his way to Pennsylvania and enrollment at Clarion State Teachers College. There was math and more math. Competing with other candidates who had two to three years of college proved to be a challenge to Tony, but he compensated by studying late into the night, long after lights-out.

Life at Clarion was not all work though, since the young navigation students were housed on the first floor of a coed dormitory. Many of Clarion's female students occupied the second floor. Tony soon grew friendly with an attractive coed who coincidentally lived in the room directly above his. The college's administrators did what they could to "protect" their female charges, including enforcement of a strict curfew. By the time Tony finished his required study time, the women's dorm floor was sealed up tight. With no telephone communication available, Tony and his new girlfriend worked out a simple solution.

Tony had noticed that a pair of steam pipes ran from his room through the ceiling. Guessing that the pipes also ran through the room above, the couple soon developed a "tapping code" that served them well. Late in the evening, Tony would often tap out a request for the young lady to sneak out of the building and meet him outside. A single affirmative tap on the pipe from above was music to his ears.

Not all of the Clarion courses were as mundane as math. Despite their designation as navigation candidates, the young men were given flying lessons at a nearby airfield. Tony finally had a chance to realize his dream. The training plane was only a small two-seater, but the instructor put it through a series of spins, stalls and dives that were designed to weed out the faint of heart. After ground school and ten hours of flight time, it was time to solo. The day he sat alone in the pilot's seat of that little airplane as it lifted off the runway was Tony's best day since the barnstormers had visited Hamden.

The eight months at Clarion flew by, and Tony advanced on to the next phase of navigation training at the University of Miami. Pan American Airways provided the airplanes and instructors, and gave the cadets their first real in-flight navigation experience aboard huge "Flying Boats." Tony scored high marks and received a certificate that was redeemable for a job with Pan Am after the war. It was an exciting prospect at the time. The possibility that he might not survive the war never crossed his mind—at least not until much later.

Next up was gunnery school at Fort Meyers, Florida. It was fast paced. There was a little in-flight practice with .50 caliber machine guns, but mostly the cadets honed their shooting skills by firing at targets while riding in the back of a bouncing truck.

The final piece of the training puzzle was in Lincoln, Nebraska. The men who had spent the past year learning their specific military skills—the pilots, navigators, bombardiers, flight engineers, radiomen and gunners—were brought together to form what was then the most educated, best trained and best prepared fighting unit ever assembled: the B-17 bomber flight crew.

Tony's crew, like most, was young and eager. They looked even younger. Lieutenant Jerome Chart from Wisconsin, at twenty-one, was the oldest and would be their pilot and crew commander. A solid chin and determined eyes gave Chart a look of confidence. Tony liked that in a pilot, although he realized Chart had no more real experience as a bomber pilot than he did as a navigator.

During their first few days together, the officers and enlisted men on the crew addressed their new pilot as Lieutenant Chart. As they began to bond during the many hours of training flights, the men relaxed under Chart's easygoing leadership, and soon he was simply "Skipper" or "Jerry," except when there were higher-ranking brass around.

In fact, it seemed as if, in no time at all, everyone was on a first-name basis and most had acquired nicknames. Their copilot, Flight Officer George Wisniewski, was "Ski." The clean-cut bombardier, Flight Officer Glenn B. Kelly, liked to be called by his given name. Tony Teta, by then a second lieutenant and navigator, was "Short Round." The radioman, Corporal Kenneth Hall, from West Virginia, answered to "Ken" or "Kenny."

Tony quickly became good friends with the flight engineer, a Texan named Carl Robinson. Sergeant Robinson had a dependable face and a receding hairline, and he did not take offense when the men nicknamed him "Baldy." Corporal William Goetz hailed from Chicago. Because his descent into his ball turret reminded everyone of a crab disappearing into its shell, he became known as "Hermit."

Corporal Thomas Christenson of Michigan was of Swedish heritage and had the rugged look of a college quarterback. He was "Big Swede." Corporal John Stiles, whom everyone called "Jack," was the right waist gunner and would later become the crew's toggler. (Once the Eighth Air Force started the system of "lead" bombers, the "lead bombardier" decided when the group or squadron should drop bombs. The bombardier position aboard most bombers was later eliminated—replaced by a toggler, who required much less training.)

Wiry John Cuffman also became one of Tony's closest pals. The little tail gunner from Tennessee somehow attained the handle of "Snuffy." This was the crew (with the exception of

Glenn Kelly) that Tony would soon rely on for survival during
air combat in the sky over Germany—the crew that would also
rely on him.

At Lincoln, Tony became acquainted with the Boeing B-17
Flying Fortress bomber for which he would soon develop a lasting respect and admiration. Designed in the mid-thirties, the
B-17 had been continually improved since America's entry into
the war in Europe. The model that served as a training aircraft
for Lieutenant Jerome Chart and his crew was the B-17G. The
most technologically advanced bomber of its day, the Boeing
B-17G heavy bomber was an awesome sight to both the men
who flew her and the men who fought against her.

Tony was indoctrinated in every detail of the B-17G. She
weighed in at 44,560 pounds, was seventy-four feet and nine
inches long, with a wingspan stretching just over 103 feet, tip to
tip. She could fly high, fast and far—having been tested at an
altitude of more than thirty-five thousand feet and at a top speed
of 302 miles per hour, with a maximum range of eighteen hundred miles. There was little doubt how she had acquired the name
Flying Fortress. The first things Tony or anyone else noticed on
first sight were the thirteen .50 caliber machine guns poking out
of the bomber's nose, top, bottom, sides and tail. To lift its own
considerable heft and a seven-thousand-pound bomb load, the
B-17G was powered by four formidable Wright engines.

Despite how large the B-17 appeared on the outside, Chart's
new crew soon learned that the aircraft was not exactly roomy
on the inside. Most available space was occupied by necessary
flight equipment and armament. The nose section, with its clear
Plexiglas cone, provided just enough space for the bombardier
and navigator and their equipment, as long as neither man attempted to stand upright. Two single-barrel machine guns and
the firing controls for the front chin twin-gun turret were also
housed in the aircraft's nose.

Above and just aft of the nose section was the bomber's cockpit, which provided just enough room for the pilot's and copilot's seats amid a seemingly endless array of switches, dials, gauges and flight controls.

Directly behind the pilot and copilot was a small space that was really part of the cockpit area. Here the airplane's flight engineer was stationed to react to any emergency situation and to serve as the top turret gunner. Moving aft from the flight engineer's space, one came to the bomb bay, with its bomb racks to either side of a small walk space and a base just a few inches wide. Anyone passing through would have to turn sideways to keep from bumping into the racks of bombs, and if the bay doors were open during flight, there would be little but sky between him and the ground.

Continuing rearward past the bomb bay, the next small compartment was the radio room, where the crew's radioman maintained and operated all outside communication equipment. When necessary, he manned a single .50 caliber machine gun which was fired through an open ceiling hatch.

Protruding out of the fuselage deck, just aft of the radio room, was the top portion and door of the Sperry ball turret. A few feet past the ball turret were the B-17's side windows, left and right, with a single-barrel .50 caliber machine gun extending from each. The windows were staggered so the left and right waist gunners would not bump into one another during combat, at least in theory.

There was a small escape door to the rear of the right waist gunner's position, and beyond that a tunnel-like entrance, which the tail gunner would have to crawl through to reach his position—the most confining on the bomber with the exception of the ball turret.

Lieutenant Jerome Chart's B-17 crew flew one training mission after another, day and night, out of their Lincoln base. With each mission Tony could tell that their Skipper was becoming a better pilot. Takeoffs were crisper, landings were smoother and their scores on the practice bombing runs were going up.

In turn, Chart was noticing his crew was starting to operate as a skilled unit. His copilot, George Wisniewski, seemed comfortable handling the aircraft when he got his opportunities to take control. Kelly was getting used to the Norden bombsight. Robinson was using every available free moment to cram his brain full of information on how to keep a B-17 flying in emergency situations.

It was more difficult to analyze the performance of the gunners. They seemed to be learning the use and care of their lethal equipment, but unfortunately the Army Air Force provided little in-flight target practice. Still, while they were in the air, Chart had his gunners tracking everything in sight—other airplanes, cars and even houses.

As commander of his aircraft, Chart knew there was no crew position more important to him than that of the navigator. Navigation of a combat aircraft in 1944 was a complicated job. The navigation methods used involved "pilotage" (the use of visual ground references), "dead reckoning" (computing ETAs to various points ahead), "radio" and "celestial navigation." The pilot and the navigator worked closely during the flight, because any change in altitude, airspeed or direction could affect the navigator's calculations. The success of the mission and—more important to the pilot—his crew's survival depended on the navigator doing his job well.

The B-17 pilot training manual pinpointed the navigator's heavy responsibility: "The navigator's job is to direct your flight from departure to destination and return. He must know the exact position of the aircraft at all times."

Chart liked his spirited young navigator from the first time they met. Teta was bright and energetic, but he was also as young and green as the rest of the crew. The pilot and navigator soon made it a regular part of their routine to get together after every training flight to discuss anything that might have gone better in the way the route was plotted or the way it was flown. This post-mission meeting was something Chart and Teta would continue even after they began flying real combat raids over Germany.

As the crew began their final week of flight training, Chart hoped and prayed they were ready for the challenges of combat. That the ten young men were bonding and that each one felt the crew was ready for "the show," there was no doubt. They would not have long to wait.

Travel orders came through in September of 1944. Missing from the crew list was Glenn B. Kelly's name. He would not be going to England as a part of Jerry Chart's crew. Trained as a bombardier, Kelly was reassigned. John Stiles would move from his waist gunner's position to take over the bombsight operation as the crew's toggler. Christenson would pull double duty as both left and right waist gunner.

A couple of days at Fort Dix in New Jersey provided Tony the opportunity to slip into New York City for a reunion with his mother and sister. On the ferry ride across the Hudson River, he spotted the *Queen Elizabeth* ocean liner docked on the New York side. Tony would get to know the ship well during the next two weeks, as he and more than twelve thousand airmen, sailors and soldiers made their crowded voyage to Scotland.

The young navigator and the crew's other three officers occupied a cabin that would have been very comfortable had not eight additional officers from other crews been assigned the same lodging. There were some moments of levity, such as when a group of Marines clandestinely changed the yellow tape on the floor and successfully misdirected a large contingent of Army nurses right into the Marines' quarters. However, most of the voyage was a frustrating and hopeless search for some little place of privacy.

A welcoming committee of small, rosy-faced children met the Americans when they arrived in Scotland. Little open palms were soon filled with whatever candy and gum the troops had in their pockets.

A few days later came the long-anticipated final leg of the bomber crew's journey. They were assigned to a base named Chelveston near Bedfordshire, England. Jerry Chart's crew would be part of the 305th Bomb Group, composed of the 364th, 365th, 366th and 422nd Bomber Squadrons. Chart and his men would fly one of the twelve Fortresses of the 366th Squadron.

By the fall of 1944, the 305th had already established itself as one of the most combative and innovative bomb groups in the American Eighth Air Force. In mid-November the unit had flown its 250th combat mission over France, Holland and Germany. A grim-faced officer named Curtis LeMay had been the 305th's original commander in England, and while he held that position he had rewritten the book on combat flying. His tactics of tight formation flying for a concentration of firepower had spread quickly from the bomb group level to be accepted as standard procedure for the entire Eighth Air Force. LeMay, who was a no-nonsense group commander, was dubbed "Iron Ass" by his men, but they respected the fact that he was always ready, apparently eager, to personally lead a bombing raid.

Respecting their leader did not necessarily mean the airmen of the 305th always agreed with his thinking. None of his decisions created more second-guessing and open grumbling than his "straight-in" bomb run. The veteran bomber pilots were convinced that flying in a straight line across a heavily fortified German city was only slightly short of suicide. LeMay believed the evasive actions of the American pilots were causing bombs to be dropped sloppily, with many missing the primary targets.

Not one to worry much about diplomacy, LeMay bluntly announced the change in bomb-run procedure at a mission briefing early one morning. Although LeMay would later deny the exchange ever happened, 305th legend supports the following account as factual.

LeMay told the assembled aircrews that for this mission they were going to give the straight-in bomb run a try. A wall of stunned silence was all he received in response. Undaunted, the stone-faced commander asked, "Any questions?" It was then that a brash young airman verbalized what most of the flyers in the room must have been thinking:

"Sir, shall we go to the stockade now or wait for the MPs to take us?"

Of course, the men of the 305th flew straight-in bomb runs from that day forward, without the threat of Military Police, and there was never any scientific way to prove who was right. Perhaps both points of view had been correct. Bombing results most likely improved with the technique, and there is little doubt more American airmen died with the introduction of the straight-in bomb run.

The worst day in the history of the 305th Bomb Group came about five months after LeMay was kicked up to a higher command position in the Eighth Air Force. During a raid on Schweinfurt, Germany, on October 14, 1943, the 305th participated with eighteen aircraft. Three of the group's bombers had to abort the mission. Of the remaining fifteen 305th B-17s that attacked the target, only two returned to England.

In all, more than sixty American bombers were lost on the day of the Schweinfurt raid as the Luftwaffe sent up hundreds of fighters to challenge the unescorted B-17s and B-24s. The raid is believed to have accounted for the heaviest single-day losses for the Eighth Air Force during the entire war. The 305th had suffered more than any other unit; 86.5 percent of its bombers had been shot down from the sky.

The Schweinfurt disaster, more than any other raid, convinced the high command of the American Army Air Force that their bomber crews needed fighter escort planes that could take the Fortresses and Liberators all the way to the target and back. By the time Tony Teta and his crewmates arrived at Chelveston Air Base early in December 1944, the new long-range North American P-51 Mustang fighters, equipped with drop tanks for extra fuel, had arrived.

The official position of the Eighth Air Force high command was that the improved fighter-escort protection would drastically reduce the number of bombers being lost to enemy fighters defending German targets. This certainly would prove to be true. It followed that with fewer aircraft losses, the airmen of the "Mighty Eighth" would stand a much better chance of surviving the required twenty-five missions that earned them a ticket back to the States. However, like many military decisions, this one was a two-edged sword. The number of required missions was promptly raised to thirty and then to thirty-five. Bomber crews with only one or two missions left to complete were suddenly told to unpack their bags.

While the American Fortresses and Liberators would no longer be sitting ducks for the German fighter pilots to just pick off, even the fast P-51 Mustangs could not completely protect the bombers. Also, one other major danger had not been reduced at all—the deadly antiaircraft fire, or flak, that awaited every mission over German cities.

The veteran American bomber airmen did not like the new thirty-five-missions rule, but they gritted their teeth and kept flying, hoping their luck would hold up a little longer. The replacement aircrews arrived at their new bases unaware of the difficulty they would face in surviving thirty-five combat missions over Germany. The veterans knew. They dubbed any man who completed all thirty-five combat missions as a member of "the Lucky Bastards Club."

This was the state of affairs at Chelveston in December 1944, when Tony and the other members of Chart's bomber crew reported for duty.

It soon became apparent to Tony and the rest of the crew that until they racked up a couple of combat missions, they could expect a continued cold shoulder from the 305th's more experienced crews. The snub was not a mean-spirited gesture, but simply an emotional defense.

Every one of the veteran airmen had lost a friend with whom he had swapped mission stories, discussed wives and girlfriends, or stumbled back to base in an advanced state of inebriation. It was hard enough to see another American bomber shot from the sky, but when the airplane was in your bomb group or your own squadron, you knew it was your friends who were dying. You counted the parachutes falling from the stricken bomber and too often there were only a few. Which friends had lived? Which had died? You would not know until you got back to base in England—if you got back. Watching friends die tended to remind one of his own mortality.

The bottom line was that few of the veteran airmen were looking for new friends to mourn. They kept the rookies at arm's length. The new guys quickly began to look forward to their first combat mission in order to get the butterflies out of their stomachs and to become real members of the 305th.

For Chart's men, their time came on Christmas Eve morning.

From out of the barrack's darkness, someone shook Tony's shoulder as he lay sound asleep.

"Gotta get up, sir; you're flying today," a sergeant with a small flashlight said before moving on to the next man on his list. Tony rubbed his eyes and looked at the illuminated hands of his watch. It was 2:30 a.m. The alerted crews dressed and stumbled to the mess hall for a hot breakfast of eggs, pancakes and coffee.

A general briefing was next. The room was large and noisy as airmen from the 364th, 365th, 366th and 422nd squadrons swapped predictions on what the day's target might be. The answer was hidden beneath a large cloth sheet that covered a detailed map of Europe.

Tony found an empty seat next to Jerry Chart and George Wisniewski. The other members of the new crew sat nearby. Their quietness was in sharp contrast to the loud chatter of the veteran crews, but a silence fell over everyone when the 305th's commanding officer walked to the front of the room. He was Colonel Henry C. MacDonald, assigned to head the Chelveston-based bomb group only two months before. Tony thought the colonel looked a little young for the job. Still, when MacDonald spoke, there was confidence and resolve in his voice. He made a few opening remarks, which somehow failed to register with Tony as the new navigator stared at the covered map. What finally grabbed Tony's and everyone's attention was when the commanding officer said, "Gentlemen, today's target is . . ." Another officer pulled away the cloth exposing the entire map. "Giessen!"

So that's it, Tony thought. His first mission—and for all he knew his last—was to Giessen, Germany. He had never even heard of Giessen. What was there? Why were they going to bomb it?

"Nidda airfield," Tony heard MacDonald say. "You are going

in at twenty-one thousand five hundred feet. Expect some moderate flak over and around the target."

Moderate flak? Tony wondered how much flak was moderate. He had no way of judging. He had heard the veterans refer to the German antiaircraft fire in terms of light, moderate or heavy flak. It was all abstract until you had experienced it firsthand. Tony also pondered if it would matter if the flak was light or moderate, if it was *accurate.*

After the general briefing, the crews broke up into specific briefing sessions. Pilots grouped with pilots, navigators with navigators and so on. In each briefing, the men received details of what to expect on the mission and what was expected of them.

A little later, Chart's entire crew piled into a truck for the short ride out to the aircraft. The chill in the predawn air helped shake off any lingering sleepiness. Tony's mission report indicated their aircraft for the mission was number 037. (The 305th used only the last three digits of a bomber's serial number, for operational purposes.) She was a lethal beauty with seven machine gun positions, and she was sitting low from the weight of a full bomb load. Tony scanned 037's armament again to reassure himself.

Two single-barrel .50 caliber machine guns defended the nose—these would be manned by Tony and the bombardier. The nose was additionally armed with a twin .50 caliber chin turret. On top of the bomber's fuselage, a few feet rear of the cockpit, twin .50 caliber machine guns protruded from a Plexiglas bubble, accompanied by a single .50 caliber poking skyward from the radio room. On each side of the aircraft, single-barrel .50 caliber weapons awaited their waist gunner. Beneath the B-17, only inches off the ground, was the sturdy Sperry ball turret with its twin .50 caliber machine guns. One more set of twin fifties stuck out of the tail section of the aircraft.

Tony knew, in theory, that with the B-17G's thirteen guns he and his crewmates could protect their bomber from enemy fighter attack in any direction. Of course, the pilots of the Luftwaffe had their own tactics and theories, not to mention some very advanced aircraft.

One after another, each of Chart's rookies climbed aboard and found his combat position. Jerry Chart would be sitting in the right-hand seat of the cockpit, serving and observing as copilot for this first mission. Carl Robinson took his place as flight engineer, directly behind the pilot and copilot. Climbing in the side door, Ken Hall went to the radio room. Tom Christenson assumed his waist gunner's position, and Bill Goetz climbed into the tight quarters of the ball turret. Another crewman crawled through the little tunnel that led to the tail gunner's space. George Wisniewski and John Cuffman were not on board for the December 24, 1944, mission.

Tony waited for the toggler, John Stiles, to board, and then he pulled himself up through the little hatch under the nose of the bomber. Stiles went to the very front of the airplane's nose compartment. Tony sat down at arm's length behind the toggler at the navigator's desk, which was really just a small wooden table that was attached to the left bulkhead. It was tight quarters, even for Tony. He and Stiles settled in and took in the view from the Plexiglas nose cone.

The first 305th bomber lifted off from the Chelveston runway and disappeared into the foggy predawn sky. Thirty seconds later, another B-17 followed. Not until all the other Fortresses in the 366th Squadron had taken off did the pilot of B-17 number 037 rev the bomber's four engines and point her nose down the runway.

Tail End Charlie, Tony thought. *Last in the formation. The new guys . . . the worst position. Dead last!* It gave the term a whole new meaning.

In General Curtis LeMay's combat box formation, each squadron had a designated position to fly—lead, high or low. The last airplane in the low squadron was also the last airplane in the entire group. Tail End Charlie.

The German fighter pilots preferred attacking either the lead aircraft (to disrupt the bomber formation) or the very last airplane because it was the most exposed. Tail End Charlie was an unenviable position that a crew could only graduate from by surviving there until an even newer crew joined the squadron.

Sitting at his little navigator's desk in the nose compartment minutes before takeoff, Tony tried to peer through the thick fog but he could see nothing. When the aircraft bounced roughly, it reminded him that only thirty seconds or so ahead of them was another bomb-laden B-17, and her engines' "prop wash" was going to make it a bumpy ascent for the rookie crew.

Earlier in the war, newer crews sometimes had drawn milk runs to France as their first mission. It was a term that veteran airmen used for an easy mission. A non-German city with little flak and no enemy fighters translated into a milk run. Tony now realized what an inside joke that was. Here they were flying blind through a foggy dark sky. Somewhere ahead, above and maybe below them, were as many as thirty-five other B-17s whose pilots were flying just as blind. On top of that, other bomb groups from nearby bases were in the same area attempting to join the 305th in a massive formation for the attack on Giessen, Germany.

Most of the American bases had their own stories of B-17s that had collided while trying to get into formation. As long as formation flying was a part of the equation, there would be no such thing as a milk run for the Eighth Air Force airman.

Tony could see more light outside, and he knew that the sunrise was right on time, but still the foggy cloud cover was present and visibility extended only a few feet in front of his airplane.

He tried to concentrate on his navigation calculations but could not. In the cockpit, Jerry Chart watched the pilot and took mental notes that he hoped he would remember when his turn came to lead his crew on a mission. Both of the pilot's hands were squeezing the controls while he tried to hold the B-17 steady as the bomber was hit by prop wash and wind pockets.

Finally, a full twenty minutes after takeoff, the airplane ascended out of the clouds and into a beautiful blue sky. Another B-17 from the 366th was just yards off the right wing. Ahead and above them, for miles, the rookie crew could see dozens of other Fortresses. It was an amazing, almost indescribable sight that Anthony Teta would never forget.

The dream a nine-year-old boy first had at a little air show in Hamden, Connecticut, had now become a reality of incredible proportions. The 366th's rookie crew got a taste of real combat that day also. When they returned to base hours later, they found their bomber had been slightly damaged by German antiaircraft fire.

Chart's gunners had been anxious for something to shoot at, but no German fighters had approached the squadron. The crew did witness a dogfight between American P-51 Mustangs and enemy fighters, but it was distant.

B-17 number 037 came back safely with a crew that was a little less green for having flown a real combat mission. After peeling off their helmets, flak jackets, heavy boots, electric gloves and other combat gear, Chart's men got their first interrogation (debriefing). Someone placed a double shot of scotch in front of Tony. He took a sip, found that he liked the brand and drank the rest in one quick swallow. When he put the empty glass on the table, the interrogation officer asked him, "What was the flak like today?"

"Too close," Tony replied with a grin.

There were lots more questions. Visibility? Bombing results?

Enemy fighters? Later, while he was having a beer with the rest of the crew at a local pub, Tony found that what he remembered most about the mission was that it was cold. Very cold! And the flak had made an impression. Bill Goetz called it "meager flak." Still at least one shell had exploded close enough to damage the aircraft. The gunners confessed they really did not mind that no enemy fighters had challenged them. Everyone laughed and they ordered another round.

Three days after Christmas came the crew's mission number two and Jerry Chart's first mission as pilot and aircraft commander. The airplane was B-17 number 571, and this time the 305th Bomb Group struck the railroad yards at Siegberg, Germany. At twenty-seven thousand five hundred feet, it was even colder than the first mission. Flak was light again, but still the enemy ground gunners managed to hit Jerry Chart's bomber. Tony had a front-row seat for the incident.

A flak burst sent a piece of shrapnel through the B-17's nose, and the fragment hit the toggler, John Stiles. The force of it knocked him backward, and as Stiles slammed into Tony, both men toppled onto the floor.

At first look, Tony thought his friend was dead. Stiles was not moving. His eyes were closed and his body was limp. When Tony could not find any trace of blood on Stiles' flight suit clothing, he realized what had happened. The shrapnel had hit Stiles in the chest, and the toggler's flak vest had saved his life. Soon he regained consciousness, badly bruised but okay.

The toggler had done his job before getting hit, releasing eighteen two-hundred-pound bombs over the target. The flak damage to the B-17s nose was only slight, but the sound of wind whistling through the hole on the return trip reminded Teta and Stiles that they were in a dangerous business.

Seven and a half hours after they had taken off, Jerry Chart's crew was back on the ground at Chelveston. After interrogation,

Tony tried to get a nap but found it difficult to sleep. The scene with Stiles kept going through his mind. Flak! It was the wild card in this game. Unpredictable, like the single bullet in a game of Russian roulette.

There must be some precaution a guy can take to lengthen the odds a little.

Tony tossed beneath his blanket and considered the problem for a while without any revelations. Finally, one of the guys suggested they head into town and find a pub. Tony gave up trying to sleep and went along. By the time he returned to the barracks late that evening his mood was considerably better, and sleep came quickly. It was a short sleep.

Early the next morning, Chart's crew was up and off aboard B-17 number 555 on a mission to Bullay, Germany. The target was a nine-hundred-sixty-foot bridge over the Mosel River. It was the only bridge between Cologne and Frankfurt, and it was extremely important to the Germans in getting supplies to the western front. Tony expected it would be strongly defended but was pleasantly surprised when the group encountered no flak or enemy fighters. During interrogation, Tony heard tail gunner John Cuffman describe it as "an extremely easy mission." Since it was the first time in three missions they had not suffered some kind of flak damage, Tony had to agree.

Still, Chart's crew had been in the air for almost eight hours on the second of back-to-back missions, and they were exhausted. They all hoped for a little downtime. They got their wish and more. After the mission to Bullay, they would not fly again for six days.

New Year's Day of 1945 began with Tony and the other members of Jerome Chart's crew starting to feel more a part of the 366th Bomb Squadron. With the completion of three missions over Germany, the rookies were beginning to be accepted by the more seasoned members of the squadron. In fact, many of the new guys were becoming fast friends with the veterans, so it was shocking when tragedy struck the 305th on the very first day of the year.

While Tony and the other members of the crew slept in after a late night of New Year's celebrating, twelve other crews of the 305th were up early to join a mission to Magdeburg. Flying without fighter escort, the American bomber formation ran into a large group of German Focke-Wulf Fw 190 fighters. In a desperate air battle, the B-17 gunners managed to shoot down seven of the enemy airplanes, but six Fortresses were also lost. Four of the destroyed B-17s were from the 305th (two aircraft from the 366th Squadron, one from the 364th and one from the 422nd). Twenty airmen from the 366th—twenty new friends— were gone in the blink of an eye. A total of forty airmen from the 305th were missing in action. Eighteen of these airmen would eventually be listed as "killed in action."

At the time, most of the men were presumed dead, since one of the 305th bombers had exploded in midair. Tail gunner John Cuffman wrote of the lost friends in his war journal:

"Lost Dilts, Dezelick, Moore, Martison, Kinder and Prehn over Magdeburg. All but Prehn are believed dead . . . Prehn bailed out. Other ship blew up. Lost twenty men in squadron and six in our barracks alone. They've had it, and a good bunch of boys went to Northampton last night with Prehn and Kinder before they got it. Also Bray(?), a boy from Bristol, Tenn. got it." (Of the men Cuffman mentions: Kenneth L. Dilts, Gerald J. Kinder and Robert J. Prehn were later listed as KIA as a result of the January 1 mission to Magdeburg. The others listed in Cuffman's journal entry—Robert S. Dezelick, Eugene M. Martison and Mark Bray Jr.—survived the mission, most likely being captured and sent to German POW camps.)

A heavy gloom fell over Chelveston air base, but operations against Germany continued on schedule. On January 5, Jerry Chart drew his fourth aircraft in as many missions. This B-17 was very different, unique in fact. The aircraft (number 501) was named *Old Miss Destry*, and she had been a very lucky bird for all of her previous crews. *Old Miss Destry* had been to Berlin nine times, and in total, the airship had flown 107 successful missions over Germany. In the Eighth Air Force's short history, *Old Miss Destry* was a legend.

Of course, there was also the theory among some airmen that a bomber with that many trips on her résumé was overdue for some bad luck. Tony figured the old girl had at least one more round-trip in her. She did. Without encountering any enemy fighters and by avoiding any flak damage, *Old Miss Destry* completed her 108th mission. Her luck would never leave her—*Old Miss Destry* would finish the war with 138 combat missions to her credit.

With four missions under his belt, Tony Teta was gaining more experience and more confidence in his ability to navigate his crew to various German targets and then back to base in England. One more mission and Chart's airmen would receive their air medals. A coveted badge of honor for any Army Air Force airman, the air medal indicated its wearer was an experienced air combat veteran and a member of a very select club.

Mission number five would make them earn their air medals and give them all a good scare in the process. At the briefing on the morning of January 6, a groan rolled across the room when the target was announced: Cologne.

Located on the Rhine River, about fifty miles into Germany, Cologne had a deserved reputation as being well protected by antiaircraft installations. Flying their fifth aircraft, the men of Chart's crew joked nervously about their new bomber's name. She was *Fancy Pantz*, B-17 number 300. How she got her name,

Tony could not imagine, but he and the rest of the crew liked the artwork on the bomber's nose—a scantily clad young lovely who could star in any airman's dream. As the young navigator worked over his charts in the cramped nose section, the sound of *Fancy Pantz*'s four powerful engines was smooth and reassuring.

The 366th Squadron arrived at the Initial Point unhindered by enemy fighters, but it soon became apparent that Cologne was all they had heard she was. The flak over the city was heavy from the very beginning of the bomb run. Tony watched the deadly black puffs multiplying at an alarming rate. In front of him, the toggler was watching the lead bomber flying ahead in the distance. The lead aircraft was equipped with smoke flares that would be fired when the lead bombardier found the target in his bombsight. Once the flares were spotted, all the other American bombers would release their bombs at once.

Fancy Pantz bounced roughly while flying through the flak-filled sky, and Tony's gaze became fixed on the lead ship. In the cockpit, Jerry Chart and copilot George Wisniewski also anxiously awaited the signal. Cologne was visible twenty-four thousand feet below, but still no flares appeared. Then as the formation began to fly past Cologne, every man on board *Fancy Pantz* began to guess what had happened. Each of them hoped and prayed they were wrong in their thinking.

Skipper Jerry Chart's voice over the interphone confirmed their fears:

"Okay, boys . . . it looks like we're going around again."

Tony bit his lower lip to keep from cursing and made the sign of the cross over his chest instead.

Either the primary target was covered by low clouds or another bomber group had clogged up the bomb run area. Whatever the reason, the pilot of the lead Fortress had made the tough decision to circle around 360 degrees and make a second bomb run on Cologne.

Now the American B-17s would be aiming for the marshaling rail yards, which were not only vitally important to the Germans but also extremely visible for attack. Tony estimated that a second bomb run over a heavily protected German city not only meant their odds of getting hit were doubled—it was like flying two missions and, if you survived, only getting credit for one.

Facing the flak again was not the only problem. A bomber formation tended to get loose or sometimes even sloppy on an unplanned second run. It was not difficult for a bomber to get separated from the group.

Chart put *Fancy Pantz* into a wide turn and followed the lead aircraft as it made a complete circle back to the I.P. The flak was just as intense on the second bomb run, but Chart took his B-17 through without a scratch. Once the bombs were released, he began evasive action, but it became obvious that his airplane was not handling properly. Sergeant Carl Robinson was sent to find the source of the problem and he soon reported back.

The flight engineer gave Chart the bad news: "The bomb bay doors won't close!"

When Tony heard his friend Robinson's statement over the interphone, he quickly got busy with his navigation tools. *Fancy Pantz* was undamaged by combat and her engines were still running strong, but if the crew could not get the bomb bay doors closed, the wind-drag would make it impossible for the airplane to keep up with the rest of the group.

In such a situation, the navigator had to know the exact position of his aircraft and he had to keep the pilot constantly informed, because as *Fancy Pantz* began to fall farther and farther behind the scattered 305th Bomb Group, simply following the other bombers back to England would not be an option. Indeed, the men on board *Fancy Pantz* were soon all alone in a German sky.

John Cuffman, in his tail gunner's position, patrolled every inch of sky within his field of vision. His hands clenched the handles of his twin .50 caliber machine guns tighter than ever before. In fact, every gunner on board the lone B-17 was feeling the pressure to stay alert for enemy fighters.

In the nose, the toggler manned the chin turret, while behind him Tony double-checked his headings. Eventually, Carl Robinson was able to crank up the bomb bay doors manually, and Tony's calculations were right on the money. Chart sat *Fancy Pantz* down safely on the Chelveston runway, successfully completing the Cologne mission.

Each member of the crew who had completed all five missions received his air medal. Tony pinned his air medal ribbon above the left shirt pocket of his dress uniform and then headed over to the officers' club for a cold ale. He knew he still had thirty missions to fly, if he could survive that many, but he did not want to think about that just then.

Fancy Pantz was all right in Tony's book. Jerry Clark agreed. Silly name and all, *Fancy Pantz* had taken them over the target at Cologne twice, and then brought them back home. Her four officers drank a toast to the gallant B-17 and hoped they would fly her again.

On January 7, just a day after the Cologne raid, Chart's crew took off on a mission bound for Koblenz, Germany, but only twenty-five minutes into the flight the number two engine blew an oil line. Engine number three was also running rough, so the Skipper had no choice but to return to base.

An aborted mission was always depressing for an aircrew. A man had to get ready for each mission, both physically and mentally. The physical part was waking up before dawn, then attending the briefings, followed by getting into the heavy combat gear. This physical routine also gave the crewman time to mentally prepare. Sometimes a preflight religious service helped.

Takeoff in a B-17, loaded with high explosives, was never a sure thing, and of course there was the dangerous job of getting the aircraft into formation. Once a man went through all of that, he wanted to complete the mission and have it credited toward his "required thirty-five." That meant dropping bombs on a target.

Three days later, the 305th Bomb Group went back to Cologne. For mission number six, Lieutenant Chart was assigned an airplane he had flown before, number 571. Bill Goetz would later write that the second strike at Cologne was "our toughest mission so far."

John Cuffman would note in his combat journal, "Boy, this one was the roughest I ever saw. That flak was intense and accurate."

It was also cold—the coldest January on record in more than fifty years. Flying at twenty-six thousand feet, the airmen's hands and feet suffered despite their electric gloves and socks. The thermometer on Chart's cockpit console read: "minus 55 degrees."

To make matters even worse, somehow the 305th Fortresses got split up, resulting in Chart's bomber and the rest of the "high" squadron (366th) flying over the target alone. John Cuffman's journal described the horrific scene: "Lost Jordan's crew over Big C. Got hit in (illegible). Saw one B-17 burning as she went down." (Flying as part of the 365th Bomber Squadron, Lieutenant R.J. Jordan's bomber was hit by enemy fire and crashed on January 10, 1945. Jordan and eight of his crew survived, but ball turret gunner, B.F. Evans, was killed.)

Despite the heavy flak over Cologne, Chart got his bomber back home, suffering only two flak holes in Ken Hall's radio room. Everyone on board counted themselves lucky, but for the 305th, it had been a rough day. One B-17 had crashed on takeoff, its crew escaping with no serious injuries. Jordan's crew had been shot down, and another 365th Squadron bomber had been destroyed by flak—this airplane was piloted by Arthur F. Leuthesser. (This is most likely the bomber John Cuffman saw "burning as she went down.") Leuthesser would survive the crash along with two other crew members. Six of his crew—William S. Butcher, Claude R. McLaughlin, Irwin Levy, Virgil H. Biggs, Marshall J. Villani and Jimmie D. Shambarger—would all eventually be listed as KIA. Three other missing bombers would be accounted for in the next few days, having been diverted to other airfields.

January 13, 1945, found the men of Lieutenant Jerome Chart's bomber crew twenty-five thousand feet over Germany in B-17 number 033. The target was another bridge on the Rhine. The structure was clearly visible to Tony as Chart started his bomb run. John Cuffman watched the bombs strike the target with "good results." Compared to Cologne, the flak was light; however, at least one or more bursts were close enough to put four holes in the aircraft, including one in the Tokyo tank. Each wing of the newer B-17Gs housed an extra Tokyo fuel tank to provide the airplane with the long-range capability needed to reach targets deep inside the Third Reich.

With his bomber damaged and possibly leaking fuel, Chart headed for England, but he was not confident they could make it back. The weather back in Britain would resolve the issue for him. Chelveston was reported to be hampered with thick clouds and low visibility—Chart's aircraft was diverted to Weston Zoyland airfield, in southern England.

The crew was glad to be on the ground anywhere but in Germany, and they soon found their stay at the Royal Air Force base a pleasant experience. The barracks were nicer, the chow was good, and their British hosts could not have shown more hospitality. Ball turret gunner Bill Goetz was the only crew

member who did not enjoy his visit to Weston Zoyland. Eighth
Air Force rules required someone must guard the aircraft. Goetz
drew the short straw.

The British ground crews worked through the night to have
the B-17 repaired by daybreak the following morning. The
Americans were in the air by 10:30, and Tony was charting a
course for Chelveston. They were back at their home base at one
in the afternoon.

After their mission on January 15 was scrubbed, Chart's crew
got a few days of well deserved rest. Some of the boys headed to
London to enjoy its sights and delights, but the normally fun-
loving little navigator begged off.

"Ah come on, Tony, you aren't afraid of those V-1s, are ya?"
one of his buddies teased, referring to the German rockets the
Nazi regime was launching against Londoners.

"You guys go ahead. I've got other plans." Tony's boyish
smile revealed more than he intended.

"Okay, what's her name, Short Round?" John Cuffman
wanted to know.

"See you later, boys!" Tony laughed and walked away in the
direction of the base PX.

Her name was Peggy. She was a pretty young English school-
teacher whom Tony had met at one of the Chelveston base dances.
On this particular day, he had been invited to have dinner with
her parents, and he did not intend to arrive empty-handed. Exiting the PX, Tony carried a large bag filled with many of the
items local citizens found difficult to obtain—including chocolate and American cigarettes. The latter item was an instant hit
with Peggy's father, who Tony would soon learn was a chain-
smoker.

It was the first of many enjoyable visits to his English girlfriend's home. Her parents liked the polite young American and

if they worried that their daughter's relationship with Tony was just a wartime romance, they kept it to themselves. After all, it *was* wartime.

Tony was not surprised on the morning of January 20, when Jerry Chart told him they would once again be flying a different B-17 to Reims, Germany. The aircraft's number was 015, and she brought Chart's crew safely home from the Ruhr Valley mission. For only the second time, there was no flak over the target, and once again, Tony and his crewmates had seen no enemy fighters. They did see a couple of American fighter planes attacking some German trains.

The Luftwaffe was down *but not out* in the early months of 1945. The constant combat against the Americans in the daytime and the British Royal Air Force at night had done more than destroy thousands of Germany's fighter planes. It had destroyed thousands of her irreplaceable pilots. Equipped with drop tanks, the new American P-51 Mustang fighters were able to escort their "big friends" all the way to the target and back. The Mustang was also faster than any fighter in the Luftwaffe's arsenal, at least until German jets started showing up in the final weeks of the war. On some missions, like the one to Reims, the Mustangs, Thunderbolts and B-17 gunners controlled the air to such an extent that the American fighters could leave the bomber formation to attack targets of opportunity on the ground.

Since the mission to Reims had been the easiest yet for Chart and his crew, some considered B-17 number 015 a lucky airplane. Tony did not dismiss anything that might help their chances and decided he would not mind flying the bomber again. There would be several more opportunities to fly 015, and the final one would test the airplane's luck and endurance, and leave the lives of her nine airmen hanging in the balance.

"You're flying again today." The sergeant's voice was quiet, but it cut the darkness of the navigators' barracks like a honed knife. It was the morning after the Reims raid, and Chart and his crew had drawn the second leg of back-to-back missions. The target of the day was Pforzheim, Germany, on board B-17 number 571. Although the mission went well, with the crew watching their bombs burst right in the center of Pforzheim's marshaling yards, it was still a difficult trip for everyone. First of all, it was extremely cold. Bill Goetz suffered the worst of any of them. There was no heat in the ball turret. In addition to the cold, at nine hours and twenty-five minutes, the run to Pforzheim was the longest mission Chart's crew had ever flown.

January 28 marked the crew's tenth mission to Germany and their third raid over dreaded Cologne. Flak over the city was no less severe than the first two times, but flying B-17 number 015 again, Jerry Chart brought them home with only one hole in the radio room. The bomber was patched up and ready to go on a mission to Koblenz the very next day. Tony figured the Fortress was in better shape than most of her crewmen. Luckily, the flak was light, and both 015 and the crew returned unscathed.

That evening Tony lay in his bunk fully clothed, covered with two blankets, and still he could not get warm. To take his mind off the chill in the barracks, he began to review the past couple of months since his arrival at Chelveston. Eleven missions completed and twenty-four to go. After what he had seen in the skies over Germany, twenty-four more missions seemed unattainable. During the first ten missions, the various B-17s his crew had been aboard had been hit by flak on five of the missions. Only the grace of God, pure luck and Jerry Chart had prevented their destruction.

The crew itself was the upside of the situation. They had

come together like brothers in a crisis, looking out for one another whether they were in combat or on liberty. They had made it through eleven missions together, why not twenty-four more? As his exhaustion began to usher him into sleep, Tony thought, *Right now, I'll settle for making it through one more mission.*

In late January of 1945, while the men of the Eighth Air Force in Europe lived from mission to mission, their leaders were busy planning an attack that might bring the staggering German government to its knees. Berlin was not only the capital of Germany, it was also the very core of her military organization. The war could not be ended without the fall of Berlin, and accordingly the American bombers had been striking the city since the first week of March 1944. Britain's RAF had been pounding the German capital long before that.

Finally the American high command felt it had the resources to hit the center of Berlin with an armada of such enormous size and destructive power, if it did not end the war outright, it would certainly shorten it considerably. On the morning of Saturday, February 3, Tony Teta sat with his friends, Skipper, Snuffy, Baldy, Big Swede, Hermit and the rest, as a briefing officer gave the airmen of the 305th Bomb Group the details of a new mission to Berlin.

Over one thousand Fortresses would take part. The American bombers would be escorted by more than nine hundred P-51 Mustangs and P-47 Thunderbolts. The target was the center of Berlin—more specifically Gestapo headquarters, the Reich Chancellery, the German Air Ministry and any other government or military building. Just as important as targets were thousands of German soldiers, who were being reorganized or were passing through Berlin—so the rail system needed to be knocked out.

The bomber crews could expect heavy flak, the briefing officer continued. "And the Luftwaffe," which had been keeping a low profile during recent raids, could be expected to be "up in force" to protect Berlin. Four hundred more American B-24 Liberators would be striking Magdeburg and should "divert some attention away from the Berlin raid." Tony doubted the Germans could miss noticing a thousand B-17s heading for their capital. He glanced at Jerry Chart and tried to read the pilot's facial expression. To Tony, their skipper seemed to have a look of resolution. He hoped he was reading it right, because that was what they would need on their first mission to Berlin.

The boys in Chart's crew were glad to see it was bomber number 015 waiting for them as they piled out of their truck. She had taken them to Reims, Cologne and Koblenz and had always brought them home. If they had to go to "the Big B," she was as good a gal as any.

Later at several thousand feet above the English Channel, Tony surveyed the scene from his perch inside the airplane's nose section. Ahead of the aircraft, as far as the eye could see on a beautiful clear day, were hundreds of gleaming B-17s. It was a sight that he knew he would never be able to sufficiently describe to anyone who was not there.

He also knew history was being made, and he was a part of it. For a while, the young navigator forgot about what he knew was waiting for them in the sky over Berlin—dense flak, a long bomb run and probably German fighters. His hunger to fly, along with destiny, had placed him on board this B-17 as a part of a massive strike at the heart of the Nazi government, and like every man on board, he planned to do his job.

Thousands of other Eighth Air Force airmen were also buckling down for the long trip to Berlin. Far below, German citizens on farms and in small villages ran from their homes to stare up at the fleet of American bombers that soon stretched from horizon to horizon. Most of the German spectators must have realized how the war must now end—if an aerial invasion of such unimaginable size could cross their homeland unopposed.

From the lead aircraft to the last B-17, the bomber formation stretched for more than three hundred miles. When the first Fortress dropped its bombs on Berlin at ten thirty a.m., the last American bomber was just passing over Holland.

Tony checked and rechecked his coordinates to the Initial Point. Then he checked them again—more to occupy his mind than for any other reason. Time passed slowly as the rumble of the bomber's engines mingled with the noise of the other 305th B-17s, flying in a tight combat box formation.

Visibility was excellent and miles away from Berlin, Tony spotted clouds of dark smoke rising from the Earth. He knew the source of the smoke was the fires burning out of control in the German capital. The first wave of American bombers had marked the target area with high explosives and incendiaries. The city's firemen would be helpless to extinguish the fires until the last bomber was gone. The attack would last for one hour and forty-five minutes. Hitler's vow that "we will raze their (English) cities to the ground" had come home to haunt Berliners.

As the 305th Bomb Group approached the Initial Point, Tony could see that despite the devastation she had already suffered, Berlin was still ready to put up a fight. Black flak bursts pocked the sky above the city. Twenty-five thousand feet below, veteran Luftwaffe gunners manned the flak towers that had been constructed to make the capital the most strongly defended of all German cities. The towers were augmented by numerous other antiaircraft installations operated by teenage boys and members of the German Home Guard.

Moments after Tony reported to Jerry Chart, "Skipper, we're at the IP," the B-17 began to get bounced around by flak concussions. Waist gunner Tom Christenson was the first of the crew to have a brush with death. A piece of shrapnel flew by him, just missing his head—but not missing him completely as it grazed him over the eye.

In the airplane's nose, Tony began his personal survival routine, which he had been using on the last several missions. Maybe it did not provide any real protection and it certainly was uncomfortable, but it was *his* routine and it had worked so far.

Tony reasoned it was his job to get his B-17 to the Initial Point. After the dangerous bomb run, it was his job to guide the pilot and the aircraft back to England—but during the bomb run, Tony's only priority was to stay alive.

The navigator held the small cross that hung around his neck with the forefinger and thumb of his left hand. He crossed himself with his right hand. Already wearing one flak jacket, he placed another on the floor beneath the navigator's desk. His friend Carl Robinson had procured the extra jacket for him. Tony had reciprocated by purchasing a new pair of officer's dress shoes at the PX and giving them to the flight engineer.

Exchanging a quick glance with the toggler who was kneeling at his bombsight, Tony tightened the strap on his flak helmet and squeezed his five-foot, two-inch frame underneath his desk. It was a tight fit even for his size.

The toggler watched Tony's routine and wished he had a desk, too. Of course, every man on the bomber knew that for the next fifteen minutes, there would be no safe place inside the B-17. Flak bursts were already starting to shake and rattle the bomber. Should the nose of the airplane take a direct hit, Tony's routine would not matter. Everything would be gone— the desk, the toggler and the navigator.

The German antiaircraft gunners in Berlin were to be respected. They had gained plenty of experience since the American B-17s and Liberators had begun flying daylight raids on the German capital almost a year before. To Allied airmen, Berlin was The Big B, and as far as Tony was concerned, the "B" stood for Bad!

As large as New York City, Berlin presented a long bomb run. Some bombers were going to be hit, and some crews would not be going home. Flying LeMay's straight-in bomb pattern, it was mostly a matter of luck or fate. So Tony had nothing to do but to ride it out. His only obligation during the bomb run was to log in the time of the bomb release, and he had even worked that out in a way that limited his exposure.

More flak bursts. Heavy impact. Very close. B-17 number 015 was a tough bird, Tony reminded himself. Jerry Chart was a top-notch skipper. He had brought them home from eleven missions and often with a shot-up airplane. Top-notch skipper.

Two loud flak explosions seemed to say, "This is different!" This was The Big B, and she had a special welcome for the 305th Bomb Group on its first visit to Berlin since December of the previous year. That mission had cost the 305th dearly, with three of its bombers being shot from the sky—one of those, commanded by pilot Charles R. Todd, had broken apart in midair, killing Todd and all eight of his crewmen.

Now Tony could hear the sound of metal fragments glancing off the airplane's Plexiglas nose cone. It sure seemed as if they had been in the bomb run long enough to be over target. Why had he not felt the bombs being released?

"What's going on?" he asked the toggler without moving from his spot below the desk.

"Lead plane hasn't dropped his bombs yet," the toggler replied, making no attempt to hide the impatience in his voice.

Tony shifted his weight to keep his legs from cramping up and freed his left hand, checking his watch. Only seven minutes had passed since I.P. Still, they had to be close to target. Then, suddenly, there it was. The airplane lurched upward as several hundred pounds of bombs fell from its belly.

As the B-17 lifted, so did the crew's spirits—at least a little. The flak was just as bad on the way out, of course, but now their pilot's flying skills could come into play. He could take evasive action and use his instincts, which they had all come to believe in. In the cockpit, Jerry Chart was well aware that evasive action was really a guessing game when the flak was this heavy.

He tried his best to find clear patches of sky but by the time an antiaircraft shell exploded, it was by then too late to avoid it. There was also the ever-present concern of collision with another bomber. Pilots had to fly evasive action as a part of their squadron. On instructions from the lead aircraft, the rest of the 366th Squadron's bombers would make turns or change altitude, sometimes dropping five hundred feet together.

The object of these coordinated maneuvers was to shake the radar fix of the antiaircraft gunners that had zeroed in on the B-17s by the time they had released their bombs. Flying evasively like a flock of geese was no easy task for the American pilots. Their combat formation placed the bomber's wingtips as close as a hundred feet from each other. One bad move by any of the squadron's pilots could result in disaster.

Assured that his bombs were on their way to Berlin, the toggler scrambled to the back of the nose compartment to make himself as small as possible. On the way past the navigator's desk he saw Tony's hand appear above the desk to write in the time of the bomb release perfectly on the log.

As Chart weaved the Fortress through the thick flak above Berlin, his crew hunkered down as best they could. The three exceptions were Chart, copilot Wisniewski and flight engineer Robinson. Robinson was busy checking the bomb bay. Everyone was listening on the interphone when he reported back to Chart.

"Skipper, we've got five bombs stuck in the bay!"

"Can you drop them manually?" the pilot asked.

"Tried it. They're stuck good!" Robinson replied.

Tony continued to listen as Chart ordered his flight engineer to go back to the bay for a second shot at manually dropping the bombs. Between the continuous flak concussions and the pilot's evasive maneuvering, it almost seemed a possibility the bombs would shake free on their own. Tony knew that was a long shot and soon Robinson was reporting back.

"I tried to kick them loose, Skipper. They're still stuck!"

When he heard Chart tell Wisniewski to close the bomb bay doors, Tony knew they would be carrying the five unwanted bombs back to Chelveston—provided they made it back to England. At the time, Berlin's antiaircraft gunners were doing everything possible to prevent it.

A strong impact shoved the B-17 to the left and almost toppled the young navigator out of his little desk fort. If that one had not hit them, it had damn well come close. Tony crawled out to investigate. Looking forward through the Plexiglas he could see flak bursts quickly appearing, one after another. How was Jerry flying them through that stuff?

Tony got to his feet and checked out the small left window. Everything looked okay. Number one and two engines were running fine. When he checked the right wing, he immediately spotted a problem with the inside engine. Number three's propellers were still spinning, but it was not the smooth rotation of a healthy engine. Moments later, the propellers stopped. Tony realized that could only mean that Chart had decided to "feather" the props of the damaged engine.

The process of feathering actually turned the propeller's blades to slice into the wind, instead of grabbing the wind when in the normal position. Left unfeathered, an engine prop could spin out of control, creating a drag on the aircraft and even causing a fire. Tony got on the interphone with his pilot.

"Everything okay up there, Skipper?"

As he asked the question, Tony discovered things were going

from bad to worse. The interphone was dead. He climbed quickly up the little ladder in the back of the nose compartment, emerging right behind the pilot's seat. A cold wind swirled blue smoke around the cockpit, sparks were spewing from a fuse box and next to the top gun turret, Tony could see blue sky. Flak had ripped away a sizable piece of the bomber's roof.

Robinson was on his feet but he looked shaky. Tony pulled down his oxygen mask and asked, "You okay, Carl?" The flight engineer gave him a thumbs-up.

Looking at the flak hole again, Tony could not imagine how his friend could have been so fortunate. Through the cockpit windshield, Tony could see only an occasional black puff of flak, indicating Chart had successfully flown them out of the effective range of Berlin's ground gunners. He figured it was as good a time as any to check with his pilot for instructions. He leaned between the pilot and copilot's seats.

"How's it going, Skipper?"

Chart glanced back at the young lieutenant whom he had personally trained until he felt Tony was a first-class navigator. Now he would find out for sure.

"Tony, you had better plot a course for Sweden . . . just in case."

The order spoke volumes to Tony. He knew Chart would prefer to nurse the B-17 back to England on three engines. They would not be able to keep up with the rest of the 366th Squadron or the 305th Bomb Group. They would almost certainly lose not only airspeed but also altitude. Staying in the bomber lanes might enable them to stay within the protective cover of American fighter escorts, but before long Jerry Chart would have to make a critical decision—to gamble on the long run back to England or to change course and land in Sweden.

Sweden was indeed much closer and their three healthy engines could probably get them there, but Sweden was a neutral country. Any Allied airplane and crew that landed there would be taken out of the war permanently. Only the survival of his crew could force Chart to make such an irreversible decision.

Tony also knew that Chart had already ruled out trying for a landing in Russia, which was an available option for pilots of wounded Allied bombers flying a Berlin raid. Eighth Air Force headquarters had given approval for emergency landings in Russian territory, but had also indicated such action was to be a last resort. The Army Air Force commanders were confident any downed American aircrews would be safely returned by the Russians, but they were not so sure about getting their aircraft back.

"Sweden. I'll get right on it, Jerry," Tony assured him as he headed back down into the nose section. As he was descending the short ladder, the navigator could hear the pilot already giving Carl Robinson an order to begin transferring fuel away from the number three engine. They would need every drop if they had any chance of making it back to Chelveston.

At the beginning of the Berlin run, Tony had crammed all his navigation charts and instruments into his navigator's case for safekeeping. Now he shoved the case on top of his desk and popped the latches open. The toggler pulled his oxygen mask down and asked, "What's up?"

Tony gave him a quick review of their situation while he located the relevant navigation charts. Once he had the picture, the toggler moved to man the nose guns, realizing the bomber crew could soon be on its own.

Tony was grateful to have some company as he dug into the job of plotting a course to Sweden. He thought about his friend John Cuffman, back in the tail section of the B-17, all alone and isolated with no communication. Tony hoped Christenson or Hall would crawl back there and let him know what was happening.

The tail gunner would eventually get the word, but until then Cuffman stuck to his post, hands locked around the handles of his twin machine guns. He watched as the other bombers of the 366th seemed to gradually grow smaller and smaller above him. From his position, Cuffman could not see the feathered engine prop on number three, but he guessed that something was seriously wrong if the airplane was starting to lose altitude.

It had been a rough run for Cuffman. Every movement of the aircraft was magnified in the tail. He had been banged around with each flak concussion the B-17 had endured. As he got his last look at Berlin, the city looked like what someone had once named the steel mill city of Pittsburgh: "Hell with the roof off." Behind his own airplane, Cuffman could see mile after mile of B-17s yet to make their bomb runs.

Down in the ball turret, Bill Goetz had sat in the choice seat to watch the nightmarish show. He had seen flak bursts everywhere among the Fortresses. Some had been so close that he could "see the cherry," the red center of a flak explosion. He had not seen the blast that sent a metal fragment slamming into his ball turret. He had, however, felt its impact and the sound of hissing icy wind had let him know his ball turret now had a hole in it.

In the cockpit, Jerry Chart could feel not only the missing power of his third engine but also the drag on his aircraft resulting from the large hole next to the top turret. As time wore on, he could see other B-17s in the bomber lanes above his airplane, some returning from Berlin and still more bomber groups heading toward the German capital. He wondered if any of the American fighter planes patrolling those lanes could see his lone B-17 flying far below.

Keeping sight of the 366th proved impossible. The pilot of the squadron's lead aircraft had wished Chart and his crew "good luck," when their condition had been reported. There was nothing else he could do for them. The men of Chart's crew knew the fighting strength of the Luftwaffe was being weakened with each Allied bomber raid, but even one or two stray German fighters could spell disaster to a wounded B-17.

Nobody had forgotten that less than three weeks before, enemy fighters had brought down Jordan's bomber, and the 305th had lost four bombers to German fighters as recently as New Year's Day. Every man on Chart's crew was on fighting edge as they found themselves alone in a vast chunk of enemy sky.

Once Tony had the coordinates for Sweden, he rechecked them quickly and then, confident they were correct, he turned his attention to reworking the coordinates for the route back to the Chelveston base. A crucial factor of navigation had changed after the number three engine had been lost. The bomber's airspeed was slower now, so all of Tony's calculations would have to be adjusted to provide a reliable course and estimated arrival time for a flight back to England.

The young navigator knew his pilot was waiting for the new information, and he had to fight the impulse to hurry the work. A navigation mistake under their current circumstances could prove deadly for everyone on board. Soon Tony was scrambling up the ladder that led to the cockpit.

Jerry Chart listened as his navigator gave him the headings, first for the neutral country and then for Chelveston. George Wisniewski jotted down the coordinates on his notepad as Chart continued to mull over his decision—England or Sweden. Tony felt the bomber commander would have to decide soon or even a run to Sweden would be in doubt. Chart ran it over in his mind.

The aircraft was performing okay on just three engines, although it continued to gradually lose altitude. He believed they could stay high enough to reach England, if the fuel held out.

The fuel transfer had gone well but it would be close. The five bombs lodged in the bay were not part of the equation, since they were an added danger no matter where he landed.

The fact that he and his crew were on their own concerned him, but they had not yet spotted a single enemy fighter. Carl Robinson, peering out of his top turret, interrupted the pilot's thoughts.

"We've got company! Two aircraft approaching!" the flight engineer shouted.

Robinson tracked the two black specks that were approaching from above the B-17. Christenson's waist gun was also angled upward to cover the unidentified planes. Cuffman, in the tail, had also spotted the airplanes, but they were too high for his tail guns to cover. They looked like fighter planes to him. *Enemy or Friendly?*

It was the fighters' movements that first gave them away, before anyone on board the bomber could identify their silhouettes. The two fighters continued to close in on the bomber, but their angle of approach had changed. Instead of diving straight at the bomber, the mystery airplanes were coming in on a more parallel route.

"I think they're ours," Robinson announced from the top turret. Then, when he could make out the fighters' distinctive shapes, he added, "Yeah, its two little friends!" Moments later two shiny P-51 Mustangs pulled alongside of Chart's number 015 Fortress—one cruising just feet away from each of the bomber's wingtips. Chart returned a friendly wave from one of the fighter pilots, and then everyone on board found himself smiling and waving.

Tony was not surprised when their skipper announced his intentions. They would be continuing back to England. Whether it was the friendly fighter escort that had tipped the scale, Chart did not say, and Tony would never know. Chart had made his decision and his men trusted him.

Long minutes, and then hours, dragged by as the B-17 labored homeward. Tony made several trips between the nose and the cockpit, consulting with Jerry Chart on the bomber's airspeed and informing his pilot of where they were and the remaining distance to Chelveston. The two P-51 "little friends" departed and returned several times as they checked on other American bombers. Finally, the Mustang pilots returned a last time to give the bomber crew a send-off wave, and then they streaked away, leaving contrails in their wake. Like everyone else, Tony hated to see them go, but he guessed they were now out of the danger area for enemy fighter attacks.

Fuel was a concern, but their altitude seemed acceptable. They were still at several thousand feet when Tony spotted the English Channel in the distance. Soon the navigator and toggler began sighting familiar landmarks of the English countryside, and they knew they were approaching Chelveston. Tony breathed a sigh of satisfaction and relief. His navigation calculations had been right on the money for Jerry Chart to get them back home.

Finally, there it was—Chelveston, with its distinctive three runways crossing one another to form a small pyramid pattern in its center. Most of the 305th Bomb Group's B-17s were visible, already parked in their assigned positions around the perimeter of the airfield. A couple of other Fortresses were just landing as Chart's aircraft turned to begin its approach. Tony thought the ugly air base, at that moment, was the most beautiful thing he had ever seen.

Sitting in the left seat, Jerry Chart was calm and confident. They were going to be okay after all. He had not forgotten about the five live bombs still on board, but that did not cause him great concern. He felt he could land the damaged Fortress safely on just three engines. The B-17 had proven to be an incredible airplane, and he was, after twelve combat missions, an experienced bomber pilot.

At an altitude of one thousand feet, Chart motioned for Wisniewski to hit the switch to lower the landing gear, and he also began to engage the landing flaps. At once both pilot and copilot knew that something was wrong.

Chart visually checked the left wing and Wisniewski checked the right wing. The landing flaps were not working at all, and even worse the pilot could not feel or hear the aircraft's wheels coming down. Since the interphone was inoperative, Carl Robinson went aft to confirm the wheels' status. Soon he was back to report that the wheels had not dropped down into landing position. Chart had already guessed where the problem was.

"It must be the fuse box," he told Robinson. "The flak hit must have burned out the fuses."

The flight engineer went to the still-smoldering fuse box and pulled out the fuses that carried current to the landing flaps and landing gear controls. He replaced the damaged fuses with the spares, which were also stored in the fuse box. Wisniewski tried the landing gear switch again. Chart tried the flaps. Nothing happened—the spare fuses had also been ruined.

Chart considered circling the airfield but that meant burning precious fuel that he could not spare. With the wheels up and no landing flaps, he might still be able to glide the Fortress in for a crash landing, but even that option was removed because of the five live bombs still on board. No, he had to somehow get the landing gear down and he had to have working flaps. How? If only he could just shove a penny in the fuse box, like he had seen his old man do once when the lights had gone out at home. Of course, the B-17's fuse-box connections were much too large for that—Chart guessed there was two or three inches of space between the posts.

"Carl!" The pilot turned to his flight engineer. "Go back to John and get an empty shell casing off the floor. Quick!"

Robinson stared back at his skipper.

"Go now!" Chart ordered.

As Robinson headed back to the waist gunner's area, across the five live bombs in the bomb bay and through the radio room, Chart's plan hit him. *It might work,* he thought. *Just might.* He found Bill Goetz and John Christenson looking out the side window, discussing why their pilot seemed to be bringing them in for a landing with the wheels still up. Robinson could spare no time for explanations. He saw a couple of dozen empty shell casings lying on the floor. The shells had fallen there when Christenson had test-fired his .50 caliber machine guns on the way to Berlin. The flight engineer grabbed a shell casing, gave his two crewmates a thumbs-up sign, and headed back to the cockpit. Ken Hall watched it all from the doorway of the radio room. After Robinson brushed by him, Hall and the two gunners exchanged looks of bewilderment.

Jerry Chart was hoping there was enough copper in the empty brass shell casing to conduct electricity and serve as a replacement fuse. He was counting on the slow-voltage electricity to not give Robinson too much of a jolt, especially since the flight engineer was wearing heavy gloves. Robinson did not wait to be told—he jammed the shell casing across the two appropriate posts in the fuse box.

"Give it a try, George!" Robinson shouted.

The copilot worked the switch that controlled the wing wheels. Back in the waist, Hall, Goetz and Christenson had been joined by John Cuffman, and they all let out a cheer when the bomber's wheels lowered and locked into landing position.

In the nose compartment of the aircraft, Tony and the toggler sat watching Chelveston airfield quickly growing closer and
closer, neither man aware of the problems with the wheels
and flaps. Once the wheels were down, Robinson pulled the
empty shell casing from the fuse box and repositioned it over
the two posts that controlled electricity to the landing flaps. He
could feel the current's pulse through his gloves but made no
complaint.

"They're working!" Chart announced as the flaps of each
wing came down and caught the wind. On the ground, other
flight crews, ground personnel and officers watched anxiously
as the wounded B-17 glided toward the runway, with just three
propellers spinning. Some with binoculars spotted flak damage
aft of the cockpit and elsewhere on the bomber.

In the nose of B-17 number 015, Lieutenant Tony Teta took
a deep breath and held it as he watched the runway surface approaching just a few feet below the Plexiglas. Jerry Chart was
holding his breath too when he eased the airplane down. As he
felt the bomber's wheels make contact with the runway, Tony
whispered a silent "thank you" and touched the cross that hung
from the chain around his neck. Chart brought his damaged
aircraft, with its crew of nine good men and five unwanted passengers, in for a textbook landing.

Berlin had lived up to her reputation as perhaps Germany's
toughest target, but Chart and his airmen had done their jobs.
Though their Fortress was severely damaged, they had lived to
tell the tale of their mission to The Big B.

There was much laughter, hand shaking and backslapping as
the airmen climbed out of their bomber, but the men grew quiet
as they got a better look at the flak damage number 015 had
sustained. Besides the major hole near the top turret and the
damage to the inside engine of the right wing, there were also
holes in the left wing where flak had punctured its gas tanks, a

flak hole in the ball turret, and numerous holes in the fuselage. Tony walked slowly around the aircraft with John Cuffman, and the two friends took their own postflight inventory. When they were done, they had counted 168 holes in their aircraft.

The Berlin mission had lasted for more than ten hours and every man who had flown with the 305th Bomb Group that day needed rest, but first there was the necessary interrogation session. There was plenty to tell. Chart's crew had been banged around, but all had survived their twelfth mission without serious injury. They had witnessed the appalling sight of other American bombers being blasted from the sky.

Later that evening, John Cuffman would open his diary and write about the Berlin mission of February 3, 1945: "Couldn't drop right side of bombs because we were all shot up. Saw 5 B-17s blow up and go down. Boy it was horrible. God, I'm glad it is over."

The massive American air raid of February 3, 1945, was the worst yet for Germany; the bombers dropped almost twenty-three hundred tons of bombs on the city of Berlin. For nearly two solid hours, the German capital was pounded by wave after wave of American bombers. Soldiers and citizens unlucky enough to have been caught in the center of their city that Saturday suffered the hardest blow. There, government buildings that had been specific targets of the American high command were struck again and again. The Reich Chancellery, including Adolf Hitler's personal residence, received heavy damage. Unfortunately for the Allies and the German people, the *Führer* survived the bombing raid unharmed in his bunker beneath Berlin.

The average Berliner had no personal bunker in which to hide. Individuals and families sought refuge in the basements of their buildings. Thousands were already homeless from previous raids, and they tried to find protection in the crowded public shelters. Overhead, they could hear the bombs exploding, at first in the distance and then seemingly right on top of them. Even the buildings that were not hit shook, windows shattered, and smoke and dust choked the lungs of the inhabitants.

When it seemed the bombing would never end, it finally did, but the surviving Berliners emerged from their shelters to find their capital in flames. Even the buildings that had been left untouched by the bombs were at great risk from the fires that were spreading almost unhindered. Earlier in the war, Hitler's bombers had killed tens of thousands of innocent civilians in cities such as Rotterdam and Warsaw, and now the Nazi leader was sentencing the German population to destruction by continuing a war that their country no longer had any hope of winning.

At Chelveston, the 305th repaired its airplanes and counted its blessings. The bombers John Cuffman had seen "blow up and go down" had been part of other bomb groups involved in the Berlin mission. Amazingly, the 305th suffered no loss of aircraft on the February 3 raid. Most of the airmen under Lieutenant Jerome Chart believed that without his quick thinking and composed flying, the 305th would have had at least one missing bomber and crew that day.

For Tony Teta, the memories of the Berlin mission, and the men who shared its perils, would stay with him for a lifetime. Yet it was only mission number twelve, and there would be many more dangerous raids for the young navigator from Hamden, Connecticut. For years in his sleep he would see flashes of those missions—like the time the 366th Squadron encountered another American bomb group during a bomb run. Approaching the target from different headings, the Fortress formations sliced through each other's airspace, and the pilots flew "by the seat of their pants," trying to avoid midair collision. Tony later recalled the frantic warnings Jerry Chart received over the interphone from his crew: "Jerry, there's one over us!" Then another crew member shouted, "Go to the right!" A third reported in, "Skipper, there's one underneath us!"

During the nervous few minutes of this midair traffic jam, the young navigator looked up through the clear Plexiglas nose cone and was startled to see another B-17 flying just a few feet above them, its bomb bay doors open in preparation for the release of its deadly payload. Tony recalled the moment forever frozen in his memory: "I'm looking at their bombs! If they had released, they would have gone right through us."

Also, he would remember the mission he never completed because his B-17 blew a tire during takeoff. Tony was flying with a different pilot that day, and for once he regretted being in the nose of the aircraft as the Fortress skidded down the runway, the metal and Plexiglas scrapping the surface the entire way.

"With the angle that we were tipped," Tony remembered, "it was like running and sliding on ice. A lot of noise like thunder and sparks flying, and we had a fire on the wing."

Tony, who had deposited himself as far to the rear of the nose compartment as possible, was the closest to the front escape door when the bomber finally came to a stop. The door was jammed. Behind him other crew members, fearing an explosion, were yelling, "Hurry up! Get the door open!"

Luckily for Tony, the jammed door did not open too soon. When the airplane had stopped moving, the pilot had left the cockpit without remembering to switch off the engines. Had the escape door in the nose section opened immediately, Tony could very well have jumped or been pushed directly into the spinning propeller blades of engine number two. As it happened, when the door jammed, enough time elapsed that flight engineer

Carl Robinson noticed the pilot's error and killed the engines himself, very likely saving his navigator friend's life.

Then there were the extraordinary missions over Germany by the 305th, armed with "Disney" bombs. Developed by the British, two of the top secret experimental bombs weighed nine thousand pounds, while the B-17 was designed to carry a maximum bomb load of only seven thousand pounds. These mammoth bombs were so large they would not even fit inside the Fortresses' bomb bays. They had to be strapped underneath the bombers' wings.

The veteran air crews of the 305th quickly named the new weapon the "Disney" bomb, because they looked like something only the imaginative cartoonist could have dreamed up. The general opinion of the combat airmen was that a B-17 would never even get airborne with two of the silly-looking bombs weighing it down.

Tony later recounted the test run:

"Our hotshot colonel . . . a young guy, about twenty-seven years old . . . they strapped two of them on his plane. He took off that morning. He used the whole runway and just about bounced off the end of the runway. Went over the English Channel . . . he dropped them off into the channel. He (then) said: 'That's it, now we can do it!' As long as he could do it, we all had to do it. We did it."

The hotshot colonel was Henry MacDonald, and his example, while daring and inspiring to his aircrews, was not very comforting. The airmen of the 305th had watched MacDonald's takeoff with the Disneys beneath his B-17's wings. He had indeed been able to get the aircraft in the air, but they had also noted that as the bomber left the ground the tail fins of the Disney bombs actually scraped on the runway, sending sparks flying. One little slip or miscalculation by a pilot and a Disney bomb mission would be over before it began.

During March of 1945, the 366th Squadron carried the heavy Disney bombs to Hamburg, trying to bust open the thick concrete submarine pens there. It was on this mission that Tony witnessed the debut of a new German weapon and got an early look at the future of aviation.

"We'd heard they had jets, but we had never seen them. We saw those jets coming through our formation one day . . . unbelievable! One went right through and you could never shoot them." Tail gunner John Cuffman fired about one hundred fifty rounds at two streaking German jets and other propeller-driven fighters, while Chart's other gunners were kept equally busy. American P-51s finally swooped in to chase the jets away.

The new technology of the German Luftwaffe was impressive, and despite the constant bombardment of its industry, Germany still managed to produce the jets and traditional fighter aircraft to defend its skies, even during the last days of the war. Thanks to the heroic efforts of the men of the 366th Squadron, the 305th Bomb Group and the thousands of other brave Eighth Air Force airmen of other proud bomb groups, the Luftwaffe finally ran out of pilots. The gunners of the American B-17s and Liberators, and their escorting Mustangs, Thunderbolts and Lightnings (along with the RAF), had simply shot all their enemies out of the sky.

In fact, Tony and his crewmates had become as much decoys as attackers during the last weeks of the war, as the American high command baited the last defending German fighters with the American bombers. Yet somehow all of the men of Chart's original crew survived the war. Chart, Wisniewski, Hall, Stiles, Robinson, Goetz, Christenson, and Cuffman, as well as a young navigator named Teta, beat all the odds against them and became Lucky Bastards.

By the end of their tour of duty, both Chart's and Teta's skills and experience had been recognized by the squadron command.

Chart had been picked to fly several missions as lead pilot of the 366th. Tony's reputation as an accurate and reliable navigator had resulted in his assignment as deputy lead navigator four times and lead navigator for one mission. Since flying lead or deputy lead was considered more hazardous, Tony received an extra credit for those five missions. Thus in the end, he had completed thirty-four combat missions over Germany, yet received credit for thirty-five missions.

When the war officially ended in Europe on May 8, 1945, Tony was a decorated veteran air combat officer and a proven navigator—he would be nineteen for one more week. The war that had accelerated a boy's entrance into manhood had not extinguished Tony's lust for adventure. Following his return to the United States, Lieutenant Teta volunteered for service with the U.S. Army Air Force in China. He served there as a navigator and backup copilot on humanitarian flights for eight months.

Flying C46 and C47 cargo airplanes, the American aviators supplied oil, food and other vital materials to both the Communist forces and the Nationalist forces, which had fought to defeat the Japanese in China and had then turned on each other. While there was no one shooting at the American airmen, flying the missions over China proved to be both challenging and dangerous.

"The navigation charts we were given were bad," Tony recalled. "The chart would say a mountain was ten thousand feet high. . . . We would be flying at fifteen thousand feet, and we'd still have to pull up to get over it."

Although the Chinese charts were inaccurate, Tony adjusted and improvised when he had to. "The Chinese railroads and the Great Wall of China were helpful navigation landmarks," said the man who had so many times before faced tougher challenges in the sky over Germany.

The completion of thirty-five combat missions (or twenty-five combat missions in the early stages of the war) in the European Theater of Operations is a heroic achievement for any man who can claim membership to that fraternity of warriors. To don the heavy flight gear and climb aboard an aircraft adorned with fresh patches of the previous day's flak damage, and to do this not once but again and again and again required resolve, dedication to duty and a special kind of courage. Later, when asked how and why they did it, many Eighth Air Force airmen would modestly reply, "I was just doing my job."

For Tony Teta, sometimes the missions had been back-to-back for two or three days in a row. Sometimes there had been enemy fighters—and almost always deadly flak. The danger of collision had been a constant presence. After his first mission, Tony had learned to look only to the end of the next. He had placed his trust in God, his crewmates and himself—in the end, it had been enough.

After the War

Anthony Teta returned home to Hamden, Connecticut, in September of 1945 with his body and spirit whole. Not long after the long-awaited reunion with his parents, Alex and Mary, and his brother and sister, John and Josephine, Tony's attention was stolen by a pretty local girl. Her name was Rosalie Sazano.

Tony and Rosey became inseparable, but in August 1946, military duty once again took the young lieutenant to a foreign land. By April of the following year Tony was back in the States, and he became a civilian two months later. The couple's relationship was rekindled, and on October 27, 1951, Tony and Rosalie were married.

Tony tried a range of occupations in the early years of marriage, including produce retailer and long-distance truck driver, but eventually he was fortunate to land a job with the New York, New Haven & Hartford Railroad Company. His natural enthusiasm and his organizational and problem-solving skills propelled Tony up the ranks at NY, NH & H. He spent thirty-six years with the company (which became Penn Central and part of Conrail), most of his career as a train master responsible for a large area of track encompassing New Haven, Danbury, Hartford and much of eastern New York State.

Retiring from the railroad business in 1991, Tony spent his days caring for the horses, ponies and various other creatures that inhabited the Tetas' small ranch in Northford, Connecticut. He and Rosalie felt blessed to have their two daughters, Mary Ellen and Dora Ann, sons-in-law, three grandchildren and one great-grandchild living close by. Rosalie was always quick to say her husband had lost none of his sense of adventure, and she marveled at his energy as he went about his ranch chores. The couple had enjoyed fifty-six years of marriage when Rosalie passed away in January of 2008. Nowadays, Tony still stables a few neighbors' horses and enjoys attending the University of Connecticut Women Huskies basketball games with his good friend and fellow Bomber Boy George Ahern.

Jerry Chart became a research biologist and pharmacologist after his return to civilian life. He spent most of his working career with Ciba in New Jersey and New York. He fell in love with a pretty girl named Therese, and the couple married in 1953. Jerry and Terri became parents in 1954 when their daughter Kate was born. Five sons (Greg, Tom, Joseph, Geoffrey and John) followed and then eight grandchildren. After retirement in 1985, Jerry and his wife, Terri, lived in the New York–Connecticut–New Jersey area for ten more years before moving to Helena, Montana, at the urging of two sons who already lived there. Jerry enjoys fishing in the cold clear Montana streams and wishes they had moved to the state even sooner.

John Cuffman returned to his beloved Tennessee after the war. He attended George Peabody University in Nashville and attained a Bachelor of Science degree. The former tail gunner's main civilian career was as a longtime agent for the National Insurance Company (which owned WSM-AM radio and *The Grand Ole Opry*). He and his wife, Virginia, had two sons, one daughter and five grandchildren. Through the years, John Cuffman and Tony Teta maintained a long-distance but close friendship that continued until John's death in 2003.

George Wisniewski, Kenneth Hall, John Stiles, Carl Robinson, William Goetz and **Thomas Christenson**: All of these airmen survived the dangerous air combat over Germany, returned to America and enjoyed the freedom they had fought so bravely to defend.

Crew Reunion: Four members of Jerry Chart's crew were able to reunite at least once to catch up on each other's lives and to remember the antics and adventures they had shared as mere boys in uniform. The mini reunion was held at former copilot George Wisniewski's Wisconsin home. In addition to Wisniewski, Jerry Chart, John Cuffman and Tony Teta attended the gathering. The four war buddies had been unable to locate most of the other crew members, and Bill Goetz was not able to attend.

Over good food and cold beverages, the four air veterans bonded again, and on the last day they talked of getting together for a second reunion. Unfortunately, George Wisniewski would pass away soon afterward and then came word that Bill Goetz had also died. With John Cuffman's passing, now only two of the original crew remain—Chart and Teta. The two friends talk on the phone occasionally, and they would like to see each other again, each knowing it may not happen.

In 2003, a writer interviewing Jerry Chart told him, "By the way, Tony and John had the nicest things to say about you, and I think they both feel that they would not be here today if you had not been their pilot." There was a pause, and then Chart quietly replied, "Well, they were a good crew."

• Escape from Black Thursday •

PETER SENIAWSKY (PETER SCOTT)
Left Waist Gunner

384TH BOMB GROUP

547TH BOMB SQUADRON

Peter Seniawsky hated the desert. More specifically, he hated the Army base outside of Clovis, New Mexico, which was smack in the middle of the desert. It was a stretch to even call it an Army base. There was nothing there except endless sand dunes and an assortment of huts where the soldiers lived.

During the day, the desert sun made working on the airplanes a miserable experience, and if a windstorm blew in, the sand got into everything—the airplane engines, clothes and, worst of all, eyes. Even Peter's thick glasses provided little protection from the relentless sand.

At only twenty, Peter was already a sergeant in charge of a company of mechanics, most of whom were into their second hitch with the Army. They had plenty of on-the-job experience and also plenty of attitude. The fact that none of them had made the rank of sergeant, despite many having been in the service for eight or nine years, said a lot about the mechanics. Peter had evaluated them after his first week and had decided: "They're a bunch of screwups!"

The thing that really made his assignment in New Mexico
unbearable was that it was halfway around the world from
where he wanted to be. There was a war going on in Europe, an
all-or-nothing, us-or-them shooting war, and Peter had done everything he could to get into it. So far, fate and the Army had
placed one barricade after another in his way.

Born in Rutherford, New Jersey, in 1922, Peter had spent his
early childhood on a farm in Lisbon, Connecticut. His father,
Gabriel, had emigrated from the Ukraine and was a tool and
die maker by trade. In search of a better life for himself and his
family, he did all he could to make a go of it as a farmer, holding
down his regular job in Jewett City and then working all weekend on the farm. After three years it became too much. The farm
was lost to creditors. Afterward, Gabriel Seniawsky was never
the same man.

Peter's mother, Eva, had come to America with her husband
and had given birth to his four children. She stood by him in
good times and bad, but when her husband began to drown
his depression in alcohol, the marriage became strained. As a
teenager, Peter escaped his parents' unsettling relationship by
going on hiking and camping trips whenever there was an opportunity. Whether it was an overnight sleep-out close to home
or a weekend outing with his Boy Scout troop, Peter loved to be
outdoors.

Sometimes the scouts would visit the highland forests in
New York State. Here, young Peter and his friends would hike
for hours along the mountain ridges of the Appalachian Trail.
He loved the woods, the mountains and the lakes. The wilder-
ness also had valuable lessons to teach him and without even
being aware of it, Peter learned skills that would one day prove
crucial.

Peter's older sisters, Alice, Vera and Margaret, were already married, and Peter was sixteen years old when their parents separated. Peter quit school and got a job to help support his mother. A little more than a year later Eva Seniawsky died.

Margaret, the youngest sister, was married to a New York City fireman named Thomas Bile, and the couple asked Peter to come live with them in Brooklyn. By the time he turned eighteen, Peter had a good job in Brooklyn, was paying a little rent to the Biles and had saved enough money to buy a used motorcycle.

Helen Stagniunas had striking good looks, and she was smart. Peter was attracted to her the first time they met. He thought she was the prettiest girl in Brooklyn. He also thought she was a little spoiled. Helen was the daughter of a tailor and the youngest of four girls. When she first met Peter at a friend's party, Helen played it cool, although she was immediately taken with him. He was tall and had that rugged outdoor look about him. Peter Seniawsky just looked like a guy who could take care of himself, and Helen reasoned he could also take care of any girl he really cared about. When she ran into him again during a not-so-chance meeting, she accepted his request for a date.

As they dated through the summer of 1941, Helen came to understand something else about Peter. There was a restlessness inside him—not just a desire, but an actual need to test what he was made of. Once discovered, this part of Peter's personality both excited and scared Helen. She was developing serious feelings for Peter and wanted to know that he was going to be around.

One night, as he walked Helen to her door, he reluctantly told her of a big decision he had made. He and a friend were going to take a tour of the western United States and perhaps Mexico—on a motorcycle.

"A motorcycle?"

"Yeah, I'm going to buy one," Peter told her.

"And tour the country?" Helen frowned.

"Well, yeah . . . I . . ."

"Peter Seniawsky, if you buy a motorcycle, then you can forget about seeing me!" Tears glistened in Helen's eyes.

Peter hesitated. God, she was pretty, but he would only be nineteen once, and if he did not go now, he never would. He went on to explain how much he cared for her, but the trip would last no more than a couple of months. He was not leaving for good. It was just something he needed to do. Helen had stopped listening. It would be several weeks before he and his friend would be prepared to leave, so he and Helen could still see each other. She did not think that was a good idea. They kissed goodbye and parted that night, not with anger but with regret.

Peter got a great deal on a Harley-Davidson that needed some repairs and soon he had it running like new. He took a solo trip on the Harley to Philadelphia as a shakedown cruise. By the first week of December, Peter and his traveling pal had stockpiled enough cash and even mapped out their western tour route, day by day. Everything was ready. They decided to leave in the early spring of 1942 once the weather turned warmer. On December 7, their plans changed.

Peter walked down to the local Army recruiting office and, catching his reflection in the glass door, he stopped and removed his glasses. As he entered he resolved to demand duty in the armored corps, thinking that he might still get the chance to drive a motorcycle. Less than a half hour later, he was back standing on the sidewalk in front of the recruiting station.

"Sorry, son. Your eyes aren't up to par," the recruiting sergeant had told him. It was a free pass, one many men would have gladly taken. But Peter did not want it and, in fact, was determined not to accept it. There had to be a way.

About two months after his rejection by the Army, Peter noticed an article in the newspaper that said the vision standards had been lowered. He was back at the recruiting office the next day. This time he passed the eye test, just barely.

"I want to get into the armored corps. I want to drive a motorcycle," Peter told the sergeant in charge.

"No problem," the sergeant responded. "Just sign right here." If Peter had said, "I want to be a general," there is little doubt the recruiting sergeant's reply would have been any different.

The Army sent Peter first to Long Island for more testing, where they informed him that he had an aptitude for things mechanical. Next it was off to an Army base in Mississippi, where he breezed through the courses of the Army Air Corps Mechanics School. Upon graduation, he was enthusiastically looking forward to at least being part of a combat aircraft ground crew, servicing the fighters and bombers that would strike Germany and Japan. Where he ended up was Clovis, New Mexico.

On an especially hot morning, Peter walked into his commanding officer's hut, determined to demand reassignment to some kind of frontline unit. Removing his cap, Peter watched as sand fell out of it. The tiny grains bouncing across the floor only strengthened his resolve.

"Sir, I've . . ."

The officer looked up from his desk and interrupted his chief mechanic. "Peter, I'm glad you're here. I need you to pick out fourteen men from your company. They will be reassigned."

"Reassigned?" Peter asked.

"Yes, I've got to provide fourteen men for gunnery school."

"What kind of gunnery school?" Peter wanted to know.

"Fifty-caliber machine guns, I believe," the officer said.

"Fifty caliber. You're talking about bomber gunners, right?"

"I would think so."

"How about putting my name down on that list," Peter said.

The officer looked the sergeant in the eyes. "Are you serious?"

"Yes, sir, I am."

"Peter, you wear glasses! I can't . . ."

Peter removed his glasses and shoved them into his pocket. "They don't know that at the gunnery school, sir."

The officer smiled. He certainly owed this young sergeant more than a favor or two. He had taken a group comprised mostly of slackers and underachievers, and he had kept them on the job and mostly out of trouble.

"You really want to go, Peter?"

"Yeah, I do."

His commanding officer wrote "Peter Seniawsky" at the top of the reassignment list. Peter did not even ask where the gunnery school was located. It had to be better than the desert.

The sergeant and thirteen other enlisted men were soon on their way to Utah. When their airplane landed at an air base that had been constructed on the edge of the Great Salt Flats, Peter began to wonder if the locale *was* any better than Clovis.

"Well, it doesn't matter," he said to himself. "I'm going to be a bomber gunner. In a few months, I'll be overseas."

The former mechanics were all pleasantly surprised when they were informed that their gunnery school was miles from the air base. It was located high in the majestic Rocky Mountains, which bordered the salt flats. For the next few weeks Peter had a wonderful time. He learned everything there was to know about the .50 caliber machine gun—how to take it apart and put it back together, even blindfolded. And if the actual target practice was not that realistic, at least it was interesting.

The new gunners assumed they would be driven down to the air base, deposited on a B-17 and allowed to acquire some in-flight gunnery experience. During their first two weeks of training, what they got was a thrilling ride aboard an open mining car. The little car was equipped with a .30 caliber machine gun and rolled—or more accurately, careened—along a narrow-gauge track. On the descent, the occupant tried to hit targets, at least when he was not holding on for his life. After a few bumpy rides, Peter figured out it was impossible to hit the target under such conditions, except by pure luck.

What Peter enjoyed most was taking solitary hikes through the Rocky Mountain forests. On his day off, he would pack a couple of sandwiches and not return until after sunset. He imagined how the legendary nineteenth-century mountain men must have felt. That was not a bad life, he decided.

During his last few days at gunnery school, Peter and the other trainees were finally given the opportunity for some actual in-flight target practice. Flying in a B-17, the men were to each have a burst or two at a target sleeve pulled by a second airplane. He watched with anticipation as the first man was unable to score a hit. *I can do better than that,* Peter thought and wiggled his fingers in preparation for his turn.

The second man to shoot began to blast away at the target, and to everyone's amazement the sleeve went down like a rock. The irritated instructor informed the jubilant marksman that although he had missed the target sleeve completely, he had managed to hit the tow cable. The sleeve was gone and so was Peter's first and last chance at air-to-air shooting practice. The first time he would fire a .50 caliber in the air, he would be heading to Germany on his first combat mission.

During his first week at gunnery school, Peter had taken great care to conceal his vision problem. However, he found it necessary to wear his glasses when he was first ordered to strip down the .50 caliber weapon and then reassemble it. He waited nervously for the instructor's negative reaction, but it never came. After that, Peter freely wore the glasses whenever he needed to. No one ever said anything about his glasses at the gunnery school, but Peter knew at his next assignment, it could be a very different story.

With gunnery school nearly finished, he would soon be headed to Washington State to join his bomber crew. These guys would be putting their lives in each other's hands, and they might not be so accepting of a gunner who wore thick glasses. He knew he could do the job, but he decided, "Why rock the boat?" Before he left gunnery school, he sent his official aviator sunshades home to his sister Margaret, with instructions to have prescription shaded lenses inserted. Those shades would help Peter hide his little secret until he got to know his new crewmates.

It was March 1943 when Peter joined his B-17 crew in Moses Lake, Washington, where they would begin their in-flight training before transferring to Walla Walla. His assignment was left waist gunner. The aircraft commander was First Lieutenant Giles Kauffman Jr. The pilot's quiet demeanor, Peter soon learned, was not aloofness. Kauffman turned out to be friendly enough once you got to know him. Casual with his men while off duty, he was a no-nonsense, get-the-job-done type of officer when commanding his aircraft. Most of the crew thought those were admirable traits for a man who was about to lead them into air combat.

One day, during a break from their B-17 flight training, one of the boys suggested a game of touch football. Although it was a typical drizzly Washington day, Peter could not remember when he had such a great time. Everyone seemed to be getting along fine. At the end of the lively game, someone asked Kauffman's crew to pose for a photo. Peter stood at the end of the back row, his baseball cap tilted back on his head.

When he was given his copy of the crew picture, Peter sent it along to his sister Margaret in Brooklyn, writing on the back of the photo: "The best damned B-17 crew in the Army Air Force! We will make history!"

Half boast and half tongue-in-cheek joke, the young waist gunner's words would prove to be prophetic.

———

Kauffman's crew received orders to report to the Eighth Air Force in England upon completing training. Luckily for Peter, he was granted a three-day pass to visit his family in Brooklyn. Returning to the East Coast, he took the ferry across the Hudson River and caught a Brooklyn-bound subway train from Manhattan.

Peter had never thought much about the concept of fate until then, but as he exited the subway at the Myrtle Avenue station, he experienced one of life's rare and mysterious moments. Walking up the stairs leading to the street level, Peter encountered a beautiful young girl coming down the steps.

"Helen!" he said, stopping so suddenly that several people behind him bumped into each other. The look of total surprise on Helen's face was quickly replaced with a warm smile.

Peter Seniawsky, she thought, *from out of nowhere and looking wonderful in his uniform.*

"Peter, what are you doing here?"

He started to explain that he was heading overseas and to tell her all about his new assignment, but he stopped in midsentence. Peter realized for the first time that he was in love.

"Helen, what are you doing tonight?" he asked.

"Nothing, I guess . . ."

"Will you go out with me?"

"Yes, you know I will." Helen laughed and hugged him. The next day Peter asked her to marry him. She said, "Yes."

Without an official engagement ring, the young airman offered his new fiancée his Air Corps wings. She proudly pinned them on her blouse. The following day Peter and his crewmates shipped out for Britain.

When they arrived in England, Giles Kauffman's crew was assigned to the 547th Bomb Squadron as a part of the 384th Bomb Group at Grafton Underwood airfield. By September they were in the air on their first combat mission. When their B-17 popped out of the clouds, Peter marveled at the blueness of the sky, which seemed filled with olive drab bombers.

"Man, I'm finally here," he said out loud. Soon Kauffman gave the okay for the gunners to test-fire their weapons. Peter stood at the left waist machine gun and rattled off a couple of quick bursts. It felt good. It was the first time he had ever actually fired a .50 caliber in the air. Underneath his goggles and oxygen mask, Peter was wearing his prescription sunglasses. He had stashed a second pair and a third, clear pair in his flight jacket and pants. He was taking no chances.

He gave the machine gun's trigger another quick squeeze and watched as the tracers streaked into the open sky. It was reassuring. He felt he was ready to deal with an enemy fighter, should one come close. Almost as soon as the bomber group cleared the English Channel, the young waist gunner found out he was very mistaken.

As Peter scanned the sky beyond the squadron's other bombers, an enemy fighter flew right through the formation.

"My God, that's a German airplane," Peter said.

There was no time to get a shot off—it was there. Then it was just a gray blur and then it was gone. There would be many other opportunities for the left waist gunner. Early in the war, the Luftwaffe command was fully aware the American bombers lost their escorts early in a mission. When the American fighters turned back to England, the bomber crews could count the seconds before German fighters appeared. If their bomber survived the trip to the target and the flak, the crew still had to fight their way home. So it went for the first two missions flown by Kauffman's boys.

On October 4, Kauffman drew one of the original B-17s assigned to the 384th Bomb Group. Stenciled on the bomber's tail fin was the serial number 42-30043, but everyone called her

Ruthless. The crew stowed their equipment on board, then gathered under the bomber's nose to wait for the signal for takeoff.

As some of the men chatted, Peter sat quietly and observed his crewmates—they had known each other only a few months, but they were a combat family now.

First Lieutenant Giles F. Kauffman Jr., the pilot, was quiet and steady. From Lewistown, Pennsylvania, he had spent a couple of years at Penn State studying chemical engineering. Kauffman's father had died early, leaving his son to go to work in his teen years—something to which Peter could relate. Most of the crew called their pilot Junior.

Second Lieutenant George Molnar, the copilot—good natured, always smiling. The men nicknamed him Happy.

Second Lieutenant J. J. Lecroix was the bombardier.

Second Lieutenant Frank Pogorzelski served as the navigator. Nobody could pronounce his Polish name, so he told the crew to just call him Pogo. The name stuck.

Sergeant William Jarrell was the crew's flight engineer. Jarrell seemed to be an expert on information about a wide range of topics. He was the crew's only Republican. The boys called him Whataman.

Sergeant Stanley T. Ruben, a Cherokee Indian from Oklahoma, was the tail gunner. Peter and Ruben had become almost instant friends back in Walla Walla.

Sergeant Jacob M. Martinez, a good-looking kid, was the ball turret gunner.

Sergeant Jules Beck was the crew's radioman.

Sergeant Paul Spodar, the baby-faced right waist gunner, stood back-to-back with Peter during air combat. Spodar was from Cleveland, and he and Peter had at least two things in common. Spodar also had a vision problem (a weakness in his left eye), and like Peter his father had immigrated to America from the Ukraine. The two waist gunners were friendly, but during off-duty time Peter tended to hang out with Ruben, while Spodar was close to Beck.

Peter had complete confidence in each of his crewmates, but after what he had seen on the first two missions, he did not expect their luck could hold up.

Kauffman and Molnar were discussing the evacuation procedure in case of a ditching. Both the pilot and copilot were supposed to leave the aircraft through the cockpit's sliding side windows. Neither man was sure that could actually be accomplished in an emergency. Some of the other crewmen expressed their opinions on the best way to quickly get out of a B-17. There seemed to be some confusion on the subject.

"We've got the time, Junior. Why don't we walk through the evac drill now?" Peter suggested. Kauffman thought it was a good idea. The crew climbed aboard their bomber and each man found his station. Kauffman read the procedure from his manual, and on his signal each crew member went to his assigned escape location. Since a crash landing and a water ditching required different escape routes, the pilot made sure each man knew where to go in either situation before he ended the drill.

Peter did a last-minute check of his machine gun. He was glad he had suggested the escape drill, but he thought it was unlikely they would ever use it. He guessed they were much more likely to be blown out of the sky by flak or an ME-109 fighter. A few minutes later, *Ruthless* roared down the runway and climbed into a cloudy sky on what would be her last mission.

The objective that day was an attack on Frankfurt, Germany. To Peter it seemed pretty much like his first two missions. The gunners were kept busy fending off enemy fighters on the way to the target. Kauffman dodged Frankfurt's plentiful flak to drop his bombs, and then he turned *Ruthless* toward home. The German fighters hit the group again on the return trip, but *Ruthless* rumbled along seemingly untouched.

The first Peter knew of trouble was when Kauffman informed the crew over the interphone: "Boys, we're going to have to lighten the aircraft. We are very low on fuel." Peter was surprised when he heard the pilot's announcement, and he looked at Spodar. The other waist gunner shook his head with a frown. He had witnessed a scene before takeoff that now seemed very important. The ground crew apparently had been given a directive on rationing each bomber's fuel supply for the mission. Spodar had been nearby when Kauffman had become engaged in a heated argument with a staff officer over the subject. The pilot made it clear that he felt they were cutting it too close on fuel, but the other officer would not relent.

Perhaps on a better day, the fuel allotted would have been sufficient, but many unforeseen factors could come into play on any given mission. Wind currents could be more severe. Getting into formation could take a little longer. Flying a "tail-end Charlie" position or a poor running engine could eat up additional fuel. Whatever the reason, *Ruthless* was almost dry.

Peter and Spodar wasted no time discussing the whys of their predicament. They began tossing anything loose and not absolutely essential out the side windows. When the crew had disposed of almost everything they could think of, Peter asked the pilot, "Junior, what about the guns?"

A few seconds of silence elapsed before Kauffman's voice came back over the interphone.

"Dump the guns, too!"

Peter reluctantly disengaged the .50 caliber and shoved it out the left window. Spodar, behind him, did the same. Then out went the remaining ammo, which was now useless to them. *Ruthless* was now flying over Belgium, defended only by her nose, tail and ball turret guns. If a German fighter came at them from above or either side, the bomber would be a sitting duck.

Kauffman took *Ruthless* down until she was flying just above the treetops. Peter watched farms and small Belgian villages pass underneath and wondered how much farther it was to the coast. Then pastures and forests gave way to marshy grasslands and rocky coves—and finally, whitecapped waves rippled below the bomber.

Now the lone B-17 would be under the wings of American or British fighters, in theory anyway. Peter kept a watch for "little friends," and sure enough an RAF Spitfire soon pulled up just off the bomber's left wing. Spodar tapped him on the shoulder and pointed to a second Spitfire to their right.

The crew waited for an update on their situation from their pilot. Could they make it back to Grafton Underwood or at least to a coastal RAF base? Kauffman's answer to his crew's unspoken question was direct, and it was also an order.

"All right, boys, prepare to ditch! Everyone to his assigned place. Prepare to ditch!"

Peter and Spodar helped Martinez out of his ball turret. Ruben joined them from his tail gun position and then the four gunners headed forward to the radio room. Jarrell and Beck were already there, preparing to go out the ceiling hatch once Kauffman put the airplane down in the North Sea. Lecroix and Pogorzelski arrived from the nose compartment.

The pilot gave them a quick "Get ready!" over the interphone just seconds before *Ruthless* touched the water. The B-17's tail hit first; then seawater came pouring into the plane before she stopped her forward motion. The aircraft's fuselage had cracked at a point right behind the radio room. Peter could see that everyone in the radio room had survived the jarring landing, but he was not sure eight men could climb out the overhead hatch before the airplane sank. The cold seawater was already swirling around his knees.

Someone pulled the lever to release the bomber's life rafts. The first two men out were responsible for getting the rafts into position. The third man out was to stay near the hatch to give a hand to the men still in the radio room.

As Pogorzelski attempted to exit, he slipped and with his right hand grabbed the first thing he could find to keep from falling back into the radio room. What the navigator's hand found was Paul Spodar's head—the right waist gunner was pushed beneath the rising water. Spodar popped back up only to have the navigator slip and grab his head a second time. Spodar had had enough.

"Lieutenant, would you please get out of the airplane or get out of the way?"

Peter knew it was taking too much time. Weighted down by their heavy flight jackets, boots and Mae West life preservers, the men moved in what seemed to be slow motion. Finally, there was only one man left in the almost submerged radio room— Peter Seniawsky. The water was lapping at his chin as Peter began to pull himself up. He managed to get his elbows over the rim of the hatch but the weight of his flight gear was pulling him down. Someone reached out a hand, and Peter summoned all his strength to climb to the top of the aircraft.

He could see the yellow life rafts rising and falling in the waves near the bomber's tail section. Peter walked along the dorsal fin until he reached the tail and then he climbed onto the rear stabilizer. Jules Beck was already there, but he was making no effort to lower himself into the sea.

Peter went in feetfirst and swam toward one of the rafts. The boys had done their jobs well, inflating both life rafts and tethering them to each other and to the airplane, but for some reason the rafts had not completely inflated. It was no easy thing to climb on board, but by helping each other, soon nine of the ten-man crew were in the rafts.

Jules Beck was still standing on the stabilizer of the quickly sinking bomber. The men in the rafts were shouting for Beck to,

"Dive in!" The radioman replied that his Mae West was only half inflated and explained, "I can't swim!"

"Tough shit!" someone yelled. "You're gonna drown if you don't."

Beck went into the cold salt water, and his friends pulled him on board a raft. Kauffman took a head count and found nobody missing. Peter scanned the faces of the men in his raft. There were no signs of relief after their narrow escape, only expressions of fear. He knew the same expression was on his face, too.

Someone cut the tether line connecting the rafts and the bomber. About four minutes after she had hit the water, the B-17 *Ruthless* disappeared beneath the waves of the North Sea. A crewman began to crank the Gibson Girl signal unit. One of the Spitfires dove down close to the surface and dropped signal flares into the water. The two British fighters made one more low pass, waved their wings and then disappeared in the direction of England.

There was nothing the cold, wet airmen could do but to pray and wait. They had no food and worse, no fresh water. Peter watched the sun descending in the west. *Only a few hours of daylight left.* After dark they would be difficult to spot—just two yellow specks on a big dark blue canvas. He checked his watch. Two hours had passed. It seemed like a day.

Help showed up about two hours later in the form of the British patrol boat *Lord Keith*. It was close to darkness when the last American airman was pulled from his raft. The English sailors provided Peter and his crewmates with blankets, food and plenty of excellent rum. Once ashore, the airmen were taken to a nearby British air station where they received a warm welcome and dry RAF uniforms. After a hearty breakfast the following morning, Kauffman's crew climbed aboard a truck and headed back to Grafton Underwood. On the ride to their base, Paul Spodar expressed the entire crew's gratitude to their pilot with a left-handed compliment: "You know, Junior, you've made some bumpy landings and that one was the bumpiest . . . , but it's the best damned landing you ever made." A couple of days later, each of the *Ruthless* survivors was granted a three-day pass to London.

Peter returned from London on the evening of October 9. He was awakened early the next day with the news of a mission to Münster, Germany. If any of the crew had butterflies about flying again, it was well hidden and soon they were in the air, all too busy to worry. The Luftwaffe put up a stiff defense to protect Münster, an important German railroad hub.

Kauffman's gunners blazed away and shouted the location of enemy fighters over the interphone. With three missions behind him, Peter felt he could bring down one of the German planes. When an attacking Me-109 stayed a little too close for a little too long, the left waist gunner watched as his machine gun's bullets found their target.

Peter could clearly see the .50 caliber rounds ripping into the enemy plane, and he kept firing until black smoke billowed through the air. The German fighter rolled over and spiraled toward the earth. Peter watched the burning plane fall until another enemy fighter flew by—that snapped the young waist gunner back into the fight. Münster was a tough run. Lots of fighters and lots of flak, but when Kauffman landed his B-17 back at Grafton Underwood, his crew agreed it was not nearly as rough as going into the North Sea.

For his action on the Münster mission, Peter was given an official kill for the Me-109 fighter he had shot down. He was also credited with the probable kill of another enemy fighter. Many gunners would go their entire tour of duty without an official kill. The boy from Brooklyn had shot down one, perhaps two German airplanes and survived a B-17 ditching in just four missions. Still, if Peter considered himself lucky, it was only "lucky so far." He always assumed that the next mission would be the worst, and on October 14, 1943, he was right.

The first indication that something out of the ordinary was brewing came early on that morning at the mess hall.

"How do you like your bacon?" the mess worker asked as he dumped a large helping of fresh scrambled eggs on Peter's plate. *Bacon? Fresh eggs?* Something was up. The crews finished their breakfast in time for the seven o'clock briefing, where they were given the bad news.

"The target for today is Schweinfurt," the briefing officer said calmly. The uproar among the bomber crews took Peter by surprise. There was moaning, yelling and cursing. What was so bad about Schweinfurt? The Germans had thrown everything at them over Münster—could Schweinfurt be worse? Peter got his explanation from a veteran member of the 384th after the briefing.

The airman explained that the Eighth Air Force had flown a dual mission to Schweinfurt and Regensburg back in August. The Regensburg formation had lost twenty-four bombers, and thirty-six more had gone down on the Schweinfurt run. A total of sixty American bombers and six hundred airmen gone in one day.

Schweinfurt was deadly for two reasons. It was deep inside Germany, requiring the attacking bombers to fly a long route directly over or in the vicinity of numerous German airfields. Hundreds of enemy fighters would be within striking distance. The second reason Schweinfurt was such a tough target was the same reason the Americans were determined to bomb it— the German city was home to three ball-bearing factories.

Ball bearings were essential to the production of Germany's aircraft, weapons and transportation equipment. To destroy these factories was to severely injure the German military's ability to wage an offensive war and defend the fatherland. Schweinfurt would be fortified with every antiaircraft gun and fighter the Luftwaffe could muster.

Peter had already written four letters home. One was to Helen, and the other three were addressed to his sisters. Regulations forbade any airman from writing any information about a particular mission. Peter would not have done so anyway. Why worry Helen and his family any more than they were already? As always, he mentioned mostly things about life on the base and the personality traits of his crewmates. Before departing for Schweinfurt, he gave the letters to a friend on the ground crew to mail. A Catholic priest was on hand to give absolution to anyone who sought it. There were quite a few takers.

Kauffman's crew climbed aboard a gleaming B-17 with the serial number 42-29870. (It was listed by the last three digits on the squadron formation plan.) There was one change in the crew for the Schweinfurt mission. The crew's regular bombardier, Lecroix, was on the sick list. Sergeant David Dannerman, a toggler, would be Lecroix's replacement.

At more than twenty-six thousand feet up, the temperature was at least thirty below zero, but Peter found he was perspiring so much that his oxygen mask was repeatedly slipping down his face. He was nervous and on edge—they all were. Waiting for the enemy fighters to appear was as bad as the combat. Then the wait was over.

From his left waist position, Peter could see almost half of the 384th Bomb Group B-17s and even some of the forward and rear groups. It was the forward groups that the German fighters struck first, flying head-on through the bomber formation in waves.

Peter watched as one American bomber after another began to roll over and go down. He wiped the condensation from his glasses and tried to count parachutes coming from the dying Fortresses. Sometimes he saw a few—sometimes he saw none. The worst feeling was to see a B-17 just disintegrate into a tomb of boiling fire and black smoke, knowing that the men inside had ceased to exist in the time it took to snap your fingers.

"They're shooting rockets at us!" It was the voice of Stanley Ruben, the tail gunner. Peter could see the source of the rocket attack. Twin-engine Messerschmitt 110s were flying well out of range of the bomber gunners, lobbing in their rockets. In frustration he swung the .50 caliber waist gun around, looking for something to shoot at. Two Me-109s came in, their machine guns and cannons firing. Peter squeezed the triggers, and his mind went blank as he became lost in the life-and-death struggle of air combat.

The American bomber force that crossed the border into Germany on that Thursday morning numbered 257 aircraft. The Luftwaffe attacked with more than four hundred fighters. Many of the enemy fighters flew initial assaults on the B-17s, then landed to refuel and hit the bomber formation again. Even this all-out effort could not stop the B-17 formation from reaching Schweinfurt, but the price paid was high. Twenty-eight bombers were shot from the sky without ever reaching their target.

During the American Civil War, one of the early battles that shocked the world was fought near the small Shiloh church in western Tennessee. More than thirty-four hundred men died during the Battle of Shiloh. Nowhere on the killing field had the fighting been more intense than around a small briar thicket held by Union soldiers. Time and time again, the Confederates charged the thicket only to be repulsed by a shower of lead.

One young rebel staggered back into his lines and exclaimed, "It's like a hornet's nest in there!"

The Confederates finally captured the Union thicket, but Southern dead carpeted the ground around it. The Hornet's Nest came to symbolize the sacrifice and brutality of war. For the American bomber crews, Thursday, October 14, 1943, was beginning to resemble a Hornet's Nest.

There was no escape from the enemy fighters. Like hornets, they were everywhere—above, below, in front, behind, on the sides and in the middle of the bombers. Even when the B-17s reached the outskirts of Schweinfurt and began to enter the heavy flak area, some of the German fighters boldly followed them.

Giles Kauffman was one of the pilots who was able to get his aircraft over Schweinfurt and drop his bombs on the target. It was no small accomplishment, since the flak over the city was the thickest he had ever seen. Some of the flak bursts came very close to his aircraft. None of the crew reported damage, but the number one engine was acting up as he banked his Fortress and headed for England.

At his waist window, Peter spotted a small stream of smoke trailing the outside engine on the left wing. He also felt something thick and wet running down his left cheek and an uncomfortable stinging sensation from his ear. When he checked the area with his hand, the fingers of his glove came back bloody. He concluded if he was still alert and standing then it was not a serious wound. Probably a nick, likely from the same explosion that had damaged the number one engine, which was now emptying a much larger amount of black smoke into the sky.

That one is finished, Peter thought.

On the other side of the airplane, Spodar was having his own problems. His machine gun was jammed and despite his best efforts, it would not function. Luckily, there was a short period of relief from attack as the bomber completed its turn and struggled to maintain formation altitude.

The German fighters were concentrating their attacks on the

loaded incoming bombers. It would not be long, though, before refueled Luftwaffe planes would be coming up to attack the homeward-bound B-17s. Spodar decided if he could not function as a gunner anymore, at least he could make sure everyone else had plenty of ammunition. He keyed his interphone mike as he tapped Peter on the shoulder.

"Pete, I'm going to get some more ammo." Then Spodar headed for the radio room.

We're going to need it all, Peter thought. *With just three engines, we'll end up on our own, and those Luftwaffe fighters are going to be all over us.*

Spodar had just disappeared when Stanley Ruben's voice came over the interphone. "Hey, guys, I'm out of ammo back here!" Peter glanced down at his feet—there was one full box of ammunition left.

"Hang on, Stan, I'll get you some," Peter assured the tail gunner.

He pulled off his headset and disconnected from the main oxygen supply. After he hooked up to a walk-around bottle of oxygen, Peter carried the heavy ammunition box to the back of the bomber. When he reached the tail section where the low ceiling would not allow him to stand, he got down on his hands and knees and pushed the ammo rearward. Burdened with dragging along the oxygen bottle, it was an awkward process. Peter had finally managed to get the box into the entrance of the tail gunner's area, when he met Ruben crawling out.

Peter pointed to the ammo box and motioned for his friend to go back, but Ruben shook his head and pointed toward the front. Without his interphone, Peter was deaf to what was happening. Something was up, and once he backed out of the tail section it was easy to figure out what it was.

Martinez was out of his ball turret, and he worked on opening the escape door behind the right waist gun position. Through his left waist window, Peter could see most of the bomber formation above them. Kauffman's B-17 was losing altitude rapidly and now two engines were trailing black smoke.

Peter grabbed his Air Force–issue shoes hanging nearby and attached them to his parachute harness. Flight boots did a nice job of keeping an airman's feet from freezing at high altitudes, but they would not be worth a damn if he had to walk, or if necessary, run.

Spodar and Beck showed up from the radio room. Like Peter, Spodar had been unaware they had been ordered to bail out until he walked into the radio room and saw Beck putting on his parachute.

As the five airmen huddled around the escape door, it somehow opened up before the hinge pin was completely removed. The outside air currents jerked the door rearward and Martinez's parachute harness became caught. The ball turret gunner was half in and half out of the airplane, with the wind pinning him against the door. If they could not get the hinge pin loose and release the escape door, each of them was going to have the same difficulty that Martinez was encountering.

Suddenly Martinez was gone. Two seconds later, Ruben gave the release pin a powerful kick—the pin popped out and the escape door fell away. Peter never saw it happen. He had been helping Ruben, trying to release the door when everything went blank. The walk-around oxygen bottle had reached empty several minutes before, but in the excitement Peter had not even noticed. Ruben bailed out and Peter, right behind him, fell out of the bomber—his crewmates never even realizing the left waist gunner was totally unconscious.

At twenty-six thousand feet, a temperature of minus thirty degrees could be an airman's friend, especially if the shock of cold air awakened him from a deadly free fall. Peter did not know up from down when he came to. He was tumbling through the air end over end. He pulled the ripcord, and for a second or two nothing seemed to happen. The jolt that followed almost pulled the breath out of him.

There was no way to judge how far he had fallen before his chute finally opened, but looking up Peter spotted three tiny parachutes. He assumed the others pulled their ripcords right away. He, on the other hand, had dropped like a rock—apparently for several thousand feet.

Drifting down over Germany, Peter knew he was lucky to be alive. One mistake and that could change. He tried to analyze his angle and rate of descent and to picture in his mind where he might land. It was a guessing game, but the wind seemed to be taking him directly over a small village. The stories he had heard of German civilians assaulting and sometimes killing downed Allied airmen made the thought of landing in the village extremely unappealing.

During his last couple of minutes in the air, Peter was relieved to find the air currents were carrying his chute past the village and over what appeared to be an area of small farms. In his first and only parachute jump, he made a rough but safe landing in a large, freshly plowed field.

While he was gathering his chute to his chest, Peter took a quick look around. There was nobody, neither civilian nor military in sight. He was certain that would change quickly enough. Where could he hide?

A small gully close by seemed to be his only immediate option. When he scrambled over its edge, he tumbled into a shallow stream. He pushed his chute into the water, weighed it down with several rocks and then climbed back up the stream bank, being careful not to expose himself. He spotted someone immediately.

The man was armed with a shotgun and from his clothing, Peter surmised he was probably a farmer. Very likely, he owned the field Peter was hiding in. Farmer or not, if the man continued walking in his direction, Peter decided he would have little choice but to kill him. He reached down to his side for his .45 automatic pistol and found it was not there. No pistol and no holster. Peter silently cursed himself for his thoughtlessness in leaving his sidearm on his bunk that morning. *What now?* The man continued walking in Peter's direction, finally stopping no more than fifty feet away.

A noise had caused him to stop—the sound of a small machine gun. It was just a short burst, but when Peter looked to the east, he spotted four German soldiers emerging from the woods. They were close to a hundred yards away, and they began yelling to the farmer in German. He responded, waving his arms and yelling back to them. Of course, Peter could not understand any of it but he was certain his whereabouts were the main subject of the conversation. If any of them reached the edge of the gully and looked down the streambed, they could not help but spot the American flyer.

Surrender became a possible solution in Peter's mind, but he quickly shoved it aside as a last-resort alternative. He could not discount being shot by the German soldiers or even the farmer if he tried to surrender. Even if he was not shot, spending months and perhaps years in a prisoner of war camp seemed only a slightly better fate. The airman took a deep breath and tried to keep his head so he would be ready for his chance if it came.

When the man with the shotgun began walking to meet the German soldiers, Peter knew he had to take a risk. On the other bank of the stream was a lone but rather large tree. It was the only cover in the field other than the gully. Peter slipped across the stream, climbed up the opposite bank and, hugging the ground as close as possible, he slowly crawled behind the tree.

Sitting with his back pressed against the trunk and his knees up against his chest, Peter stayed motionless when the farmer returned to the area, now accompanied by the soldiers. He could tell from their voices and movements that the Germans were checking the streambed. He prayed his parachute remained wedged beneath the rocks.

The Germans stayed close by for several minutes, and when they moved to the north, Peter quietly slipped around the tree to the south. If they had spread out or even crossed the stream, his location would have been discovered. Luckily his pursuers went off in another direction. Peter remained frozen in position, his back to the tree. The searchers came back one more time before deciding the American must by then be far away. Dusk was beginning to fall when they left for good.

Peter had not been idle while he was clinging to the big tree. He had used the time to decide on his route of escape. When it was dark enough, he crawled on his stomach for almost a hundred yards to the protection of some woods to the west—the exact opposite side of the field from where the German soldiers had disappeared.

Peter stayed in the small woods until it was completely dark, and then he walked until he came to a road. It seemed to run north and south. Not knowing where either direction led, the downed airman headed north on a whim. He still held on to the diminishing hope of finding one or more of his crewmates but realized now it would be a miracle. If any of the others had managed to avoid capture, with the coming darkness they would be on the move trying to get as far away as possible. The truth was, as Peter Seniawsky walked along the German road that night, he was the only member of his crew who was still free.

The nine other men of Giles Kauffman's crew, including the

pilot himself, had been captured within minutes of their parachute landings. Paul Spodar was almost glad to see the German
soldier who showed up to take him prisoner. On the way down,
Spodar had barely avoided being killed by a civilian who
took several rifle shots at him. The right waist gunner was sure
he would not have been given the chance to surrender had that
civilian been the first to reach him.

Spodar was taken to a farm shack and locked in. About fif-
teen minutes later, another prisoner was shoved into the shack.
It was Stanley Ruben. The tail gunner produced a couple of
Camel cigarettes, and they smoked to celebrate being alive.

William Jarrell got out of his parachute harness quickly after
landing and tried to make it to the cover of nearby woods. A
German soldier's bullet brought him down on the run. Jarrell
felt his left leg collapse and watched his chance for escape disappear. The wound in his thigh would make the long walk to
prison camp even more miserable.

Giles Kauffman landed and immediately reached for his .45
automatic. Several German soldiers were running toward him as
he pulled the pistol from its holster. The pilot knew there were
too many. He might have been able to shoot one, perhaps two
of them before the others shot him down. He let the .45 fall to
the ground and slowly raised his hands above his head.

As the sun set on Thursday, October 14, 1943, the Germans
were rounding up hundreds of downed American airmen from
Schweinfurt to France. Only a handful avoided capture on that
Black Thursday to stay free for even one more day.

The temperature was falling quickly, and Peter was more occupied with keeping warm than concentrating on where he was
going. He had left his heavy flight jacket hidden in the woods. Its
loss was regrettable but necessary. If anyone spotted him wearing
that jacket, it would be a dead giveaway to his occupation.

Pulling his Army issue sweater up over his ears and head gave

Peter a little relief from the cold as he trudged along in the darkness. Without even noticing, he walked right up on a German
antiaircraft installation. He could see enemy soldiers behind a
camouflaged fence, perhaps some of the same soldiers who had
earlier searched the farmer's field for him. Peter carefully turned
and walked back in the direction he had come, praying that he
had not been spotted. With each step, he expected to hear a German voice commanding him to stop, or worse, the sound of a
rifle firing.

When no soldiers followed him, he just kept walking. In
about an hour he spotted something shining through the trees.
Leaving the road to investigate, he discovered the source was
moonlight reflecting off a large river. *It must be the Rhine,* he
thought. The wide river was beautiful under the moon's glow,
and it was possibly disaster for him. If he had landed on the
eastern side of the Rhine, he was as good as done.

Dejected, the young American airman sat down and opened
the small escape kit that the Army Air Force had provided. He
had to take stock of his situation, evaluate it and work out a
plan for survival. Before any of that could be accomplished, he
had to stop his mind from racing. Clear, logical thought was
what was needed now. Carefully, he placed each item of the escape kit on the ground in front of him.

There were only a few items he felt would be useful. Peter
picked up the small compass. Three greenish dots glowed in the
moonlight. Two of the dots at the end of the compass needle indicated north. The single dot at the other end of the needle stood
for south. He tucked the compass into his pants pocket, aware
that nothing in the escape kit was more valuable to him.

Next, he unfolded a silk handkerchief. On one side was a
map of Germany, and on the opposite side was a map of France.
Major cities, towns and larger roads were included on the maps.

Missing were numbers for the roads. Peter failed to notice this omission, but later it would cause him to curse the men who designed the escape maps.

There was a photo of Peter in civilian clothing—white shirt, tie and an ill-fitting jacket. Soon after he had sat for the photo session, someone had explained that the "escape photo" was useless. It was meant to help convince any enemy authority who might conduct a personal search that a downed American aviator was simply a harmless civilian. The Germans had taken so many of the pictures off captured American airmen that they could guess the number of the bomber group just from looking at the clothing in the escape photo. Peter tucked it back into the kit.

When he found a chocolate candy bar among the kit's contents, he was tempted to eat it right then. Instead, he broke off a small section to nibble on and put the remainder in his shirt pocket for later. He had no way of knowing how long it would be before he could find any other food.

As for the rest of the things in the escape kit, only five French notes struck Peter as being of any eventual use to him. Each note was one hundred francs. *So that's it,* he thought, *a compass, a map, some French money and a candy bar.* Then he remembered the hunting knife that he always carried in a scabbard on his belt. Still, it was not much. He could speak neither German nor French, and he was wearing olive drab clothing that could hardly be mistaken for anything but a military uniform.

Little could be done about his language limitations. Perhaps he would pick up a few necessary words if he avoided capture long enough, but in order to do that, he would have to find some civilian clothing as soon as possible. Until then, he would travel by night, and hide and sleep in the daytime. His first objective had to be getting out of Germany. France was somewhere to the west. If he traveled the roads leading southwest or northwest but always in that general direction, he had to come to France eventually—that is, if the river did not block his way, if he were not spotted by a German civilian or picked up by a military patrol.

When and if he reached France, what then? From Air Force briefings, Peter knew the northern two-thirds of the country was occupied by the Germans, and the lower third was under the rule of the Vichy government, which had a policy of total collaboration with the Germans. His only hope would be to connect with a member of the French resistance. How he could accomplish this, he had no idea, but that was not his problem at the moment. Reaching France was what mattered first. Peter stuffed the escape kit into his back pocket and checked his compass. He walked for the rest of the night, always heading west.

As Peter Seniawsky stumbled along a lonely German road on the evening of October 14, the survivors of the Schweinfurt raid were relating the gory details of the day's combat and praying their missing comrades would somehow miraculously return. As the reports from the various American bases in England began to be compiled and evaluated, the full cost of the great air battle became clear.

That morning, 291 B-17s had departed for Schweinfurt. Mechanical, engine and formation problems had reduced the American bomber force to 257 aircraft by the time the formation had crossed into German territory. Messerschmitt and Focke-Wulf fighters along with twin-engine rocket planes had swarmed the Flying Fortresses, knocking twenty-eight of them from the sky before they could reach Schweinfurt.

Intense flak over the target and almost constant enemy fighter attacks on the return trip had destroyed another thirty-two B-17s. Sixty American bombers were lost! Another five bombers

crashed after making it back to English airspace. Of the returning Fortresses, 138 suffered some kind of battle damage, and
seven of those would never fly again. Some of the aircraft that
made it back carried dead or severely wounded airmen.*

There were 594 American airmen missing in action. When
the surviving crews began to relive the mission during their in-
terrogations, it became apparent that many of the missing were
most likely dead. Too many explosions and burning bombers,
and not enough parachutes spotted. Friends were gone, many
forever.

The target, the three ball bearing plants in Schweinfurt, had
indeed been hit and badly damaged. Albert Speer, Hitler's
Minister of Armaments and War Production, estimated that 67
percent of German ball bearing production had been lost as a
result of the Schweinfurt raid. Speer and the surviving Schweinfurt factory workers braced for the follow-up American raid
that would bring the German ball bearing industry and perhaps
its military mobility to a halt. But the shaken American Eighth
Air Force could not follow up. American newspapers were soon
telling the story of the second air raid on Schweinfurt, a city that
had spelled disaster to more than one hundred twenty B-17
crews in just two months.

The American bomber airmen in England would gladly wait
until the new P-51 long-range escort fighters arrived before re-
suming their missions deep into Germany. In the meantime,
fathers, mothers, families and fiancées waited anxiously for
some word from their dear airmen. A letter saying, "I'm alive
and okay," was an answered prayer. Helen had managed to land
a job with the telephone company, where war news and gossip
was always plentiful and often unreliable. She heard the rumors
of the great losses the American Air Force had suffered at a

---

* Aircraft loss numbers were taken from *Flying Forts: The B-17 in World War II*, by Martin
Caidin, and a copy of the official report on losses, provided by Peter Scott.

place named Schweinfurt and tried to tell herself that the numbers were too outlandish to be true. Soon she was reading the front-page newspaper headlines that confirmed what would be called Black Thursday.

Had Peter been on the raid? Had he survived? Helen waited for word from England. A V-letter (censored photocopy) arrived in the last week of October. It was from Peter. Tears of joy began to slip down her cheeks. Then she noticed the date on the letter—October 14, 1943. She guessed Peter had written the letter just before takeoff to Schweinfurt.

Helen touched a fingertip to the "I love you" at the bottom of the page and whispered a prayer. A few days later, on October 28, as her family gathered to celebrate her father's birthday, the bad news arrived. Peter's sister Margie had received a notice from the War Department. Peter was "missing in action."

The sun rose behind Peter on the morning of October 15, casting a soft orange hue across the roofs of the little German village. He had walked through the night and was not sure where he was, but he was at least confident that he was far from where his bomber had gone down. His encounter with the Rhine had not proven insurmountable. What he had seen was merely a bend in the majestic river. Luckily he had landed on the western side of the Rhine.

A few vehicles had passed along the road during the night, forcing him to scurry into the woods. Thankfully none of the cars and trucks had borne any military markings.

The village, a half mile ahead of him, was comprised of a dozen or so houses, all clustered close together on either side of the road. Pastureland covered the remainder of the immediate area. Peter was still damp and almost completely exhausted. Sticking to his plan, he looked around for someplace to hide where he could sleep through the day. A comfortable-looking haystack in an adjacent field seemed perfect. He could get out of his damp clothes and let the sun dry them while he slept.

The side of the haystack opposite from the village would be best, Peter decided. He soon discovered that although the haystack was soft and dry on the outside, it was wet and firmly packed underneath. Simply sleeping on top of the hay risked a visibility he could not afford. He had no choice but to burrow into the damp hay and cover himself as best he could. He ate a meal of another small piece of the chocolate bar and a condensed-milk cube that he had discovered in the escape kit, and then the weary airman tried to get some sleep.

As tired as he was, sleep came only in short intervals that day. Still in his wet clothes, he was cold and miserable. As dusk began to fall, Peter spread his handkerchief map out and tried to figure out where he might be. It was a hopeless effort. Without numbers for the routes, the road signs he had encountered meant nothing. *Keep heading west,* he thought, as he crammed the handkerchief back into his pants pocket and climbed out of the haystack.

His second night in Germany was much like his first. Peter walked all night. At least his clothes were mostly dry now. The weather was chilly again. During the night he came upon another small village, similar to the first. Taking to the fields, he walked around the village, rejoining the road on the other side.

Early the next morning Peter began to scout the fields for another haystack. None was to be found, but he did spot a small clump of trees in the middle of a field. Peter guessed he could sleep the day away there without being discovered. He was mistaken.

That afternoon two men walked into the woods. Peter got to his feet and sized up the strangers. They looked to be farmers. Neither of them spoke or made an aggressive movement even though they saw him. Peter used his right arm to shield his hunting knife from their view and with his left hand he made a circular movement over his stomach.

"*Glodny*," he said, using the Polish word for *hungry*. Peter remembered a little of the language he had learned at his Ukrainian grandmother's knee.

There was no response. The men looked at one another, then walked away without ever saying a word. Peter watched them leave and resigned himself to capture. German farmers would certainly report such a discovery to the military. He was too exhausted to run, and he would not get far in the daytime wearing his uniform. He sat down and waited.

Half an hour later, Peter spotted two men approaching his clump of trees. It was the same two villagers. They walked up to him, handed him a small flask and walked away, again without speaking. Peter unscrewed the flask's cap and smelled the contents. It was a sweet alcohol aroma. A short sip revealed it was a rich, smooth whiskey. He wondered about the two men and finally came to the conclusion that they were Polish forced-labor workers. He nursed the whiskey through the rest of the day, napping between drinks.

By his third night in Germany, Peter was having severe hunger pains. He consumed the rest of the chocolate bar as he walked, but when it was gone he felt no relief. Foraging in a farmer's field, he dug up what appeared to be some kind of turnip. As hungry as he was, Peter could not stand its bitter taste and had to spit it out. Back on the road, he continued west.

On night number four the young airman's pace slowed as both hunger and thirst began to take their toll. When he came upon a creek, Peter decided to risk getting sick. He just could not go on without water. Filling a rubber pouch from the escape kit, he dropped in a purification tablet and took a deep drink. The water's taste was awful and he could not keep it down. Several minutes of heaving left him even weaker. Vowing not to try that again, he made up his mind to find some fresh water, even if he had to risk being seen. His opportunity came later that evening.

Railroad tracks crossed the road, their twin ribbons glowing beneath a bright moon. Peter checked his compass. The tracks ran to the southwest. Up ahead, beyond the tracks, was a crossroads with a single house. A little light was coming from downstairs. He could follow the railroad tracks and avoid the house, but that would not satisfy his thirst. So he kept walking toward the crossroads.

In front of the house there was a hand-cranked water pump. Peter could not resist it. As carefully as he could, he brought the pump handle up and then down. A rusty squeal broke the quietness of the night. He knew it would take two or three pumps of the handle before any water would flow, so he tried again. Again the pump refused to be quiet but a small trickle of water appeared.

Peter was just getting set to give the handle a third try, the one he was sure would send water gushing out of the pipe, when the front door of the house swung open. Light silhouetted a figure in the doorway. It was a woman. She was wearing a military overseas cap. Peter could see its German eagle emblem clearly in the moonlight. She said something to him in German.

"*Woda,*" Peter replied in Polish.

She did not answer.

"*Français?*" Peter tried.

Again the woman spoke words in German; then she retreated inside the house, closing the door behind her. Peter abandoned the pump and hurried down the road. The woman was either a member of some kind of military unit or the cap belonged to her husband, brother or some other family member. Peter had no way of knowing if anyone else was in the house. Even if the woman was alone, he had to assume she would be spreading the alarm.

About a mile away from the house, he abandoned the road and cut across a field. He walked until he came to the railroad tracks and followed them southwest. Near daybreak he slipped inside a railroad culvert and was soon asleep.

He was awakened later by the sound of children's voices. It was a pleasant sound. *German or American, the sound of children at play is a sweet thing,* he thought. Peter smiled and began to drift back into sleep. When the children's voices grew closer, he sat up and began to listen intently. These kids were having fun at some sort of game, but there was something else going on. They were searching for something. Teenage male voices shouted above the younger ones. It struck Peter with a chill.

They're looking for me!

For more than an hour, the children searched the surrounding fields and woods, but none of them ever approached the culvert. The young Germans left as they had come, their happy voices trailing into the distance. Peter surmised the woman at the crossroads house had reported their encounter. Luckily there apparently had been no soldiers in the area to search for him. Peter fell back to sleep, grateful he had not seen any enemy soldiers since his narrow escape on the first day. The downed aviator's luck was about to change.

As darkness fell, Peter crawled out of the railroad culvert and resumed his journey west. His hunger and thirst stalked along the tracks with him, and he tried to put them both out of his mind. Focusing on keeping a slow but steady pace helped a little. *Keep moving. Get out of Germany. Get to France.* Still, the question kept intruding on his resolve—*Can I do any of these things if I can't find something to eat?*

Late that evening, the American airman followed the railroad tracks into a darkened train yard. Any hope of finding a boxcar full of rations was quickly dispelled. Peter had walked into the middle of an impressive display of German military hardware. Flatbed cars on each side of him were loaded with deadly cargo—artillery, tanks and other armored vehicles.

Peter's first thought was how he could destroy at least some of the enemy's war materials. What Kauffman and the boys would have given to get this juicy target beneath their aircraft—but what could he do? His only weapon was his hunting knife and he had absolutely no training in espionage. In fact, Eighth Air Force briefings had instructed airmen who found themselves behind enemy lines not to do anything but try to escape. "Do not try any espionage. Do not do anything you are not supposed to do. Avoid capture—that is your job." The instructions had been firm.

Hearing the conversation of guards nearby, Peter realized if he stayed in the train yard too long, he would surely be captured. Such a stockpile of military equipment would require a substantial number of soldiers close by. Reluctantly, he walked quietly out of the train yard. He was far away before the first hints of sunrise.

Before it grew dangerously light, Peter spotted a haystack that he hoped might provide a bed for the day. Once he had climbed to the top, he was happy to discover it was pleasantly soft and dry. He covered himself with loose straw in preparation for much-needed sleep.

Forcing himself to stay awake for a few extra minutes, Peter opened the small black prayer book that he always carried. With a stub of a pencil he made a mark on one of the pages. Altogether there were now six marks, one for each day he had been on the ground in Germany. *Six days,* he thought. *How far have I gone? How much farther to France?* He could not know.

Day six provided Peter the best sleep he had gotten since leaving England. He woke in the late afternoon, still hungry and thirsty but noticeably more rested. His mood was improving. If he was not close to France, he was getting closer each day. Maybe this night he would finally find food. He took out his map and compass to plan the evening's journey.

Perhaps it was the effects of his ordeal—a man could get jittery from not eating for days—or perhaps he just got careless, but Peter let the little compass slip out of his fingers. He grabbed to save it, but the little compass tumbled down into the hay and disappeared. Peter had been scared when he had parachuted into the farmer's field, and as he hid behind the tree, eluding the man with the shotgun and the German soldiers, and during his encounter at the water pump, but the thought of losing the compass brought him to near panic. Without the compass, he could wander the German countryside for days on end. His empty stomach was a reminder that he did not have days to spare.

Praying the compass had not fallen too deeply into the straw, Peter gently began digging. He forced himself to remain calm and go slowly. As he concentrated on retrieving the compass he heard someone speaking German. Looking up, he spotted two German soldiers walking across the field and heading right for his haystack. Peter flattened himself on top of the straw. He thought of pushing himself backward to the opposite side of the haystack but he remembered the compass. Any additional movement could send it farther down into oblivion. Peter lay as still and quiet as he could.

The soldiers continued toward the haystack, but Peter could tell from the manner they carried their rifles, slung casually on their shoulders, that they had not spotted him. Soon they were close enough that he could see their faces. They were young, about his age, he guessed. One took a pack of cigarettes from inside his jacket and offered one to his friend, who produced a book of matches. As they walked the last few feet to the base of the haystack, the two soldiers disappeared from Peter's line of sight. However, he could still hear their conversation, their friendly laughter and he could smell the aroma of their cigarettes.

Many thoughts raced through Peter's head—none of them good. *What if I sneeze? What if the soldiers accidentally set the haystack on fire? What if they hang around until after dark? How will I ever find the compass then?* And in fact, the soldiers were in no hurry to leave. They enjoyed their break for more than an hour. By the time they picked up their rifles and wandered across the field, it was dusk.

Peter watched the two Germans until they were out of sight, and only then did he begin to look for the compass again. It was hopeless. There was just not enough light. Peter decided to wait until nightfall, another half hour or so, before moving on. The moon rose slowly above the horizon, and its soft blue hue fell across the German countryside.

Thinking a short prayer might help a lost soul without a compass find his way, Peter took a few moments before beginning his night's journey. As he finished the prayer, something beneath the straw caught his eye. A soft spot of greenish light beckoned Peter to the place where the compass was resting. A random ray of moonlight had connected with the tiny dot that indicated *south* on the compass dial.

His heart pounding, the young airman carefully retrieved his most important possession and placed it safely inside his pants pocket. Once on the ground, Peter took the compass out again, gave it a glance and once again he headed west.

———

Peter stuck to his established routine and walked all night. Just before sunrise, he began to scout around for a potential hiding place. An old barn near the road seemed to be a good choice. It crossed his mind that he might even find a potato or an ear of feed corn inside, but a search of the barn produced nothing edible. He settled for a soft bed of hay in the loft. He fell asleep, thinking the barn was the best shelter he had yet found, but his rest was interrupted in the early afternoon.

Peter was awakened by the sound of someone climbing up the ladder to the loft. The man who ultimately appeared was the biggest human he had ever seen. The giant held a horse collar in his right hand like it was a weapon.

"American!" Peter blurted out. When the man did not strike him, Peter continued, *"Glodny. Glodny."*

The stranger smiled and spoke to him in Polish. Neither man was a master of the Polish tongue, but they communicated well enough for one to express his situation and for the other to indicate his willingness to help. After a short time, the man left, but he soon returned with an armload of apples. It was the closest thing to a real meal Peter had had in a week. He ate until he was past full.

That evening, the big man returned to guide the American to an undisclosed destination. The stranger led Peter along forest trails, avoiding the main roads. Finally, he indicated that Peter should get down on his hands and knees, and from there on the two continued in that fashion, sometimes dropping to their stomachs. Every once in a while, when voices could be heard nearby, a huge hand would grab the back of Peter's neck and shove him facedown into the ground. After the two men had crawled underneath a barbed-wire fence, the man motioned for Peter to get to his feet.

His guardian angel pointed to a road and gestured in the direction Peter should take. Then he shook Peter's hand, smiled and turned to leave.

"*Nazwa?*" Peter asked.

"Walter," was the answer.

Peter started to ask him for his last name. If he made it back to the States alive, it would be nice to know the name of someone who had risked his life to help. For that very reason, Peter stopped himself. *If I'm captured, it will be better for Walter if I don't know who he is.*

"Thank you, Walter," he said. The big man smiled again and said something in Polish. Peter did not understand, but he took it to mean, "Goodbye" or "Good luck." Then Walter was gone.

Peter walked to the road and started hiking in the direction Walter had advised. In less than a mile, he came upon a road sign. He could not read what it said, but the color and shape were different from the signs he had encountered during the past week. It was at that moment that Peter knew for certain he had reached France.

As he walked deeper into France that night, Peter rethought his plans. He knew he was still in great danger of being captured. This was France, but it was the occupied part of the country. Running into German soldiers was a certainty. If he continued to travel only at night, he would also continue to go hungry, and there would be no opportunity to connect with anyone in the resistance movement. No, he would have to take some chances. Somehow he would get some civilian clothes and try to blend in. He would have to trust someone. It was risky, but it was the only way.

On the following day, the airman had his first encounter with a French civilian. The man was a farmer who came out to work in his field near where Peter had once again found a haystack in which to sleep. Smaller than Peter, the farmer posed little physical threat to him. Still, Peter approached him cautiously.

"*Français?*" Peter asked, trying to appear as nonmenacing as possible.

At first, a frightened expression crossed the farmer's face, but then he answered, "*Oui. Oui.*"

"American aviator," Peter said in English, pointing a finger to his chest.

"Oh yes. *Oui!*" The farmer dropped his rake and threw his arms around Peter.

"*Faim. Faim,*" Peter said, using the French word for *hunger*, one of the few he knew. His new friend motioned for him to follow, and soon the two men were walking through a small village. In his olive drab clothes, the young airman might as well have been carrying a large sign promoting his identity. He was just about to try to communicate his concern when the farmer began to shout enthusiastically, "Hey look, American! American!"

Peter quickly clamped his hand over the farmer's mouth. With no additional incidents, they made it to the man's house, where he fed Peter well and gave him an old suit to wear. It was a faded shade of black and the pants were too short, but Peter accepted it gratefully.

To cover up his army shirt and sweater, Peter ripped the colorful lining from the suit jacket and used it to form a makeshift ascot. The farmer donated a beret that fit nicely. When he resumed his journey, Peter Seniawsky looked very much like a poor French civilian. Now as he walked through the village no one seemed to give him a second look. Peter began to feel a little better about his chances. He reasoned that if a German soldier walked though Times Square in New York City while in civilian clothes, who would know? Nobody, as long as he did not speak.

Back on the road, Peter soon fell in with a talkative Frenchman with a suitcase. Peter responded with nods and an occasional, *"Oui,"* when it seemed appropriate. The man did not seem to mind carrying the conversation once Peter offered to carry the suitcase. Before long, the man had hitched them a ride on a passing truck. It carried them all the way to the city of Nancy.

Peter discovered Nancy was large and beautiful. Planned in the mid-eighteenth century to serve as the capital of the Lorraine region of France, Nancy had grown and prospered along the Meurthe River. As Peter walked through the magnificent Place Stanislas city square, he began to feel a little like a tourist. In fact, the square, with its surrounding ornate gates and fences, had been the destination of thousands of tourists before the war.

Peter's sightseeing was interrupted when the Frenchman pulled the suitcase from his hand. The man waved goodbye and began to walk away. Peter grabbed him and whispered, "American aviator." The Frenchman's eyes grew large with fear, and he broke loose and started to flee. Peter was able to grab him again, and this time he was more demanding: "American aviator . . . hungry!"

Evidently, the man decided there might be more danger in ignoring the desperate American than in risking being caught aiding him. He motioned for Peter to follow. Peter did so without ever letting go of the man's arm. Guiding him to a small café, the Frenchman said a few words to a young waiter and then left quickly. The waiter led his shabbily dressed customer to a table near the back of the restaurant.

As the waiter walked away, a feeling of isolation swept over Peter. He had no way of knowing whom he could trust. The stranger with the suitcase had been very afraid of being around him. Would he contact the German authorities? Even the young waiter might be betraying his identity, because at that very moment, he was talking in hushed tones to three men in their thirties or forties seated at a nearby table.

When the waiter went into the kitchen, the three men approached Peter's table. They were talking in French among themselves as they sat down without an invitation. Soon the waiter was back carrying a large bowl of soup.

"*Merci beaucoup,*" Peter said. He had only taken two or three spoonfuls of soup when his three new companions began to sing a bouncy French song. Peter, more focused on his food than his companions' behavior, continued eating until one of the men poked him in the ribs with an elbow. He nodded toward the front door where two serious-looking strangers had just entered.

It was quite obvious the men were not there to eat. They strolled through the restaurant with a slow and deliberate pace. Despite their civilian clothing, Peter knew they were police of some kind—German Gestapo or French collaborators. Another jab from his companion, and Peter put an arm across the fellow's shoulder and joined loudly in the singing. Of course, not knowing the song or the language, Peter's contribution was more humming than actual singing.

The two detectives paid little attention as they walked past the singers' table and exited the restaurant through a rear door. Peter and his new friends kept up their singing until the policemen were well out of earshot. Peter smiled and shook hands with the men at his table, then quickly returned his attention to the soup.

The American airman assumed someone would eventually ask him to leave the restaurant, but instead the waiter brought more food and indicated for him to stay. He killed the entire afternoon and much of the evening there, relaxing over coffee. When the café closed, the waiter took Peter to a small two-room flat, loaned him a razor and offered his bed to the weary American.

Before falling asleep, Peter tried his best to inquire about the French resistance movement, but the waiter claimed he knew nothing about it. The next morning Peter woke to the sound of church bells ringing all across Nancy. His host shared a sparse breakfast with him, answered Peter's questions about the location of Nancy's train station and then showed him to the door. Thanking the young man, Peter walked out into the warm sunshine of a Sunday morning.

At the train station he found the posted French schedule too confusing to fully comprehend. He was able to conclude that there was a train heading to Dijon early that evening. He would have to find some way of blending into Nancy's Sunday routine until departure time. The sound of another ringing church bell gave Peter an idea.

He went to mass at a beautiful old cathedral. It felt good to be in church, and even better to lose himself in the crowd of worshipers. When the first mass ended, the young airman stayed for a second mass and then a third. It was after one in the afternoon when he walked back onto the street.

Strolling around Nancy, nobody seemed to notice him, and Peter began to enjoy his tour of the old French city. As it happened, he became a little too at home in his new surroundings. Walking past a sign that said FORBODEN, he found himself in a section of the city teeming with German military activity. He left the area quickly, deciding it would be wise to once again try melting into the civilian scene.

As he was walking past a busy bar, he saw his opportunity to not only get off the street, but to quench his thirst too. Inside, he found the saloon's patrons were mostly French civilians, but several German soldiers were enjoying drinks at the bar. A large advertisement sign caught his eye. The sign was an illustration of a cold sudsy glass of beer, with the word **BIÈRE** in bold letters.

Peter walked casually to the bar and told the bartender, *"Bière."* The airman was relieved when the bartender simply nodded and began filling a mug with the cold brew. When the beer was placed in front of him, Peter confidently handed the bartender a one-hundred-franc note. He was not prepared for the man's reaction.

Obviously irritated, the barman began complaining loudly in French. Peter instantly realized he had given the man far too much money, but he was at a loss to respond to the protest. People were beginning to turn their attention his way and worst of all, the German soldiers were taking notice. A young soldier standing to Peter's left gave him a long look, and then glanced at the one-hundred-franc note lying on the bar. Peter felt a chill climb from between his shoulder blades to the back of his neck. Reaching into his pocket, the German retrieved two coins and tossed them onto the bar in front of the still-jabbering bartender.

Peter managed a smile and said, *"Merci beaucoup."* The soldier nodded and turned back to his friends. Under the circumstances, it was the best beer Peter had ever tasted. He drank it slowly and enjoyed his secret. When he was done, he placed the empty mug on the bar and left quietly, with a new sense of confidence. If he could pass as a Frenchman, as he had done this day in Nancy, he might have a chance.

Back on the street, he spotted a line of people waiting to buy tickets in front of a movie theater. When he reached the ticket booth there was no complaint about his one-hundred-franc note. As the blue-tinted images began to flicker on the movie screen, Peter fell fast asleep.

———

The noise of the other movie patrons exiting the theater woke Peter from his nap. It was growing dark as he walked outside and made his way to the train station. The evening train to Dijon would take him southwest. Once he arrived there, he would have to make a decision—head northwest to Paris or go south to Marseilles.

Peter bought his ticket with no problem, found a seat on the train and considered his options. Continuing to Paris was a possibility that greatly intrigued him. When would he ever have another opportunity to visit the City of Light? Also, as large as Paris was, there had to be a large resistance movement there. His chances of making contact and being smuggled back to England could be better there.

On the other hand, he could not rule out the possibility he would never make contact with the French resistance. *What then?* Paris was only a hundred miles or so from the coast, with England just across the channel, but how could he get there on his own?

If instead, he went south through Marseilles and then traveled east to Perpignan, he would be within walking distance of the Spanish border. Spain, though cozy with the German government, was officially a neutral country. The route would be a long one, nearly five hundred miles. But Peter had seen Marseilles listed on the railroad schedule posted in the Nancy train station. He could take the train there, perhaps even as far as Perpignan, saving his energy for the final hike into Spanish territory.

Besides its length, there was one other obstacle on the southern route, and Peter was not sure how daunting it would be. He could not risk a look at his handkerchief map while on the crowded train, but he remembered that the map indicated a line of mountains running along the French and Spanish border. The range was named the Pyrenees. The map provided no information on how high or how rugged these mountains were, but if he chose to head for Spain, there would be no avoiding the Pyrenees.

By the time his train pulled into the Dijon station early the next morning, Peter had made his decision. He would try for Spain. After the rest of the passengers had departed, he sneaked a quick peek at his map. Lyons would be his next destination— Lyons, Avignon, Marseilles and Perpignan, then on foot to Spain. Tucking the map away, the American airman went in search of something to eat, feeling better than ever about his chances now that he had a solid plan.

Peter had no way of knowing that the escape route he had chosen was one of the most traveled escape lines used by the French underground movement. Because of its popularity, it was also one of the most dangerous. The route was inhabited by fearful civilians, French resistance patriots, turncoat collaborators, Vichy spies and German Gestapo agents. From outside appearances, there was often little indication who was who.

There were two types of activity that the French resistance forces engaged in along the Dijon to Marseilles-Perpignan route. One side of the resistance forces concentrated on sabotaging the German army that was occupying their country. The assassination of German officers and the destruction of enemy personnel and equipment became the French saboteurs' primary mission. Supplied with weapons, explosives and training from Britain's Special Operations Executive, these French resistance members were a constant and deadly threat to the German occupation troops.

If caught, the resistance fighters paid the ultimate price, and when they were not caught, often French civilians were made to pay. Frustrated by their inability to stop the assassinations and bombings, the German high command took brutal countermeasures. If a German officer was killed, dozens of local residents could be sentenced to death by firing squad.

The second mission of the French underground forces was to aid Allied airmen who had been shot down and the few soldiers who had escaped from German imprisonment. The escape-line resistance fighters also received training and aid from a British intelligence organization named MI9. The risks taken and the secrecy surrounding this side of the French resistance was perhaps even greater than those involving the saboteurs.

In many instances, the various underground agents who escorted the "evaders" along the escape lines did not even know each other. They might drop off an airman at a café, where he would be picked up by a different agent for the next leg of his journey. In this manner, if one agent was captured and tortured, he could not betray anyone beyond his own cell.

The Germans made great efforts to infiltrate the escape-line organizations, and when they were successful, the French resistance members were often never heard from again. During the war, hundreds of these patriots would give their lives while helping thousands of Allied airmen and soldiers make it back to safety in England.

Most Frenchmen were not part of the resistance movement, nor were they Vichy collaborators. They were simply trying to survive the war. With the threat of removal to a concentration camp or even death for himself and possibly his entire family, the average French citizen's emotions ranged from nervousness to outright terror. Peter had seen it in the eyes of the man with the suitcase. He would see it again.

Peter had observed that in order to buy almost any kind of food in France, one needed a government coupon. One of the few exceptions to the rule seemed to be simple bouillon soup, so that is what he ordered in a Dijon restaurant. Afterward, he strolled through the narrow streets of old Dijon's outdoor markets and managed to swipe an apple. As hungry as he was, he did not dare to take more.

Dijon was larger than Nancy, and Peter thought it even more beautiful. During the fifteenth century, the state of Burgundy had been one of the most influential in all of Europe. Dijon had been Burgundy's capital and had attracted many of the best artists and architects. With time to kill before his train left for Lyons, the young American airman became a tourist again, wandering the city, enjoying its cathedral and the magnificent Palais des Ducs.

An uneventful train ride south to Lyons only enhanced Peter's good mood. Things were going well now. He had encountered no German soldiers since his free beer in Nancy, and as he walked out of the Lyons train station and confidently down the street, his mind was on reaching Spain, England and eventually Brooklyn. He was daydreaming when he passed along a street bordered on the left by a high brick wall. It was a jarring shock when the German soldier stepped into his path. With a rifle in one hand, the soldier threw his other hand out in an unmistakable signal for Peter to halt.

Peter's heart accelerated with a quickness he could never have imagined before. *If he asks me anything, I'm caught,* Peter thought. But the soldier did not speak. He just stood staring at him, as Peter's heart pounded. Then turning to his right, the soldier motioned to some unseen person behind the wall. Seconds later a large German army truck rolled into the street and was followed by a second. Once the trucks had passed, the German soldier nodded for Peter to continue on his way. Peter managed a smile and forced himself to keep a casual pace as he passed by. It was several minutes before his heart rate fell back to normal.

During the train stop in Avignon, Peter elected to stay on board. It was early in the afternoon when the train rolled into Marseilles. As he walked off the platform and into the station, the line of departing passengers came to a halt. Up ahead a German officer, accompanied by several soldiers, was checking identification papers. Peter had no choice but to slowly retreat.

Back on the platform he looked around for other avenues of exit but quickly spotted soldiers stationed at each end of the rail yard. However, he also spotted a half dozen railroad workers walking past. With lunch pails in their hands, they were heading out of the yard. Peter did not waste any time thinking over the wisdom of his decision—he just hopped down from the platform and fell in step with the workers.

The men noticed him but pretended not to. He tried to match the pace and manner of their strides. By the time they reached the German soldiers, Peter was right in the middle of the workers. Accustomed to seeing the railroad men every day, the Germans paid them little attention. So it was that Peter passed safely into the seaport city of Marseilles.

Marseilles was big and busy, its harbor full of open-air markets. Peter was able to purchase food and even a couple of souvenirs—a pipe and a small knife. With the Germans checking papers at the railroad station, he decided to wait until the following day before catching the train to Perpignan.

When he cautiously entered the station the next day, Peter was relieved to see there was no activity involving the German military. Everyone seemed to be coming and going as they pleased. He was well aware that that did not mean the station was free of surveillance by Vichy spies and German agents. He vowed silently to keep his guard up. He had been lucky so far and did not intend to blow it with only one French city left between him and the Spanish border.

Getting to Perpignan presented a small problem to Peter—he had no idea how to pronounce it. Finally he decided to write the word on a small piece of paper. When he got to the ticket booth, he shoved the paper across the counter along with a one-hundred-franc note. The man in the booth handed him a ticket to Perpignan and his change, without comment.

On the train, Peter pulled his beret down over his eyes and was soon asleep. The warmth of sunshine on his right cheek awakened him an hour or so later. He immediately was overcome with a feeling that something was wrong. The sun was on the wrong side of the train.

He had a ticket to Perpignan to the south. The morning sun should have been on the left side of the train. Sunshine coming from the right side could only mean that he was heading north. Soon his fears were confirmed when the train pulled into Avignon station. Peter looked at his ticket. "Perpignan" was stamped across the top. He was still trying to understand what had gone wrong and how to fix it when the conductor asked for his ticket. When he handed the ticket back, the conductor said something in French and pointed out the window at another train on an adjacent track.

Unable to ask for clarification, Peter switched trains and was soon heading south to Perpignan. On the way he figured out what had happened. Apparently there was no direct train service between Marseilles and Perpignan. Traveling between those two cities required a traveler to head north and make the southern connection in Avignon. Had the conductor not happened by while the train was still at Avignon station, Peter would have ended up back in Lyons. He had been graced with good luck for his entire journey so far, and he could only hope it held up.

Peter got to Perpignan late in the evening and slipped beneath the station's passenger platform, where he spent the night. No time for sightseeing this time. Early the next day, hungry but rested, he began his hike to the Spanish border. From looking at the map, he judged the distance to be only thirty to forty miles. Of course, it was all uphill, but even in his weakened condition, he made good time through the foothills, spurred on by the excitement of being so close to freedom.

He had made up his mind to surrender himself to the authorities in the tiny principality of Andorra, which was to the southwest, nestled into a Pyrenean valley between France and Spain. Andorra maintained a long tradition of neutrality that was not stained by any ties to Germany. Peter was counting on fair treatment there.

His enthusiastic pace came to an end as he topped the crest of a hill and got his first look at the majestic Pyrenees Mountains. These were not the gentle sandstone mountains of the Connecticut River Valley that he had grown up with—not even the larger ranges of New York's Hudson River Valley, where he had hiked as a Boy Scout. The Pyrenees were imposingly high peaks, snowcapped and jagged. They seemed to go on forever.

What Peter was looking at was just a portion of the great mountain range, which covered twenty-one thousand square miles from the Atlantic to the Mediterranean. At least forty of the Pyrenees' peaks topped ten thousand feet, with the highest reaching an altitude of more than eleven thousand feet.

"I'll never make it," Peter said softly and sat down in the middle of the road. He had not eaten since Marseilles, two days before. In fact, everything he had eaten since he had been shot down had not amounted to much. His feet were so swollen, he could not get his shoes off. He finally had to cut them off with his hunting knife. He had no idea how he would ever get them back on.

For a while, there alone on a road in the foothills of the Pyrenees, the young American's mind simply ceased to function rationally. Hopelessness, desperation, hunger and exhaustion took over. But only for a while. Finally, he looked back down the road to Perpignan and thought of all he had been through since bailing out of the B-17—all the close calls, lucky breaks, answered prayers and the pure determination that had brought him into the shadow of these mountains. If he could not make it to Andorra, he would turn south to where the eastern end of the Pyrenees hugged the sea. These mountains, while rugged, were not as elevated as their cousins to the west. Spain was just on the other side of their peaks. There was no going back.

Peter rested long enough for some of the swelling in his feet to lessen. His shoes were a disaster but they would have to do for a little while longer. Each step was painful as the road led him higher and higher into the Pyrenees.

A little later, as he hobbled along, Peter heard a noise behind him and turned to see a puzzling sight. It was a man with two bicycles. He was riding one of the bikes and steering with his left hand, while holding the handlebars of the second bicycle with his right hand. Traveling uphill in this manner, the cyclist was barely making better time than Peter.

As the stranger approached, Peter pointed to the second bike and then to himself. "*Oui. Oui!*" the man said. Peter climbed on the bicycle and the two travelers headed up the road, each making better time than before. They rode for about three miles in silence and then the Frenchman asked, "*Français?*"

"No," Peter said. He was reluctant to take any additional chances with the locals. He was so close to being beyond the reach of the Germans, but he was still starving and not really sure how to proceed once he reached Spain. He could still use the help of the French resistance. Perhaps the cyclist would be his last opportunity.

"American aviator." Peter spoke the words with his hand flattened on his chest. The man's reaction was immediate. He nearly shoved the airman off of his bike and once Peter had relinquished it, he hurried away, taking both bicycles with him.

"You son of a bitch!" Peter yelled after the frightened Frenchman. He could only hope the cyclist would not report the incident to any German border patrols. Peter found a grassy shade near the side of the road and sat down to give his feet a short rest. Only a few minutes had passed when he heard the sound of singing. It was a German song.

Up the road, Peter could see the soldiers marching in two columns. There looked to be about a dozen or so. It was too late for him to hide. If he could see them, then they had also spotted him. If he tried to walk away, it would seem suspicious and he would not get far in his condition.

It was almost a certainty that the soldiers had passed the French cyclist along the road. Had he talked? Peter guessed he had not. If the patrol was searching for him, then why were they singing? Peter picked up a piece of grass straw, stuck it between his teeth and tried to look like a local. The Germans smiled and waved to him as they marched past. Peter smiled and waved back.

After putting a few more hard miles behind him, Peter spent the night in some woods near the road. He had been unable to find any food and woke the next morning with pains in his belly. Continuing into the mountains, he came to a farmhouse. It was not a peasant dwelling but rather a comfortable-looking home. Cattle grazed in an adjacent pasture. Peter was sure he could find something to eat at such a place.

He knocked. When a man opened the door, Peter smiled and got right to the point. *"Faim . . . faim."*

The man answered his request quickly, reaching behind the door and brandishing a large club. The hostile rebuff shocked and angered Peter. As hungry as he was, it crossed his mind to try to overpower the farmer and take what food he needed. A combination of exhaustion and moral conviction stopped him. Peter left with anger and an empty stomach.

Later in the day the young airman stumbled into a mountain crossroads village of about thirty dwellings, one of them housing a restaurant. Peter ordered bouillon from an elderly waitress, but when she returned, she placed a large plate of kidney stew and fresh bread in front of him. Peter looked into her kind eyes. She smiled at his surprised expression. He thanked her and wasted no time in devouring his meal.

As he left, the old woman was standing at the restaurant's door. Again, she smiled and then pointed to a small road leading deeper into the mountains.

"Thank you," Peter said to his benefactor. She squeezed his hand and made the sign of the cross. Peter knew he would never forget her wrinkled face. The meal she had provided in a simple act of kindness had given him the strength he needed to complete his journey.

Peter walked for hours. The little road became a mere path. Darkness fell on the mountains and still he walked on. When he had nothing left in him, he lay down by the path and fell asleep, wondering how close he was to the border.

Sunshine spread across the Pyrenees the next morning, and Peter awoke to a spectacular vista. His resting place was right on the crest of one of the highest peaks in the area. Looking in one direction, far below, he could see the little village where the old woman had befriended him. That was France. Turning the other way, he gazed on the smaller mountains and lush valleys of what he knew must be Spain. He had spent the night sleeping right on the border of the two countries.

A grateful young American aviator kneeled at the top of the Pyrenees Mountains to thank God for his deliverance from the hands of his enemies. After his prayer, Peter took out his little prayer book and turned to the page where he had made a mark for each day of his journey. He placed the fourteenth mark on the page. It was October 28. He had escaped from Germany and made his way through enemy-held France in just fourteen days.

Peter wiped away a last tear of joy and started down the mountain into Spain. Barcelona was somewhere fifty or sixty miles south of him. There he hoped to find an American or British consulate and Allied officials who could help him. As the sun set to the west of the Spanish Pyrenees, he came to a small cabin tucked into the forest. The occupants turned out to be an old woodcutter and his striking teenage granddaughter.

The two showed him warm hospitality, including a hot meal and fresh goat's milk. He spent a comfortable night sleeping on the floor close to the cabin's fireplace. Early the next day, he was off again with directions from the woodcutter on the shortest route to Barcelona. Before long he came to the town of Gerona, just as the old man had told him.

Peter decided it was best to leave the road and take a wide route around Gerona, in the same manner he had avoided German villages. Spain was neutral, but she did not enjoy the friendly reputation of countries such as Sweden. It was a good decision, but he was not quite careful enough.

When he rejoined the road on the other side of Gerona he encountered a military guard. Peter was not sure if the soldier was a member of the local militia or part of the Spanish Army, but he was smartly dressed and looked official. The man wore a three-sided hat and black knee-high boots. He was armed with a heavy-looking bolt-action rifle. Peter nodded in the soldier's direction and turned to head south again.

"Señor."

Peter continued down the road.

"Señor, alto!" The soldier's voice was louder than before.

Peter kept walking, pretending not to hear. But he did hear and the next sound was unmistakable. It was the sound of metal sliding across metal . . . followed by the distinctive sound of a rifle bolt inserting a bullet into a firing chamber. Peter stopped in his tracks.

Once he had explained that he was an American aviator, he hoped the soldier would lower his weapon. Instead, Peter was marched into Gerona and locked in a tiny cell. No bigger than eight feet by eight feet, the cell had a dirt floor and no furniture at all. The only light came through a small window with bars. Peter spent the night there without being offered anything to eat.

The next day, two soldiers escorted him via a log truck to a prison about forty kilometers from Gerona. A man in civilian clothing was the first to interrogate the American airman. Peter's feeling of relief that he might finally have found a friendly official evaporated as soon as the stranger spoke. He asked questions in English, but his accent was German. Peter refused to say anything but, "I'm Peter Seniawsky. I'm a sergeant in the U.S. Army. My serial number is 12060630."

The German soon gave up. After he had left, Spanish guards came into the room and cut off all of Peter's hair and then took him to a twelve-by-eight-foot cell. There were two other men already occupying the cell. One claimed to be a deserter from the Italian Army, and the other was a Frenchman. Peter did not trust either.

The guards provided two blankets to their new prisoner and a meal of thin soup. It tasted so awful that Peter could barely keep it down. There were no bunks, so the prisoners slept on the floor. In the middle of the night, the Frenchman quietly woke Peter and gave him a small piece of banana. He whispered that he did not trust the Italian. Peter gladly accepted the morsel of food but secretly he still did not trust either of his cell mates.

Coffee and bread were provided as breakfast. The Frenchman and the Italian were taken out for fresh air and exercise, but it was three days before Peter was allowed to leave the dark cell. Outside, he walked about a small walled-in yard. There were bullet holes in one section of the stone wall, where he guessed many men had been victims of firing squads. He could only hope that the executions went back to the days of the Spanish Civil War and that none had been conducted recently.

After a week of imprisonment, Peter reached the conclusion that his captors were making no effort to report him to the Allies. Unless a miracle happened, he might spend the remainder of the war in a Spanish prison. Thin and weakened from his escape from Germany and France, and living on the sparse prison food, Peter's health was quickly going downhill. He tried to keep his spirits up, but as day after day dragged by his hope was also growing weaker.

On the seventh or eighth day, Peter, the Italian and the Frenchman were joined by a fourth prisoner. He was a British officer of the Royal Air Force—a wing commander by the name of Griffin. The commander's airplane had been shot down on a mission over France while dropping supplies to the resistance. On the ground he had been luckier than Peter, being picked up quickly by the same underground forces he had been aiding.

When the prisoners were allowed to go into the yard, Peter stayed behind in the cell to talk with Griffin.

"I think that Frenchman is very likely a spy," the commander said.

"I don't know, I sort of like him," Peter replied, not mentioning that he had wondered the same thing.

"What's your story, Yank?" the Englishman wanted to know.

When Peter related the highlights of his long journey, the British officer shook his head in amazement. Then he told Peter why he was probably in deep trouble. "My guess is the Americans don't know you are here . . . or even alive." Griffin went on to explain that the French resistance workers who had smuggled him across the border had by then already radioed the details of his situation to Allied authorities in London. Since Peter had been unable to make contact with the resistance movement, those same authorities were most certainly unaware of his incredible escape or his present whereabouts. To them, Peter Seniawsky was one of hundreds of American airmen who had either died over Schweinfurt or who had been captured during the raid.

Commander Griffin expected he would be freed from the prison in a few days. He promised Peter that he would make sure the Eighth Air Force was informed that one of their own was wasting away in a Spanish cell. Two days later, people came to get the English officer out and, good to his word, he told of Peter's plight as soon as he reached the British consulate.

When American officials in England heard the story of an American airman who had escaped from Germany and then evaded capture unassisted on a six-hundred-mile adventure through western Germany and France, they were more than skeptical. For one thing, it had never been done before, at least not by an American. Only two members of the British military held the distinction of having escaped from behind the German border to make it back to freedom, without receiving any help from the French resistance.

If the Peter Seniawsky in the Spanish prison was really one of their airmen, then the Americans wanted him back, but the belief of at least some of the American officials was that he was something else entirely . . . a German spy. They sent a man to investigate.

A few days after the departure of Commander Griffin, Peter was interrogated again. Peter could not determine whether the questioner was British or American, but he sensed the stranger was legitimate, so he told his story freely. As the interrogator finished the session and turned to leave, he hesitated and looked directly into Peter's eyes.

"Tell me, Sergeant Seniawsky, do you think Daisy Mae will ever catch Li'l Abner?"

The question made Peter chuckle. "You mean the comic strip? No, she doesn't have a chance."

The man smiled. "We will be in touch." Three days later, a Spanish Air Force officer arrived to escort Peter out of the prison. He gave the American airman some Spanish currency. Peter slipped a few bills to the French prisoner as he shook the man's hand. Maybe the Frenchman was a spy, like Griffin thought. Maybe not. He had been kind to him; that was all Peter knew for sure.

The Spanish escort officer took Peter to a respectable hotel in Gerona. Two Canadian servicemen and a British officer were already there. After a long-awaited bath, Peter put on clean clothes that were provided. The four allies were allowed to roam the town freely that afternoon. In the evening, their Spanish hosts treated them to an expensive seafood dinner. All four men ate with abandon, but Peter's body had grown unaccustomed to fare of such quantity and richness. He became very sick after dinner.

The four escapees spent about a week enjoying the hotel and its restaurant as guests of the Spanish government; then they were escorted by train to Madrid. There they were welcomed like heroes by the staff of the British consulate. Several days and nights of wine, fine food and festivities followed. Peter was enjoying his new freedom, but his body had not recovered from almost a month of near starvation. What he needed was rest.

The last leg of the allies' tour of Spain was a long trip to Gibraltar, the gateway city of the Mediterranean Sea and the Atlantic Ocean. In Gibraltar, the Spanish relinquished control of the four men to a group of Royal Air Force officers. Peter felt a rush of relief. *Finally, I'm free.* The feeling was short-lived.

The RAF officers quizzed Peter about every detail of his story and then told him they did not believe him. The odds were too long for a man to make such a perilous escape and in only two weeks' time. They suggested the real Peter Seniawsky was locked away in a German stalag.

"I'm Peter Seniawsky, and if you get me back to Grafton Underwood, I will prove it." Peter was beginning to realize he was in reality still a prisoner. In the next few days, his health declined dramatically. The RAF men became alarmed. He could very well be who he said he was. If he was telling the truth, they had damned well better get him back to England alive. On December 1, 1943, a month and a half after his bomber had been shot down, Peter was put on a flight to the United Kingdom.

By the time his airplane landed in London, Peter was very ill. An ambulance was waiting to take him to a hospital. Under the watchful eyes and care of English doctors and nurses, his health rebounded in a matter of days. He began to count his blessings. He was back on Allied soil. He was beginning to feel rested and stronger. He had been able to write short letters to his sister Margaret and his fiancée, Helen, to let them know he was alive and safe. Only one thing bothered him. There was a U.S. Army military policeman stationed just outside his hospital room.

The presence of the guard could only mean there was still

some question of his real identity by Army authorities. Peter laughed out loud.

"They still think I'm a German spy, don't they?" he asked a young nurse when she popped in to check on him.

"Don't be silly, Sergeant," the nurse replied and quickly changed the subject. However, a visit from a staff officer of the 384th Bomb Group confirmed Peter's suspicions. The two airmen knew each other, and even though the officer did not say as much, Peter knew he was there to confirm his identity. Shortly after the officer left, Peter noticed that the MP was removed from outside his door.

In a matter of weeks, Peter's health had improved enough for him to rejoin the 384th Bomb Group at Grafton Underwood, where he immediately requested a waist gunner position with a new B-17 crew. The request was promptly denied. The headquarters of the First Bombardment Division felt that Sergeant Peter Seniawsky could be more useful by sharing his story with other airmen who might someday face the same fate he had lived through. Peter was asked to travel to various American air bases and conduct a series of lectures on evading capture.

Major Edward S. Dodge recommended him for the Army's Officers Candidate School: ". . . the case of T/Sgt. Peter Seniawsky is outstanding for the year 1943," Dodge said. "Alone and practically unassisted, he evaded out of Germany and effected a safe crossing through three closely guarded borders, finishing in a neutral country.

"His quick thinking, wise planning and ability to overcome seemingly insurmountable obstacles have stamped him as officer material. Which the writer believes should afford him a chance at this advancement.

"Lectures given by the subject to Air Corps personnel in this theater will result, it is believed, in many more of our personnel following the trail he blazed." Dodge finished by writing that it was " . . . an honor to recommend him for OCS."

Peter was not a born public speaker and more than a little uncomfortable talking about his own accomplishments, but it soon became apparent that the airmen in his audiences wanted to know what to expect. Any of them could find themselves in Peter Seniawsky's shoes, and, indeed, many eventually did. Peter quickly became an effective and confident speaker.

During one lecture, he found himself talking in front of a group of airmen that included an officer named James Stewart. The Hollywood actor was serving as a bomber pilot and was on his way to becoming a mission commander. Stewart listened as intently as the rest.

The commanding general of the Eighth Air Force, General Ira C. Eaker, was so impressed with the story of Peter's survival and escape that he awarded the young waist gunner one of America's most prestigious military honors, the Silver Star. Eaker's chief of staff, General C.C. Chauncey, wrote in the official Silver Star award notice: "His gallantry, skill and fighting spirit serve as an inspiration to his fellow flyers and reflect highest credit upon Sergeant Seniawsky and the Armed Forces of the United States."

Once his lecture series ended, the Eighth Air Force decided to send its celebrated evader home to the States. Peter hitched a flight into Washington, D.C., and took the train up the Atlantic coast to New York. When he arrived in Manhattan on February 12, 1944, the first person he called from Grand Central Station was his fiancée, Helen.

As he rode the subway to Brooklyn to meet her, Peter thought of all the places he had been, all that he had experienced and somehow managed to live through. He closed his eyes and could see the faces of the men he had fought alongside of—"Junior"

Kauffman; that wonderful Cherokee Indian, Stanley Ruben; the good-natured Paul Spodar and all the others.

Where are they? Are they in some prison camp or dead? Why did God spare me? Some questions would take years, even decades to answer. Some could not be answered in a lifetime.

The subway train jerked to a noisy halt. It was his stop. He stepped into a mild night in Brooklyn and the excitement of being home pushed aside any lingering thoughts of enemy fighters, German soldiers, damp haystacks and starvation. Those things would revisit his dreams in the future, but this night was about a different kind of future.

He bounded up the apartment building's steps with the ease of a young man eager to get on with the rest of his life. He paused at the top only long enough to adjust his Air Corps cap and then he knocked on the door. Seconds later it opened, and Peter was looking into the eyes of "the prettiest girl in Brooklyn." Peter and Helen were married on April 9, 1944.

After the War

Peter Seniawsky returned to civilian life with a stunning list of accomplishments during his short military enlistment:

- He was the first American airman (and perhaps the only one) to escape from Germany, evade capture in France and reach Spain—entirely through his own efforts, with no help from the French Resistance movement.

- He was one of only 817 U.S. airmen to be awarded the Silver Star during the war.

- He is a member of the Caterpillar Club, for having bailed out of a combat-damaged aircraft; a member of the Winged Boot

Club, for walking from behind enemy lines to freedom; and a member of the Gold Fish Club, for surviving an aircraft ditching in water. Only one other individual is known to be a documented member of all three honorary clubs.

Peter and his new bride lived in Brooklyn while he searched for employment. It was not his war record but his Army Air Force training as a mechanic that landed him a job with American Airlines. Through the years, he worked on American airplanes at all three major airports in the New York City metropolitan area.

In 1951, Peter legally changed his last name to Scott. Although extremely proud of his heritage, Peter chose to Americanize the family name for the sake of his young daughters. In school, and later in the service, he had been forced to listen as others mispronounced or "butchered" the name Seniawsky.

"I decided to give the girls an easier time of it," he said.

During the Vietnam War, Peter volunteered for service with the American Airlines Cargo unit operating in Alaska. With the rank of first lieutenant, Peter served as chief mechanic there, supervising the maintenance of aircraft flying cargo to South Vietnam.

Eventually, he became American Airlines' shift supervisor of mechanic operations at JFK International Airport, in New York. In this position, he and his crew received numerous commendations for service beyond ordinary duties.

On one occasion, Peter spotted a DC-10 airliner coming in for landing with some unusual vapors trailing one of its engines. Acting quickly, he called for firefighting equipment, and when the airplane rolled to a stop, he and two of his mechanics reached the engine just as it burst into flames. The three men were able to extinguish the engine fire, saving the aircraft and possibly preventing loss of life.

Few people he worked with at Kennedy knew anything of Peter's war experiences, but in the summer of 1977 they got a firsthand look at his courage and coolness under pressure. An American Airlines jet was inbound to JFK when airport officials received an alarming telephone call with someone claiming a bomb had been placed on the flight.

The pilot was notified immediately, and upon landing he brought the airplane to a standstill at the end of the runway and then activated the emergency exit chutes. As passengers slid down the chutes and ran away from the jet, an army of airport fire and rescue vehicles and personnel surrounded the aircraft. Soon a New York City Police Department bomb squad team arrived.

Once the jet had been evacuated, the bomb squad captain ordered his men onto the darkened airplane. Peter stepped in front of the police commander and told him to keep his men on the runway until someone could board the airliner and turn on the interior lights. As the supervising mechanic, he was responsible not only to American Airlines but to the Federal Aviation Administration for anything that happened to the aircraft and anyone who might board it at that point. He was not about to stand by while the men of the bomb squad stumbled about in the dark, ripping apart one of his airplanes as they searched for a bomb. It was not safe for the aircraft or the police officers.

The police captain tried intimidation: "Listen, I am the captain of the NYPD bomb squad, mister!"

"And when that airplane is sitting on my runway, I'm captain of that airplane!" Peter responded. The policeman, no longer sure of his authority in the situation but suddenly very sure of Peter's resolve, relented. Peter turned away and began to climb up one of the emergency exit chutes. He would never have asked one of his crew members to board an airplane with a possible bomb on board.

Once he had located and activated the auxiliary lights, the police officers swarmed onto the aircraft and conducted their search. No bomb was found, but anyone who had witnessed his actions that day knew Peter could handle a crisis with coolness and control. His old friends in the 384th Bomb Group would not have been surprised.

Peter and Helen lived in Queens for most of the thirty-nine years of Peter's American Airlines career. In 1983, the couple moved to the picturesque shoreline town of Old Saybrook, Connecticut, where they still live today. They are most proud of their daughters, Helen and Barbara, and their four grandchildren.

Lieutenant Giles F. Kauffman Jr. was captured by the Germans on October 14, 1943, and spent the remainder of World War II in a prisoner of war camp. In later years, he would remember that he was "treated fairly" by his captors, although he thought the enlisted men in the stalags probably had it rougher.

One of the first things Kauffman did after returning to the United States was to get married. He wed Kathryn Bean on June 14, 1945. During the first ten years of their marriage, the couple added two sons and a daughter to their family. Giles (Jeff) Kauffman was born in 1945, Karen in 1949, and Michael in 1955.

As a civilian, Kauffman once again entered Penn State University and graduated with a degree in chemistry in 1947. He spent most of his working career as a chemist in the atomic energy industry.

The Kauffman family moved to Chillicothe, Ohio, in 1954, and Giles and Kathryn lived there until his retirement in 1981. They moved to Florida ten years later to enjoy their golden years in the sunshine.

Once on a trip back home to Ohio, Giles, his son Jeff, and his grandson Christopher visited the Air Force Museum at Wright-Patterson Air Force Base near Dayton. The elder Kauffman agreed to be escorted around the museum in a wheelchair to avoid tiring his legs. As the three Kauffmans turned a corner, they were delighted to see a beautifully restored B-17 bomber.

Without saying a word, Giles Kauffman raised himself from the wheelchair, removed the rope barrier that protected the Fortress from museumgoers, and walked toward the airplane. He was standing underneath the B-17's nose when Jeff Kauffman called out to his father, "Hey Dad, I don't think you're supposed to get that close."

The museum's director happened to be standing nearby. He told Jeff, "It's okay." Then walking to the senior Kauffman, he asked, "Would you like to go on board?"

Kauffman smiled as the curator opened the hatch beneath the bomber's nose. To his son's and grandson's amazement, the former World War II bomber pilot climbed into the airplane as if he were in his twenties again. Moments later, Giles F. Kauffman Jr. eased himself into the left seat of a B-17 for the first time in more than five decades.

Kathryn Kauffman died in 1997, and Giles passed away two years afterward.

Frank Pogorzelski was captured soon after parachuting from Kauffman's crippled B-17 and was a POW in Germany for the rest of the war. Upon his return to the United States and civilian life, he attended Carnegie Institute of Technology in Pittsburgh, Pennsylvania, on the GI Bill. Graduating with a degree in civil engineering, Frank began what would be a long and successful career in chemical plant design.

He married Rita Ejchost on July 23, 1946, and in 1950 the couple's first child was born—a daughter named Carol. Frank and Rita later had two sons, Frank and Paul. In 1966, Frank changed his last name to Porell. His wife, Rita, had already passed away when Frank Porell died in September 2007.

Paul Spodar was imprisoned in the infamous Stalag 17 until the German surrender in 1945. After his discharge from the Army, he returned to Cleveland, Ohio, where he had been born and raised. For two years, he worked as a machinist for the White Truck Company, but in 1947 he jumped at the opportunity to join the Cleveland Fire Department.

Spodar had known Anne Sheyka for most of his life, because their parents were close friends. In 1947 he and Anne were married. They raised three children—Ronald, Sharon and Raymond. Two grandchildren followed.

In 1978, Paul Spodar retired from the Cleveland Fire Department after thirty years of meritorious service. Later that year, the Spodars bought a home in New Port Richey, Florida, where they lived until Anne's death in 2005. Paul now lives in an assisted living facility in New Port Richey. His daughter, Sharon, has created a very interesting Web site named Paul's Sentimental Journey (http://members.cox.net/paulspodar/), which pays tribute to her dad, his B-17 crewmates and all American and British WWII veterans.

Jules T. Beck, David D. Danneman, William Jarrell, Jacob M. Martinez, George Molnar, Frank Pogorzelski and **Stanley T. Ruben** were all taken prisoner shortly after they bailed out over Germany. Like Spodar, the enlisted men were imprisoned in Stalag 17. Molnar and Pogorzelski, who were officers, may have been placed at Stalag 17 or sent to a different prison camp. Each of these men remained a POW until the war's end, when they all returned to the United States. William Jarrell died in December 2000 and George Molnar died in March 2002.

Crew Reunion: It seems that Lieutenant Kauffman's crew members lost contact with each other after returning to civilian life. Very likely some members of Kauffman's crew may have bumped into each other at Army Air Force or Bomb Group reunions over the years. There are at least three known instances of crew contact.

Paul Spodar visited several times with Frank Pogorzelski in Pennsylvania in the 1990s, and he also paid a visit to his old pilot and commander, just before Giles Kauffman Jr. died in 1999.

Through the research efforts of the author, in April 2002 Peter (Seniawsky) Scott and Spodar were reunited in a long-distance phone call. The two former waist gunners, who had fought side by side during violent air combat and who had survived nearly drowning following the ditching of the Fortress *Ruthless*, reminisced and made plans for an in-person reunion. In 2003, Peter visited Pogorzelski at his home and later that year met with Spodar. It was the first time he had seen either of his wartime comrades since they had bailed out of a burning B-17, fifty-nine years before.

• Without a Parachute •

ART FRECHETTE
Navigator

301ST BOMB GROUP

419TH BOMB SQUADRON

Art Frechette was falling through a cold December sky, not so much like a rock as like a rag doll, arms and legs loose and useless. His fall had begun at around fifteen thousand feet, when his B-17 bomber exploded into flames. The blast hurled the young navigator clear without leaving a scratch. His parachute was undamaged and in perfect working order—yet, it remained unopened as he fell toward the Italian Alps at the rate of 150 miles per hour. Art Frechette was totally unconscious.

If he did not wake up, he would crash into the mountains in less than two minutes. Even if he did regain consciousness, he would still need to be five hundred to a thousand feet high for the parachute to significantly slow his fall.

Art sailed past one thousand feet. Now, because of the cold air that was stinging his face or for who knows what reason, he began to awaken. He had only a few more seconds to realize his situation, a few more seconds of paralyzing shock. He could see the earth right below him—just a blur of green and white.

His right hand grabbed for the parachute ripcord and found it.
Too late.

Only two years before, at the age of eighteen, Art had dropped
out of the University of Connecticut and joined the Army. He
volunteered for the Air Corps, hoping to be trained as a navigator. Fate stepped in and took him in another direction.

"How would you like to be a pilot?" the officer asked Art
after he had successfully completed several days of difficult testing. Normally the Army Air Corps was overstocked with pilot
candidates, but in the fall of 1942, it was the navigation schools
that had no vacancies.

"Okay," Art replied, thinking it was what was meant to be.
It was not. At pilot training school in Camden, Arkansas, Art
did the one thing that was almost certain to get an air cadet
kicked out—he crashed an airplane.

Actually, his initial weeks of pilot training had gone extremely
well. He passed primary training with ease and then soloed in a
cumbersome bi-wing trainer that the cadets had nicknamed the
"Yellow Peril." Despite the shortcomings of the airplane, his
maiden solo flight went smoothly. Soon he was flying daily training missions over the Ouachita delta. He loved being up there
all alone. It was a dreamlike world, but Art never forgot that the
purpose of every mission was to make him a better pilot. Ultimately it was his dedication to improving his skills that got him
into trouble.

On one particularly gusty day, he decided to make an unauthorized landing at a seldom-used airfield. His instructor's orders
before takeoff had been clear. "Fly to this point, turn, fly to here,
and then return to base." Art was not one to willfully disobey
orders, but the winds that day provided what he saw as a rare
opportunity to learn more about flying.

He assumed correctly that weather conditions in Europe might not always be ideal. One day he might be called on to land his aircraft in strong crosswinds. Art reasoned that it would be better to learn how now rather than later, when it could cost more lives than his own. What he did not know was that the Yellow Peril was a bear to land in a crosswind situation.

The landing approach that day seemed little different from any other he had made, with the exception of an occasional burst of wind buffeting the airplane. Art kept both hands firmly on the controls and brought the biplane down purposefully. A satisfied smile crossed his face as his airplane sailed only a few feet above the runway, in that wonderful period of anticipation just before the wheels make contact. Seconds later, the airplane crashed nosefirst into the runway.

The crosswind had tossed the twin-winged little aircraft as if it were a mere leaf. There was no time for Art to make any attempt to right the airplane. Any such effort would have been useless anyway at almost zero altitude. The aircraft skidded a short distance along the runway with its nose down and its tail up, finally coming to a rest at an almost perfect ninety-degree angle to the ground. There was hardly time to be afraid. It crossed Art's mind that he had just come close to dying, but the thought was only a matter-of-fact conclusion.

After lowering himself out of the aircraft, he began to assess his situation. To his amazement the airplane did not look that bad. In fact, it looked about as well as an airplane could look while standing on its nose. Maybe there was a glimmer of hope that he would not be kicked out of the pilot program.

Art thought of his father back in Groton, Connecticut. What would his dad think if he was booted from pilot training? Arthur Frechette Sr. was a tough man. As a child, Art had sometimes found him hard to please. He had always tried to live up to his father's high standards. He had never felt those standards were unreasonable, but they weighed heavy on his mind as he stood next to his damaged trainer. *What will Dad think of this?*

Arthur Frechette Sr. and his wife, Margaret, were proof that different personalities and backgrounds could make a good marriage. Arthur Sr. was French and Jewish. His wife, a Hogan by birth, was Irish. She had a wonderful sense of family, visiting several days a week with various members of the Hogan clan who lived in the Groton–New London area.

Art's father was more reserved—no less caring than the mother but always the seemingly unemotional head of the Frechette family. Later, in December 1944 when the news came that his son had been shot down over enemy territory and was missing in action, it would become clear to everyone how emotional Art Sr. could be.

For the time being, any concern about what his father would think about his crashing the trainer plane was shoved aside. Air Cadet Art Frechette had bigger problems. In the distance, he could see a Jeep speeding in his direction. The vehicle was still too far away for Art to identify any of the passengers, but he knew one would be a very angry flight instructor.

Art was not automatically booted out of the pilot training program, but he certainly had two strikes against him. One: He had crashed his airplane. Two: He had done it during an unauthorized landing. He had little doubt that the latter upset his superiors more than the former. This was the Air Corps, but it was still part of the old Army. Army training was not about initiative, it was about following orders.

A few days following the crash, Art was informed he would be given a "check flight" by the chief pilot. Art knew it would be strike three unless he flew perfectly. He made up his mind to do just that. Soon into the flight, it became apparent someone had already decided that the Air Corps could do without the services of Art Frechette as a pilot. During every maneuver of the check flight, the chief pilot chewed out the young cadet pilot. When Art touched the airplane down for a landing, he knew it would be his last.

Getting booted from flight school was a disappointment, but Art shook it off with the resiliency of an eighteen-year-old. Within days he was offered admission into the Army Air Corps navigation school in Monroe, Louisiana. He gladly accepted the chance to become a combat navigator, which was what he really wanted from the beginning. It also provided some good news to write in a letter to his father: "Dad, sorry to report I washed out of flight school, but I'm going to become a navigator." Art left out the details of why he had "washed out."

After graduation from navigation school, it was off to Tennessee, where Art joined a replacement crew commanded by pilot Lieutenant Elliot Butts. Butts's new crew went through two months of intensive combat training before heading to Lincoln, Nebraska, to pick up a new factory-fresh B-17 bomber. About a week later, the crew was aboard the Fortress, flying it to Italy for assignment with the 301st Bomb Group.

Their route hopped from Lincoln to Bangor, Maine; Newfoundland; the Azores; Marrakech in North Africa; and finally to Gioia, Italy. By the time they landed in Italy, the new crew had chalked up almost thirty hours of flying time, and Art had gained plenty of valuable navigation experience before being plunged into the pressure of combat missions.

It was at Gioia that Butts's crew discovered the cruel joke the Air Corps played on most of its replacement crews. Their shiny new B-17 was taken away from them, and they were placed aboard an old battle-worn bomber for the trip to their new air base. The base, like several other United States air bases in Italy, was near the city of Foggia. Art had heard descriptions of the conditions at Eighth Air Force bases in England. Surely the barracks were cold, but there were good points: liberty in nearby London, local pubs and friendly English girls. Art knew at first glance that life with the Fifteenth Air Force at Foggia was going to be much more unpleasant than a similar assignment in England.

There were few buildings at all. Several Quonset huts housed the operation facilities of the 301st and a dismal structure built from lava rock was designated as the Officers' Club. Officers and noncommissioned crew members alike lived in army tents amid a sea of mud.

It was October 1944 when Art reached the Foggia base, and there was already a chill in the air. His tent mate, a navigator from another crew, gave him the short tour of their home. There was a brick floor, which was a luxury since Art would later learn many of the other tent floors were simply packed dirt. For heat, a homemade burner had been fashioned from a metal spray bottle in which holes had been punched to serve as flame jets. The burner was fed by a line that ran underneath the tent to a one-hundred-octane gasoline tank outside.

Art concluded his new home was a firetrap, and during his first week there was tangible proof of it. Early one morning, Art heard a commotion outside. He stuck his head out of the tent flap to see members of a nearby tent scurrying about in their underwear. They were desperately trying to extinguish the fire that was quickly consuming their tent. It was a losing battle.

"That happens about once a week," Art's tent mate informed him before going back inside to make coffee.

On November 22, Art flew his first combat mission as a B-17 navigator. It was nothing like he had expected. At seven fifty a.m., the first of the 301st Bomb Group Fortresses lifted off the runway. The target for the day was the marshaling yard at Regensburg, Germany. By the time the formation was over enemy territory, the weather was turning bad. Snowflakes blew in the side openings and began to build up on the gunners and their weapons.

In the nose, the bombardier motioned for Art to look down through the Plexiglas. Through a break in the clouds, he spotted what his crewmate wanted him to see. They were flying directly over a German airfield. Art could see the enemy fighters lined up neatly along the sides of the runways. There was no activity down there. Not one fighter was taking off to confront the American bomber force. In a few more seconds, the airfield disappeared as the snowstorm intensified.

Art guessed the weather conditions were going to get much worse. If the Luftwaffe was not going to risk flying, what chance did the B-17s have of hitting an unseen target? By the time the bombers reached Regensburg, the crew members could barely see the airplanes flying right next to them. Midair collisions became a bigger worry than the German defenses. However, the enemy antiaircraft gunners soon gave the Americans a hot welcome.

Black pocks of smoke punctured the pure white sky as the B-17s blindly released their bombs. Art doubted the marshaling yards were suffering any damage at all. The 301st was more likely plowing some German farmers' fields.

Before the empty bombers could find their way out of the danger area, the air became filled with almost as much flak as snow. One burst just ahead of Art's aircraft sent shrapnel flying into the Plexiglas nose. Some of it blasted clean through and ricocheted around the bombardier-navigator compartment. One piece, almost spent, bounced off Art's flak vest.

Those people are trying to knock me down! Art thought. Reason told him the German antiaircraft batteries were firing blindly into a snow-filled sky, but to Art the war had just become very personal. It was a long and cold flight back to their base for the airmen of the 301st, knowing their efforts had accomplished little on that miserable day.

Art soon learned the weather was going to be a constant problem for the Fifteenth Air Force crews flying out of the Foggia region of Italy. After completing his second mission into Germany on December 2, Art's crew took off with the 419th Bomb Squadron the following day. They were forced to return with an incomplete mission. On the sixth the results were the same; and again on the tenth, another "incomplete." Finally on December 11, Art navigated his B-17 crew to a bomb drop on an oil refinery in Austria and received credit for his third mission.

Of course, bad weather was not the only thing that could force a bomber still fully loaded with bombs back to base. Mechanical problems were also common. On one mission, Art was the navigator for a B-17 when it lost oil pressure in one of its engines. Since they were not that far from their target, everyone hoped to finish the mission, but when it became apparent the aircraft could not keep up with the rest of the formation, the pilot reluctantly turned back.

Within minutes, the pilot was on the interphone requesting that Art find an alternative target where they could unload their bombs and get credit for the mission. Zagreb, Yugoslavia, was on the alternative list and pretty much on the route home. Art gave the pilot coordinates for Zagreb, and the lone bomber headed off for its new target on just three engines.

Since the crew had not been briefed for Zagreb, they did not know much about it, beyond the fact that it was occupied by the Germans. Art's maps indicated a bridge spanning the Sava River. His pilot liked the idea, perhaps for no other reason than the challenge involved in a single heavy bomber trying to hit such a small target.

As they approached Zagreb, luck was with them—both good and bad luck. The weather around the city was beautifully clear.

The bridge stood out like a bull's-eye as the B-17 started its bomb run. Art soon realized that his bomber also stood out like a bull's-eye too. Zagreb, it turned out, was strongly defended with numerous antiaircraft batteries, and all of them were trying to train on a crippled B-17 that had appeared out of nowhere.

Now as black flak explosions with fiery red centers began to appear all around his bomber, Art felt foolish for having thought the war was *personal* on his first mission. *This* was personal! These German ground gunners were not putting up a wall of flak, hoping to hit any American bomber formation. These gunners were specifically trying to blast Art and his nine crewmates out of the sky.

It was the most concentrated flak Art would ever see, but somehow they flew through it completely untouched. As soon as the last bomb fell from the bay, the B-17's pilot turned sharply away from the city. The first few bombs fell short of the bridge, producing harmless geysers in the river, but a few seconds later the Zagreb bridge was rocked with devastating explosions. Art's crew had scored an improbable direct hit.

For the American bomb groups flying out of the air bases around Foggia, the Adriatic Sea was the pathway to their targets. After six missions, Art knew the route well. The formations flew northwest up the length of the Adriatic, with the backside of the Italian boot (the eastern coast of Italy) visible to their left. They crossed the Gulf of Venice into northern Italy, where the Germans still held on stubbornly; then they flew across the breathtaking Italian Alps into Austria. If the target was in Germany, the American bombers would usually make a turn over the Austrian Alps.

As Art saw it, this route had its advantages and a major disadvantage. The upside was that more than half of the U.S. bombers' route was over water, which meant there was no threat of enemy antiaircraft fire. Also, there was little chance the depleted

Luftwaffe would risk venturing very far over the Adriatic, where American fighters ruled the skies and where a clear view of the eastern coast of Italy made navigation uncomplicated. The downside was the predictability of the bombers' route. The Germans in Austria and northern Italy knew in advance the path of the American formations, and they positioned their antiaircraft batteries accordingly.

Beginning on December 21, Art got four days off from flying. He was bored by the second day. In Foggia, the Italians were not friendly to American aviators and soldiers. There was little to do on the air base but talk, play cards and drink gin. By the time Christmas Day arrived, he was not so disappointed when he got an early wake-up. He was very aggravated when an hour and a half into the mission the bombers were called back to base because of bad weather. He had by now flown twelve missions and half of those had been aborted, most due to weather conditions. After being credited with only six combat missions for a month's worth of flying, Art was eager to get on with it.

The sky cleared on December 26 for the 301st to make a bomb run on an oil refinery in Blechhammer, Germany. The following day, the unit struck the marshaling yards in Linz, Austria. On December 28, it went back to bomb Regensburg again.

Art and the rest of the men of the 419th Bomb Squadron had flown three straight days of combat missions. They had been long and cold flights, each one lasting eight hours or more. After Regensburg, Art went to bed that evening expecting there was little chance of being called on to fly the next day. To his surprise, the duty sergeant woke him with the news before dawn. There was yet another surprise in store for the young navigator that morning—he was assigned to fly with a different crew.

Until December 29, Art had flown most of his missions with pilot Lieutenant Elliot Butts. This day he would be flying as the navigator for Lieutenant Lyle C. Pearson's crew. Art knew Pearson,

but not well. The two men had run into one another at the Officers' Club. In fact, Art had also met Pearson's copilot, Sam Wheeler,
and the bombardier, William Ferguson, at the club.

Art knew little about the officers, except that Pearson and
Wheeler were married men and Ferguson was single. The pilot
was from Minnesota. The copilot and bombardier both had
Southern accents. Art seemed to remember that Wheeler was
from Alabama and Ferguson came from Missouri. Though he
had seen some of their faces around the base, Art had not really
met any of the enlisted crewmen until the morning of December
29. He soon discovered that Pearson was also unacquainted
with these airmen.

Lyle Pearson had grown up in the small town of Montevideo,
Minnesota, the son of a mechanic. He enlisted in the Army in
May 1942 at the age of twenty-one. When four months passed
and Lyle had not been called to active duty, he and the pretty
Katherine Fuller were married. The newlyweds enjoyed five
blissful months together before Lyle's orders arrived in February
1943.

By the summer of 1944 the young pilot had completed his
training and was flying a new B-17 overseas. Trouble brushed
Pearson and his crew before they could even reach the war in
Italy. While taking off from a base in the Azores, Pearson's
bomber suffered a mechanical failure that prevented the aircraft
from gaining sufficient altitude. The fuselage of the Fortress
barely cleared an embankment at the end of the runway and the
landing gear was sheared off completely, sending the B-17 skid-
ding across an open field. Miraculously, every member of Pearson's crew walked away uninjured. It was a rocky start for a
young man who would go on to become one of the 419th Bomb
Squadron's most reliable pilots.

Pearson's very first combat mission was a brutal lesson for
the rookie pilot. For months, the bombers of the Fifteenth Air

Force had been attacking the oil refineries of Ploesti, Romania, which supplied the German war machine with much of its fuel. Before Ploesti's oil production was knocked out in August 1944, 223 American bombers and crews were shot from the sky. Pearson made the round-trip to Ploesti on July 31, through some of the most intense antiaircraft defenses of the war.

By December, Pearson had gained a reputation as a pilot who looked out for his men but one who was also determined to get the job done. During one mission, his aircraft had lost power in one of its engines while approaching the initial point of the bomb run. With reduced power, the bomber soon fell behind the rest of the formation, but Pearson refused to turn back. He took the lone Fortress over the target with only three working engines and dropped his bombs. After weaving through the flak area, Pearson and his crew flew the long and lonely route back to their base in Italy and landed safely. For this action, Lieutenant Lyle Pearson was awarded the Distinguished Flying Cross.

In fact, many times Pearson had landed at Foggia, his B-17 riddled with flak holes (fifty-seven hits on one mission), but never had one of his airmen been injured. They loved and respected him for that.

Since individual crewmen would occasionally be assigned to fly with other crews, fate played a strange trick on Pearson and his boys. By December 29, eight of his crewmen had finished their required fifty missions. Unlike the Eighth Air Force, which required thirty-five combat missions of its airmen, the Fifteenth Air Force required fifty missions, but an airman was given credit for two missions on longer raids. Only Pearson and his bombardier, William "Jack" Ferguson, had one more mission to fly before they could go home.

Pearson and Ferguson were tent mates and close friends. When Ferguson was assigned to complete his rotation with a different pilot and crew on December 28, he pulled strings to be reassigned to the December 29th mission instead. The bombardier was determined to finish up the war with his pal Lyle Pearson. Every bomber returned safely from the target on December 28.

Pearson was not all that edgy about his pickup crew. Although he had not previously flown with his new copilot, he knew Sam Wheeler had a good reputation around the base. His buddy Jack Ferguson would drop the bombs on target. Pearson knew and liked his new navigator. Art Frechette, with nine combat missions under his belt, could be trusted to find the way back home. When the day's target was announced during the early-morning briefing, Pearson felt even better. Their target was the rail yards and workshops of Castelfranco, in northern Italy. They would not be flying into German or even Austrian airspace. There was no doubt there would be some flak, as there always was, but it should be light.

After his crew assembled at their bomber, Pearson took time to introduce the officers and then asked the enlisted crewmen to introduce themselves and say where they were from.

The flight engineer, Sergeant Farrell B. Haney, was a Texan. Radio operator Staff Sergeant Robert J. Halstein was from Meriden, Connecticut, not far from Art's hometown of Groton. Staff Sergeant Charles A. Williams was the ball turret gunner; Panama City, Florida, was his home. Waist gunner, Sergeant Mitchell Vuyanovich came from Pennsylvania. The other waist gunner, Sergeant Charles T. Lyon, was from Iowa. The crew's tail gunner was Sergeant Grant M. Dory; his hometown was Seattle.

Art thought they seemed like a good bunch of boys, but he surmised they were feeling the same way he was—as though he had been yanked away from his family. His new pilot and commander, Lyle Pearson, made things easier on everyone. They were all aware of his record of bringing his crews back unharmed. Pearson was confident, even cheerful as he chatted with them before takeoff.

As Pearson was preparing to get his crew on board, a Jeep drove up with an officer in the passenger seat. Pearson smiled as he recognized his regular copilot, Lieutenant Harry Livers, who had come by to see his old friend off. The men talked briefly, shook hands and then as Livers climbed back into the Jeep, he yelled back to Pearson, "See you when you get back, Lyle!"

Pearson smiled again and waved goodbye to his friend:

"Harry, I've got it made!"

The weather was beautiful, with maximum visibility. There was still lots of chatter on the interphone as Pearson's bomber left the Adriatic behind and entered the airspace of northern Italy. The boys were getting to know each other, so Pearson decided to let them talk until they reached the initial point. Seated at his navigator's desk in the nose compartment, Art could see the magnificent Alps in the distance. The mountain range never failed to leave him in awe, but on this clear morning, the Alps were especially beautiful—their peaks a brilliant white under the morning sun, their valleys deep, green and welcoming.

Pearson's aircraft was a B-17G, serial number 44-6652. She was in the deputy lead position, just to the left and rear of the lead aircraft. There were seven silver B-17s in the 419th Bomb Squadron diamond formation. Art notified Pearson when they reached the initial point. Seconds later, Art watched the lead bomber turn slowly, signaling the beginning of the bomb run. He began to store away his navigation instruments, in anticipation of encountering flak within five to ten minutes' time.

"Flak! Nine o'clock!" the tail gunner, Grant Dory, yelled over the interphone. No sooner had he given the warning than an explosion shook the aircraft violently. Art knew instantly they had been hit, but he still found it hard to believe. Reality sank in quickly when he heard Pearson order Ferguson, "Get rid of those bombs!"

Ferguson hit the salvo switch but the bombs would not release. The bomber was shaking and seemed out of control. Art scrambled up to the cockpit to see if he could help. He found Pearson and Wheeler fighting a losing battle to regain control of the aircraft. With the big *thud* that signaled the bomber had been hit, the flying controls had gone dead. The pilot knew what the problem was. The control cables, which ran the length of the airplane, had been severed by the flak explosion.

Art looked toward the bomb bay and saw nothing but flames and smoke. Wheeler climbed out of his seat and grabbed a fire extinguisher, but when he pressed the handle, it only dribbled out its contents uselessly. Art remembered the fire extinguisher in the nose compartment and he headed back down to retrieve it.

The bomber was already sliding into a flat spin by the time Pearson climbed out of the pilot's seat. He hit the bail-out alarm and then snapped his parachute onto his chest harness. Looking back at the bomb bay he could see a wall of fire that reminded him of a flamethrower: *Fed by a fuel line,* the pilot reasoned. Smoke was rolling into the cockpit area. How many of his crew were still alive, he could not know—perhaps only Frechette and Wheeler, who was standing next to him. The bomber was spinning faster now. Pearson saw a view of the Alps flash across the cockpit windshield. *That's where we're going,* he thought.

On the other side of the bomb bay fire, Robert Halstein was forced out of his radio room by the thick smoke. He fastened his parachute onto his chest harness and headed for the rear of the bomber. Right waist gunner Charles Lyon saw the young radioman attach the chute, and it reminded him to do the same. He snapped the parachute onto his harness just in time.

In the nose of the Fortress, Ferguson had given up on getting the bomb salvo switch to work and was unfastening a fire extinguisher. Art knew in his heart the bomb bay fire was far beyond control, but he reached to get the extinguisher from Ferguson anyway. The bomber lurched suddenly and began a sharp spiraling descent that flung both the bombardier and navigator off their feet.

They were going down like a bath bubble goes down the drain when the plug is pulled. Art was sure they were all going to die if they did not bail out quickly. He was only two or three feet away from the escape door but the centrifugal force of the spinning aircraft would not allow him to reach the door's handle.

This is it, Art realized. *We're going down and there is nothing I can do about it.*

When the bomber exploded the young navigator did not hear a deafening noise. The sound was more of a *whoosh*. Then Art felt the concussion hit him in the stomach and he was gone—out of the airplane and out of the conscious world.

Lieutenant Herbert Heilbron was piloting a B-17 in the 352nd Bomb Squadron, which was flying somewhat behind and below the 419th formation. He saw Pearson's bomber when it was hit by flak. Pearson and Heilbron were close friends, and the latter watched in horror as the crippled B-17 spiraled toward the Alps and then exploded. He immediately told his gunners, "Look for chutes!" No one spotted any.

Crewmen aboard other 419th bombers also strained their eyes, hoping to identify a parachute against the snowy white backdrop of the mountains. At the end of the mission, they would report to the interrogation officers that sadly no parachutes were seen emerging from Pearson's dying Fortress. Some had witnessed the disturbing sight of the bomber being ripped apart by a fiery explosion—a wing breaking off—but no sign of chutes.

Incredibly, five of the airmen who had been blown out of Pearson's bomber managed to awaken in time to pull their rip-cords. All five of the parachutes opened properly. A sixth survivor was not as lucky. Art Frechette was alive but unconscious, and he was falling just as fast as any of the inanimate debris that had once been part of the B-17.

Like Art, Lyle Pearson had been rendered unconscious by the blast, but the pilot had regained consciousness seconds later. *"Oh my God, I'm still alive!"*

He pulled his ripcord and felt the reassuring jolt of the white silk catching the wind. Above him, he could see the rest of the bombers in his group flying on to their target. Something else was also above him and it was coming closer.

By the time Pearson had identified the falling object as a large portion of one of his B-17's wings, it was almost on top of him. He jerked at the parachute lines hoping by some miracle to steer out of the wing's path. The wreckage sailed past, missing him by no more than fifty feet. A small piece of trailing debris hit the top of Pearson's parachute, then slid away harmlessly.

Art Frechette would never know just how far he fell before he woke up. The bomber formation had started its bomb run at twenty-five thousand feet. The falling B-17 had most likely blown apart somewhere between fifteen thousand and twenty thousand feet. Art certainly had no time to consider such calculations when he woke up in midair. He was bleary but recovered quickly as information raced through his mind almost quicker than he could process it: *I'm alive! Colors . . . white and geen. The mountains! The Alps. So close! My chute is not open!* The last thought shocked Art fully awake. His right hand grabbed for his ripcord. His fingers touched the metal ring . . . and gripped it. But before he could pull the ring, Art Frechette slammed into a mountain.

———

The fallen navigator could not see a thing, but he could feel his body being tossed about. He was turning and rolling for what seemed like a long time and then nothing. The only sensation he was aware of was that he had stopped moving. He could not see anything, hear anything and strangest of all: He could not feel anything—not even pain.

So this is what death is like, Art thought. *Not what I expected.* For a while he waited to see what would happen next. He faded in and out of consciousness. Time passed. He could not tell how long, robbed of all his senses. Slowly he began to feel something. The sensation intensified, especially on his face. He was cold.

He could feel his face. *I'm not dead!* Art found he could wiggle around a little bit, even turn his head. Then he realized, he was lying facedown in snow. With great effort, he was able to roll onto his back.

"How can I still be alive?" he muttered. "Must have pulled the ripcord somehow. The chute must have slowed me a little." He raised his head slightly and could see his right hand still clenched around the ripcord ring. His parachute, he realized, was still unopened.

Overhead, Art spotted B-17s flying in formation in a sharp blue sky. It told him only minutes had elapsed since his impact with the mountain. He had not been certain before if he had been down for minutes or hours. Now he began to take an inventory of his body. He had no use of his right arm. There was no pain in the arm, but he could not move it. Both of his legs also seemed useless.

His feet felt colder than any part of his body, and when he looked, both of his boots were missing. The glove that had been on his left hand was gone. The exposed extremities soon began to ache from the cold. Art used his left arm to get into a sitting position and in doing so, he began to feel some pain coming on. He remembered the morphine in his first aid kit but quickly dismissed the idea of giving himself a shot. Morphine would make him sleepy and he could not afford that.

Would someone come looking for him? He assumed German soldiers were already searching. The Germans would want to round up the survivors as quickly as possible. *Survivors?* Art wondered how many of the guys had made it out. He could not be the only one. Then again, maybe he could be. The B-17 had exploded so suddenly. Could any of them have managed to bail out?

Art looked around, hoping to spot someone, even an enemy soldier. There was nobody in sight. Looking at the surrounding terrain, he began to envision how he had survived his terrible fall. He had landed on a steep mountain slope, packed with thick wet snow. As severe as the impact had been, it could have been worse. Striking the mountain at a bit of an angle, he had tumbled helplessly down the slope. If he had landed on flatter terrain, he would have almost certainly been killed instantly.

Art knew he might yet die there on the mountain. And if he did not die, there was a strong chance he could lose his feet or hands to the cold, unless he was discovered soon. He did another 360-degree survey of the area. He saw no one, but this time he spotted some smoke off in the distance. It was coming from somewhere down the mountain. He could not be sure how far away the smoke was, maybe a quarter of a mile.

Another painful effort to try standing proved hopeless, so Art began to wiggle and pull himself down the mountain slope, using his *good* left arm. His progress was frustratingly slow, but after a half hour or so, he reached a drop-off where he could go no farther. The first thing he saw down below was a little wooden hut. Smoke was coming from its small chimney. He guessed it was a structure used by farmers during the summer, when they brought their cows up to graze in the mountain pastures. Why it would be occupied during the winter, Art was not certain. Perhaps a hunter was using it. It did not matter—someone was either in the hut or close by. Art's spirit began to brighten.

Then the crippled airman spotted something off to the right of the hut—something that did not belong in the wintry Alpine scene. There in the little valley, little more than a hundred feet away from him, rested remains of his B-17 bomber. The airplane's wings were missing, but otherwise the crumpled fuselage seemed fairly intact. The body of one of Art's crewmates lay a few feet from the wreckage.

From where he was, there was no way for Art to identify the dead airman, nor could he tell if there were any other members of the crew on the other side of the bomber's wreckage. He was exhausted from the crawl to the ledge but the pain in his feet and legs had mostly disappeared again. He knew this was a bad sign. Art drew on the little remaining energy he had left and began to yell.

Slow minutes, which seemed like hours, passed. Art's attempt at yelling for help was slightly more than a whisper now. He saw someone coming toward him. It was a German soldier.

The soldier had been relieved from his duties at the antiaircraft battery to search for the *Luftgangsters* (air gangsters). He was sure there would be at least one dead body to retrieve, since he had watched one of the airmen falling through the sky without a parachute appearing. That could not be the man lying in the snow, who was in a bad way but obviously alive. The soldier pulled back the bolt of his rifle and pointed the weapon at the airman.

Art could not understand the German's instructions but it was clear he wanted the American to stand up and come with him. Pointing to his legs, Art said, *"Kaput. Kaput."* The soldier understood. He disappeared but soon returned with a civilian. The two men placed Art on a homemade litter and then took him down to the little hut. The warmth of the hut's small fireplace felt wonderful to the nearly frozen airman.

Not far away from the hut, Lyle Pearson was trudging through knee-deep snow. Even with a fully operative parachute, the pilot's landing had been a rough one. His back and one knee were causing him pain, and his right arm was bruised and bloody. He had shoved his right hand inside his flight coveralls to protect it from the cold. Pearson had no specific destination in mind; he was simply working his way down the mountain in the hope of finding someplace warm.

No more than ten minutes after his landing, he heard a rifle shot. It was near him. Pearson turned and spotted two civilians—an old man and a boy. The man had a rifle aimed in his direction.

"*Italiano?*" the pilot asked hopefully.

"*Nein. Deutsch!*" came the man's reply.

Pearson knew better than to take any chances with an enemy civilian. He raised his left arm into the air in surrender, but as he attempted to remove his injured right hand from inside the chest area of his flight suit, he found the blood had dried and adhered to the fabric. When he began to use his left hand to free his right, the old man fired again. Pearson heard the bullet buzz past his ear. The bloody hand was free and both arms were quickly extended above his head. The old man's perception that the American was trying to pull out a pistol had almost gotten the pilot killed.

Actually, Pearson *was* armed. He carried his regulation .45 automatic pistol in a shoulder holster underneath his flight suit. He wore the weapon on missions for only one reason—the holster and the metal of the .45 provided a little protection from a stray bit of flak striking him in the heart. He also carried a bowie knife in his boot. Although the knife looked menacing, it was there mainly to cut parachutes lines, if necessary.

Pearson sensed movement behind him and turned to see a German soldier, who struck him hard on the side of the head with a rifle butt.

"*Kaput?*" the German inquired as Pearson lay bleeding in the snow.

"*Ja, ja,*" Pearson assured him.

The soldier helped the American to his feet and relieved him of the .45 automatic pistol. Then he found the bowie knife and flung it away. The German also tried to remove Pearson's wedding ring from his left hand. The pilot balled the hand into a tight fist and pulled away, saying, "*Nein! Nein!*"

The German clutched his rifle with both hands as the American braced himself for another blow. Instead, the enemy soldier waved the rifle barrel, indicating the American should head down the mountain.

Art Frechette was not allowed to enjoy the coziness of the hut for long. Soon he was placed in a toboggan-type sled for transport down the mountain. It was a thrilling ride. The civilian from the hut stood at the front of the sled and steered it with his feet. It quickly became apparent the driver was an expert at his task, as the sled sailed along at a fantastic speed. Several times, Art was certain they were about to slip over the edge of a cliff and plunge to their deaths, but the driver smoothly swung the sled back on course just in time.

Their destination was the antiaircraft battery that had been responsible for downing Art's B-17. Two German soldiers carried him into a wooden building where he found a bittersweet surprise. Already in the room were his pilot, Lyle Pearson; the copilot, Sam Wheeler; the bombardier, William "Jack" Ferguson; and the bomber's tail gunner, Grant Dory.

The five airmen were not allowed much time for a reunion and were careful not to talk loud enough for their guards to overhear anything of importance. Art whispered that he had seen one dead crewmate next to the bomber's wreckage. None of the others had seen any additional crew members. One dead for sure. Five of them at the antiaircraft battery. Four men unaccounted for.

Art looked at the bruised and bloody faces of his fellow prisoners. *What a miracle,* he thought, that any of them had survived when their airplane blew to pieces. It was unlikely that any of the others were still alive . . . yet hope was all any of them had now.

In reality, only one other member of Pearson's crew was still alive, and he had so far evaded capture. Right waist gunner Charles Lyon had landed farther up the mountain than any of his crewmates. After a painful fall through the limbs of a tall pine, Lyon's parachute had become entangled, leaving him hanging fifteen feet above the ground. Shock brought on temporary blindness. The airman fought off panic and soon his sight returned, allowing him to cut the parachute lines and drop into a cushion of deep snow.

The bruised gunner began a difficult trek down the mountain. At times the snow was nearly waist high. As darkness fell and temperatures plunged, Lyon's wet clothing began to freeze. Far down in the valley, he could see the lights of a village. He trudged on, knowing his chances for survival were dwindling.

Lyon's capture, and rescue, came when a civilian with a rifle intercepted him. The man directed the shivering airman to a nearby farmhouse. Once inside he placed his rifle in a rack over the fireplace and offered Lyon a seat at a kitchen table. Soon a woman appeared with a large bowl of hot soup. Lyon smiled his thanks.

The airman was joined at the table by the entire family, as they shared their evening meal. Three young girls, whom Lyon estimated to be between five and nine years old, stared across the table at him, giggling occasionally. After dinner, he took a chocolate bar from his escape kit and divided it between the three grateful children. Later he was given dry clothing and shown into a room with a large feather bed. He was asleep in two minutes.

Lyon was awakened the following morning by the inviting smells of a country breakfast cooking in the kitchen. His "captors" seemed delighted to see he was thawed and well rested. After breakfast, the airman sat with the man and tried to communicate. Lyon spread his handkerchief escape map on the table.

"Where are we?" he wanted to know.

The man understood and pointed to a dot on the map labeled Brixen, Italy. Encouraged, Lyon inquired, "And how do I get to Switzerland?"

His host smiled and shook his head. The airman could not tell whether the man was indicating that such a winter's journey across the Alps was impossible, he was unwilling to aid in any escape plan, or he simply did not understand the question.

Since he had entered their home, this Austrian family had treated the young American flyer like a welcome guest. Lyon was beginning to allow himself to believe there was hope they would not turn him into the German Army. Lyon was churning butter for the wife when there was a hard knock at the front door. The two visitors were both in uniform—a teenage boy garbed in Hitler Youth attire and an armed German soldier.

Before he was led away, the young airman shook hands with the couple who had brought him in from the cold and had very likely saved his life. Positioned between his two guards, Lyon headed down the mountain to Brixen, or Bressanone, as it was known in Italian. He allowed himself one glance over his shoulder. The three little Austrian girls stood on the front steps of their house waving goodbye.

In the building at the antiaircraft battery, five bloody and wounded American airmen could find at least two things to be grateful for. They were alive and for the time being, they were still together. Their training had prepared them for the fact the Germans would interrogate each of them personally. When a German major entered the room the Americans became silent.

Art was the first to be questioned. Before asking him any questions, the German officer opened Art's coveralls. He found the navigator's escape kit, which contained, among other items, a map, a compass and fifty dollars in U.S. currency. He also discovered a pack of Camels. The German smiled and tucked the cigarettes inside his jacket. "Thank you. I accept this as a gift."

"You're welcome," Art responded. He had no intention of giving the Germans any information except his name, rank and serial number, but he did plan on being polite and nonconfrontational in his refusal.

The German major slipped up on his first question: "Well, you might as well tell us . . . we know you came from Foggia. And we know you were flying B-24s."

Art repressed the impulse to smile. "I'm sorry, Major. I can't tell you those things. I am Second Lieutenant Arthur Frechette Jr. My serial number is 02065531." Art answered each of the German officer's questions exactly the same way. Grant Dory was the next to be interrogated. He followed Art's lead, politely giving only his name, rank and serial number. And so it went with the other three captured airmen.

The German interrogator did not seem surprised or angered at the American bomber crew's lack of cooperation. At the end of the questioning, he ordered the guards to take the prisoners to another room where there were some cots. Grant Dory helped carry Art. Beyond cuts and abrasions, the tail gunner was the only one of the five Americans who did not seem to have suffered any serious injury.

Art was not only the most severely wounded, he looked terrible. He had banged his head while he had been tumbling down the mountain—a gash on his forehead had caused him to bleed "like a stuck pig." The injury looked worse than it was. What really concerned Art was the lack of feeling in his feet. The Germans put a heating element near his feet, but he could sense no improvement. He tried to keep the thought from developing, but Art knew if he did not get medical attention, he could be facing amputation.

Later in the day, Art was placed in a horse-drawn cart, along with Wheeler and Ferguson. As soon as the men realized they would be transported some distance, they urged the guards to allow Pearson to also ride in the cart. For some reason, the Germans refused to believe the pilot was really injured. Pearson was made to hobble along behind, with the aid of Dory.

The journey down the mountain was a painful one for Art. His feet finally began to thaw, and the pain was like none he had ever experienced. Each jolt of the cart added to his misery.

One of the guards was able to understand when the Americans inquired about where they were being taken. "Brixen," was the German's reply.

When they reached the town, the first thing Art noticed was that Brixen did not look like an Italian village. The houses and shops all had an Austrian or German appearance. Indeed, though it was on the Italian side of the border, Brixen's inhabitants were mostly Austrian.

As the prisoners passed down the street, civilians began to gather around the cart. Each of the American airmen had heard stories of downed airmen being killed by angry German civilians. Could it also happen with Austrians? At this point in the war, Brixen's residents were mostly women, old men and children. It was the women who ventured closer to look at the prisoners.

What Art saw on the women's faces as they gazed at him was not anger—it was pity. Some shook their heads and made the sign of the cross as they looked at his bloody head and mangled clothing. As the women turned away with sad faces, Art wanted to tell them, "Hey, I'm going to be okay!" Just then his feet throbbed with intense pain. Maybe the women of Brixen were right.

The prisoners spent the night in the Brixen jail. They were fed a meager meal by their guards but were given no medical attention. Art found he was able to use his fingers well enough to hold a piece of black bread. He still worried about losing his feet or toes, which continued to feel cold and numb. At the same time, there was ever-increasing pain.

It was nearly dark the following day when three of the American aviators were loaded into an ambulance. Lyle Pearson and Grant Dory were missing. Art wondered if he would ever see the pilot or the tail gunner again. The going was slow over the narrow Alpine roads. The driver had to find his way without the use of headlights. Art knew, at this point in the war, the Germans could not risk traveling during daylight hours. American fighters flew in almost daily to shoot up anything that moved—trains, troops, trucks and even ambulances. A red cross on the top of a vehicle did not mean much to the Thunderbolt and Lightning pilots. The Germans had a reputation for painting the medical designation on just about any type of truck.

After around two hours, during which Art judged they had covered some twenty-five miles, the ambulance arrived at the town of Bolzano. The Germans called it Bozen. The town was large enough to have a hospital, and the men received some medical aid there. Art desperately needed painkilling medication but he was given none. He guessed the drugs were as scarce as fuel for the Germans, but he would have welcomed even an aspirin. His feet continued to thaw, and the warmer they became, the more unbearable was his pain. The navigator's one night in Bolzano was agony.

The next morning, Art was feeling surprisingly better. The pain in his legs, feet and right arm was ever-present but the worst seemed to have passed. Again about dusk, the Americans were put into an ambulance for a two-hour ride to the city of Merano, which lay even deeper in the Alps than Bolzano.

For decades before the war, Merano and its valley had been a favorite resort for skiers, winter sportsmen and tourists. The town was completely Austrian in appearance and mood. In fact, Merano had once been the capital of the Tyrol region of Austria. At the end of the First World War, the Treaty of Versailles had made Merano part of Italy, at least officially. Art thought the town, with its narrow tree-shaded streets, inviting resort hotels, and old Gothic cathedral, was one of the most beautiful places he had ever seen.

But even this remote part of the Alps had become engulfed by the war. The German military had taken control of all the hotels and had turned most of them into hospitals and convalescent centers for its wounded.

Now the three American airmen were separated. Art was

saddened to say goodbye to Wheeler and Ferguson, holding on to the faint hope they might be reunited later, if only in a prison camp. At the same time, he was very hopeful that at last he might get the professional medical attention he so badly needed. It was between eight and nine in the evening when he was taken from the ambulance. Almost immediately he found himself in an operating room, surrounded by German doctors and nurses.

Three hours later, Art was awakened by the sound of laughter and singing. He discovered that most of his body was now in casts—one covering each leg and an upper-body cast that encompassed his chest and right arm. The doctors had left an opening in the cast, near the elbow, so they could change the bandage there. He could smell the sulfur-based medicine they had applied to his arm wound to fight infection.

There were two other patients in the room, wounded soldiers, Art assumed. The happy voices, both male and female, that had awakened him seemed to be coming from somewhere down the hall. And they were coming closer. Minutes later, the door opened quickly, and several German officers and civilian women entered the room. The officers were wearing their dress uniforms, and the women were in evening gowns. They were all very happy and brought with them the not unpleasant smell of alcohol and perfume.

Everyone was speaking at once but seemed to be saying the same thing. Art knew very little German but immediately understood what they were saying: "Happy New Year!"

It had completely slipped his mind that 1945 had arrived. One of the officers came to Art's bed and spoke to him. In the best German he could speak, Art replied, *"Ich bin Amerikaner."*

The German's smile grew wider. He clicked his heels together and gave Art a crisp salute. The officer's companion had overheard Art, and she reached out to shake his hand. "How do you do?" the beautiful woman asked in perfect English.

"*Fräulein.*" Art smiled back, enjoying the opportunity to meet someone who spoke his language. "You speak English, *Fräulein*. Where did you learn how?"

"How do you do?" the woman said and smiled.

Art soon discovered that "How do you do?" was the extent of her English skills. As soon as the other officers and women heard that Art was an American, there was a great excitement and everyone had to meet him. He was amazed at the friendly welcome he was receiving but thought the whole scene a little surreal and amusing. Three nights before, he had been drinking gin with his buddies in Foggia, and now he was in the middle of a New Year's celebration with the enemy.

So it was that Art Frechette headed into 1945, seriously injured albeit on the mend and a prisoner of war—but for the time being, in the hands of friendly captors. What did this year have in store for the Allies, the Germans and him personally?

January 1 brought another encounter with German civilians. The two wounded soldiers in the room were visited by friends and family members. One of the visitors was a girl around seven or eight years old, and she was dressed in a colorful wide skirt and a crisp white blouse. She carried a basket of apples and after giving one to each of the room's other occupants, she approached Art. He smiled at her and held up his hand in mild protest.

"*Ich bin Amerikaner.*"

If the little girl felt any apprehension, Art did not see it. She smiled and placed an apple in his hand.

By the end of the day, Art was beginning to feel extremely warm. His mind seemed to be working in slow motion and his vision was blurry. His fever grew stronger, and he lost track of time and his surroundings. It was two days before the fever broke and his head cleared. The head physician of the hospital was standing by his bed when Art awoke.

The doctor spoke English well enough to give Art a description of his wounds. He had sustained a fracture of the left knee-cap, torn ligaments in the left knee area, a severely sprained right ankle and a fractured right elbow. In addition to the broken bones, he had suffered a concussion, lacerations to his forehead, and all of his fingers and toes and his face showed the symptoms of frostbite. He was going to live but recovery from his injuries would be slow.

When the doctor informed Art he would soon be transferred to a room where "you can be with your comrades," the navigator felt better. But when he was taken to his new room, the two other men there were not members of his B-17 crew after all. They were American airmen, however—two crewmen of a B-24 Liberator that had been shot down a day or two before Art's bomber had been hit.

His two new roommates turned out to be godsends. Confined by his wounds and casts, Art could clumsily hold a fork with the frostbitten fingers of his left hand, but he could do little else for himself. The two other Americans were not badly injured and took it upon themselves to help their brother airman. For two weeks, they cut his food, shaved him, washed him, and sat him on the pot. When the B-24 crewmen were deemed healthy enough to be sent to prison camp, Art hated to see them go, but they had seen him through the initial bad days.

Without his two friends, the hospital room felt lonely. Rarely would a nurse stop in to check on him. His convalescent care was minimal. Art estimated there were more than two hundred wounded German soldiers in the hotel-hospital. The small medical staff was overwhelmed.

One pretty young nurse, however, seemed particularly attentive to Art's needs. He asked her if she might find something for him to read. She agreed to try but soon reported back that she was having difficulty locating a book written in English. She vowed to keep trying, and one day she walked proudly into Art's room carrying a thick book with a very worn cover. She assured him it was the only English-language book in the entire hospital.

Art looked at the contents. The book was a collection of poetry and essays. The copyright date was 1870. Not exactly what he had been hoping for, but it would help pass the time. He thanked the nurse, who appeared happy that he approved. Over the next few days Art found himself memorizing a few of the book's poems, for lack of any other mental stimulation. One poem by Henry Wadsworth Longfellow, entitled "A Psalm of Life," became his favorite. The young airman especially liked the two opening verses:

> *Tell me not, in mournful numbers,*
> *Life is but an empty dream!*
> *For the soul is dead that slumbers,*
> *And things are not what they seem.*

> *Life is real! Life is earnest!*
> *And the grave is not its goal;*
> *Dust thou art, to dust returnest,*
> *Was not spoken of the soul.*

Within a week, Art was assigned two new roommates. They were German soldiers, both of them named Hans. The older of the two referred to the other as "Hanslow," or Little Hans. Art's knowledge of the German language increased dramatically in the following days. Both of the Hanses were eager to hear about life in America. Art was equally interested in Germany and its people. All three men stayed away from any talk of their military jobs out of respect for their patriotic duties. However, the hospital staff provided current newspapers and sometimes, if the paper contained a story about an Allied air raid, the younger Hans might ask, "Why are you bombing Germany?"

Art refused to be pulled into an argument about the war, and the conversation soon returned to safer topics. He quickly grew to like his new roommates. They helped him do some of the things he still could not do for himself. On the day he took his first feeble steps, supported and encouraged by the two Germans, Art was only slightly happier than Hans and Hanslow. In return for their help, Art gave the two Hanses his daily ration of four cigarettes, which the nurses brought him the same as they did for each of the German patients.

Hanslow even gave Art a sponge bath once, after a nurse ordered him to do it. The young German, however, exercised the soldier's universal right of complaint. He griped about it in German the entire time it took him to give the bath. Art was surprised at how much he was able to understand. His German language skills were rapidly improving because of his interaction with his roommates.

As the weeks of recovery passed, Art had the opportunity to get to know other German soldiers. One was an eighteen-year-old Austrian who was assigned as the room's fourth patient. The young man was a draftee, and he hated life in the German Army. He was not reluctant to tell Art, "The war is lost for Germany. The sooner we get out of it, the better we will be."

The unhappy soldier became silent when a wounded German officer began dropping by to chat with Art. The officer spoke excellent English and the two men enjoyed their friendly conversations. As with Hans and Hanslow, Art was careful not to talk about his crew or its operations. The topics usually were confined to the American and German lifestyles. But the German officer did express one political belief that Art was to hear repeated many times by other Germans: "When are you Americans going to realize that the real enemy is the Russians? Why do you not join us and we will defeat the Russians together?"

Art was also visited by an English-speaking stranger who

claimed to be a representative of the International Red Cross. Something about the man did not seem right. Art's suspicions were confirmed when the stranger showed more interest in details about other crew members than in Art's health. His inquiries left Art with the impression that some of his B-17 buddies might have evaded capture.

Of course, he knew at least four other crewmen were in custody, and he had personally seen the body of another of his bomber mates. He provided no information to the "Red Cross representative." Each time the man asked him a question, Art shrugged and replied, "I don't know." It did not take long for the impostor to realize he was going to get nothing from the American airman. Art was glad to see the pretender leave, but it was disappointing that he could not speak with someone who was actually with the Red Cross.

All things considered, his life as a prisoner in the enemy hospital was not so bad. His roommates and the hospital staffers were friendly, the food was passable, and seated in a wheelchair, he was even allowed to attend nightly movies with the other patients.

There was one thing that bothered him greatly. He wished there was some way to get word to his family that he was alive. When the fake Red Cross man had introduced himself, Art's hopes and prayers appeared to have been answered. Back in Groton, the Frechettes received official word from the U.S. government that their son was missing in action, but few details were provided. Soon afterward, a follow-up letter from the acting commander of the Fifteenth Air Force, Brigadier General C.F. Born, arrived. As Art's parents read Born's letter, his horrific words stunned them: ". . . the bomber received a direct hit by flak in the bomb bay . . . No parachutes were seen . . . His personal effects have been assembled . . . they will be sent to the designated beneficiary." The general's final sentence left the Frechettes little hope: "I am proud to have had him in my command."

By mid-February, Art had recovered well enough to hobble around the hospital hall with the aid of crutches. He had become a familiar sight to the doctors and nurses who greeted him with smiles. On the morning of the fifteenth, everything changed. When he said a friendly, "Good morning," to his roommates, they ignored him.

Taking his morning exercise walk, he encountered nothing but silence and angry expressions from the normally genial hospital staffers. Many of the nurses seemed to be on the verge of tears and some wept openly.

The American could not imagine why he was suddenly being shunned, but he decided it was probably best to stay in his room as much as possible, at least until he had an understanding of what was going on. Later that day, one of his roommates silently handed Art a German newspaper. Art read the front-page story: British and American bombers had struck the old city of Dresden with devastating results.

The German news writers were notorious propagandists, and when Art read that as many as one hundred thirty-five thousand Germans had died in the raid, he had his doubts. Still, he also knew that aside from the expected political slant, the German newspapers were generally accurate when recounting events. There was little doubt that a terrible tragedy had befallen the people of Dresden, Germany.

Even as the young American aviator sat in an Italian hospital bed reading of Dresden's fate, the city was still in flames. The fires would rage for four more days until there was nothing left to burn.

Dresden had very little military or industrial capacity. The historic old city was a cultural center that was world-famous for its Dresden porcelain. Many of the Allied airmen who were ordered to carry out the raid could not understand why Dresden was targeted. The *why* would be debated for decades or longer, but the *who* responsible for the controversial bombing was easier to identify.

British Prime Minister Winston Churchill had long guided his Royal Air Force commanders in the strategy of the general bombing of German cities, as opposed to the American Air Force theory of "precision bombing" targets of military significance. Of course, the American bomber crews tried their best to be precise on their bomb runs, but there was often collateral damage and the unintentional killing of German civilians. Churchill and his RAF bombing chief, Arthur "Bomber" Harris, saw the demoralization of the German population as a way to bring about a speedier Allied victory. Also, the German V-1 and V-2 rocket bombings of London and other English cities very likely ignited in Churchill a basic human emotion—revenge.

It appeared that Churchill had convinced U.S. President Franklin Roosevelt of the usefulness of firebombing German civilians, or perhaps Roosevelt had his own reasons. Churchill and Roosevelt communicated constantly with each other throughout the war. With the end of the fighting in sight, it was the third Allied leader who worried them as much as the crumbling German army. Joseph Stalin's massive Russian army was closing in on Germany from the east, and its troops would be the first to reach Berlin. With much of Europe in ruins and chaos, could the ruthless Stalin be counted on to be satisfied with the conquest of eastern Germany?

Two days before the Dresden raid, the three Allied leaders had concluded their conference at Yalta. The main topic of discussion was how to divide control of the occupied countries in Europe. It was a poker game in which the Russian leader held a strong hand. If the firebombing of Dresden had been planned before Yalta, Churchill and Roosevelt saw no reason to cancel it afterward. The almost complete destruction of a major German city would certainly show Stalin the kind of military power the Americans and British possessed. And that they were not reluctant to use it.

More than seven hundred RAF bombers struck the heart of Dresden on February 13. The majority of the British bombs were incendiaries. Much of Dresden was constructed of old wooden buildings. By the time more than three hundred American bombers reached the city the next day, Dresden was already an inferno.

Besides Dresden's population of approximately six hundred thousand, up to four hundred thousand refugees fleeing from the advancing Russian army were also in the city when the bombs began to fall. The resulting fires created hell-like windstorms that roared through Dresden's streets. Tens of thousands died. The exact death toll would never be known, since many bodies were incinerated or buried in the ruins. After the war, the figure thirty-five thousand would become the (Allies') accepted Dresden death count.

In the days following the Dresden bombing raid, a nurse came into Art's room on her usual rounds. He could tell she had been crying. In German, he asked her what was wrong and she broke down in tears. She explained between sobs that she had family in Dresden.

One by one, Art's roommates and hospital staff members began to speak to him again. He tried to find the friendliness they had once enjoyed. It seemed to him that they were also trying, but the moment was gone. The feeling that, American or German, they were after all just human beings had been lost somewhere in the Pandora's box of war. Sadly, they were enemies again.

Art had reached the point in his recovery where two of his casts could be removed. Afterward, only the cast on his left leg remained. This allowed him to move around easier on his crutches, although his pace was still slow. He expected any day to be sent off to a prisoner of war camp. From what he read in the German newspapers, in the days following the Dresden raid, the young aviator had to face the possibility that his fate might turn out to be much worse. The news stories quoted Adolf Hitler, who was enraged at the attack on Dresden. The German dictator was threatening to order the executions of captured Allied airmen.

A few days later, Art was ordered to dress in his ragged flight clothes; then he was escorted to the street. There was no firing squad awaiting him there. In fact, there was not even an armed guard. He was simply instructed to walk to the corner and "Wait there for the van."

Art did as he was told. What else could he do? Any thought of escape was laughable. He could barely walk without his crutches. He waited on the street corner in Merano and soon a Volkswagen van arrived. As he struggled into the vehicle, an American officer greeted him, "Hi, Art, how the hell are you?"

Art studied the man's face. He had never seen him before. "How do you know who I am?"

The man smiled. "Sam Wheeler was in my hospital, and he told me about your fall. And I noticed your uniform is all ripped and shows signs of friction burns. I figured you had to be Art Frechette."

The officer was a B-25 Mitchell pilot who had been flying for the Twelfth Air Force when he was shot down. As he and Art chatted, the van stopped at other hotel-hospitals around Merano picking up additional prisoners. One man in particular caught everyone's attention. He was a black soldier wearing a

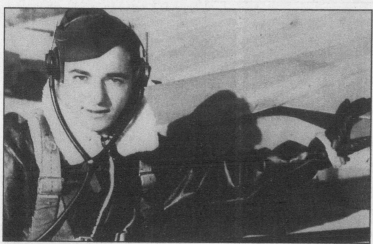

U.S. Air Force

An eighteen-year-old Aviation Cadet named Anthony Teta. Although he was in navigation training at Clarion State Teachers College in Pennsylvania, Tony also received small plane pilot training and soloed.

U.S. Air Force

Chart's bomber crew: (*standing, left to right*) Jerome J. Chart, George Wisniewski, Glenn B. Kelly, Anthony Teta; (*kneeling, left to right*) Kenneth Hall, John Stiles, Carl Robinson, William Goetz, Thomas Christenson, and John Cuffman.

U.S. Air Force

Giles F. Kauffman Jr.'s bomber crew, after a touch football game near Walla Walla, Washington: (*standing, left to right*) William Jarrel, Kauffman, unidentified, Stanley T. Ruben, J. J. Lecroix, Peter Seniawsky; (*kneeling, left to right*) Paul Spodar, Jacob M. Martinez, Jules Beck.

Courtesy of Peter Scott

Sergeant Peter Seniawsky and "the prettiest girl in Brooklyn," his future wife, Helen.

Courtesy of Peter Scott

Sergeant Seniawsky, waist gunner, in full flight gear. Note the sidearm, which Peter would forget to take along on the Schweinfurt mission.

U.S. Air Force

Arthur Frechette Jr., along with an instructor and fellow cadets, at pilot training school in Camden, Arkansas. Art is standing, third man from the left. The airplane is a Stearman PT17.

Eighteen-year-old Aviation Cadet Arthur Frechette Jr. in Montgomery, Alabama, during the summer of 1943.

U.S. Air Force

U.S. Air Force

Lieutenant Frechette, several months after VE Day, 1945. He had, at this point, regained some of the weight lost during his time as a POW, but he would never completely rid his body of the pain resulting from injuries caused by his fall into the Austrian Alps.

German military photo

Lieutenant Lyle C. Pearson, Art's pilot, in a photo taken by the German military soon after his capture.

Waist gunner Charles Lyon, shortly after bailing out of his B-17 over Austria and his being captured by the Germans.

German military photo

U.S. Air Force

Marvin R. Walker's bomber crew: (*standing, left to right*) William R. Schneider, William W. Weaver, Charles S. Armstrong, George E. Ahern, Paul A. Schrader; (*kneeling, left to right*) Walker, Maurice E. Joncas, Donald E. Knuepple, Daniel L. Rader. (Not shown in this photo is Philip Duke.)

Minutes before a V-2 rocket strike in London, the gunners of the B-17 *Torchy Tess* pose for a photo in front of Big Ben on a September day in 1944. The airmen's decision to stop their tour of the city to have this photo taken may have saved all of their lives. (*left to right*) Philip Duke, Charles Armstrong, William Schneider, George Ahern, Paul Schrader, William Weaver.

Courtesy of George Ahern

U.S. Air Force

Michael Swana's *Stork Club* bomber crew: (*standing, left to right*) Al Hareda, Leonard Weinstein, Charles DuShane, William Wells; (*kneeling, left to right*) Marvin Hydecker, Robert Valliere, Wallace MacCafferty, Michael Swana.

Stork Club copilot, Wallace Mac-Cafferty, examines the ragged hole left in his aircraft's wing by German antiaircraft during a mercy flight over Hilversum, the Netherlands, on May 2, 1945.

U.S. Air Force

Courtesy of the author

Veteran airmen who took part in Operation Chowhound and Manna are greeted by appreciative Dutch crowds during a 1995 parade. The former navigator of *The Stork Club*, Bob Valliere, waves as his wife, Nancy, watches.

Peter (Seniawsky) Scott at home in Old Saybrook, Connecticut, in 2002.

Courtesy of the author

Peter Scott (*left*) visiting Frank Pogorzelski in the latter's Pennsylvania home in May 2003. The former waist gunner and former navigator had not seen each other since they had bailed out of their burning B-17 sixty years earlier.

Courtesy of the author

Paul Spodar at his New Port Richey, Florida, home in 2002. Spodar and Scott had fought side by side as B-17 waist gunners, but each was unaware if the other had survived the deadly "Black Thursday" bombing raid until the author's research led to a telephone reunion in 2003.

Courtesy of the author

(*left to right*) Art Frechette, Lyle Pearson, and William "Jack" Ferguson during a 301st Bomb Group reunion in 1990. Almost forty-six years before, the former navigator, pilot, and bombardier had miraculously survived the explosion that had destroyed their B-17 over the Italian Alps.

(*left to right*) Bob Valliere, George Ahern, author Travis L. Ayres, Anthony Teta, and Thomas Ayres. Valliere, Ahern, and Teta, veterans of the Eighth Air Force, met and became best friends years after World War II.

German military uniform. Art introduced himself and then asked the soldier his name.

"George Smith. Good to meet you."

"George, I'm guessing you're not really in the German army."

Smith chuckled. "No, I'm from Virginia." He told Art he was an enlisted man, and he had only been in the Army for six months before being captured in Italy.

Frechette and the other prisoners were driven to the local train yard, where they were ordered into boxcars already crowded with Allied POWs. There were Americans, British and lots of Russians. The train did not move until darkness began to fall, and then it did not stop until first light the following morning.

The boxcar doors were opened and the prisoners were allowed to stretch their legs outside, but they were warned to stay close to the train. Art could see why the engineer had picked the place. Their section of track was deep in a heavily wooded valley. It would be difficult for Allied airplanes to spot them. There was a little Austrian village there but nothing worthy of the American Air Force's attention.

However, later that morning, Art had a chance to witness the awesome sight of an American bomber armada from the German's point of view. The sound of Fortress and Liberator engines rumbled through the Alpine valley long before anyone saw the first bomber. By the time the first wave of aircraft was overhead, even the train was rattling from the sound waves. Art began counting the bombers as they stretched from horizon to horizon. There were hundreds of them. He had been part of such a formation before, but seeing it from the ground was a rare experience.

The massive bomber show was also having an impact on the German guards. Art could see the fear in their eyes and could understand some of their muted comments, not meant for their officers' ears. The guards assigned positions on top of the boxcars scurried to the ground. Art felt they were ready to run and were only restrained by fear of their own officers.

One of the guards near him nervously asked Art what kind of airplanes these were. Art knew that unless a sharp-eyed P-51 escort pilot miraculously spotted the train, they were in no real danger of being bombed, but he decided not to share that information with the frightened guard.

"Those over there are B-24s. They're loaded with bombs. Just one of those B-24s could destroy the train and this town. And you see that group of planes over there?" The guard followed Art's gesture with wide eyes. "Those are Flying Fortresses. They're even more deadly than the Liberators!"

At nightfall, the train headed eastward and it reached its destination before dawn. One of the guards provided the name of the place—Spittal, Austria, somewhere near the Yugoslavian border. The railroad tracks ran right next to the prison camp, no more than a hundred feet from the gate. Art got his first look at Stalag 18 as he jumped down from the boxcar.

Eight- to ten-feet-high poles strung with barbed wire formed the outer fence of the compound. Another identical fence had been built ten feet inside the first. Wooden guard towers commanded each corner. The guards in the towers nearest the train had their machine guns aimed at the arriving prisoners. Rows of single-story wooden barracks looked cold and bleak on the treeless terrain. In fact, even on the outside of the camp, there were no trees for more than a hundred yards.

Once inside the camp, the new prisoners were separated by nationality. The Russians were sent to an adjoining compound. The Americans and Brits stayed together. There was also a compound housing only French captives. The interior of the barracks were much as Art expected—rows of upper and lower bunks.

Each prisoner had his own mattress, such as it was. The mattress was simply a large bag made from ticking fabric and filled with straw. A metal stove in the center of the barracks provided inadequate heat.

Art was directed to the end of the barracks, where there was a small room. "You will be living in here with us," a British officer told him. The "us" included three British officers and two American officers. The little room looked no different from the main barracks, except that Art noticed there was an electrical outlet on one wall. Nothing was plugged into the outlet, and Art could not imagine what electrical appliance the Germans might allow the prisoners to possess. For light, a single bulb dangled at the end of its cord, hanging from the ceiling.

Later, Art got a sample of the prisoners' menu. The meal consisted of a bowl of soup, a piece of coarse black bread and a dab of jelly. The general opinion of the prisoners, and also some of the guards, was that the bread was made of sawdust. One of his new American roommates urged Art to eat it all.

"This is your ration for the day," he said.

"It's not much to get by on," Art commented.

"We have found ways to supplement," the officer assured him. "The Brits sometimes go out to the local farms on work parties. They smuggle in what food they can get their hands on."

"What about the Americans?" Art asked. "They don't go along on the outside work parties?"

"No. The Germans don't trust us. The Jerries always demand a promise not to escape. Once the Brits give their word, the Germans know they won't go back on it."

Art smiled.

"And to get extra food," the officer added in a whisper, "we also have Wally."

"Who's Wally?" Art asked.

The officer went on to explain the remarkable abilities of

Sergeant Wally Tempest. Before the war, the sergeant had been an electrician in his homeland of South Africa. Now he was assigned as a sort of orderly to the three British officers in Art's room. Though the American officers refused to treat Wally as a servant, they did enjoy the benefits of his amazing talent for scrounging and trading with the guards.

Not only could Wally procure food and coffee, he somehow managed to obtain the components needed to make a heating appliance. As a trained electrician, it was easy for him to build the little water heater, which once plugged into the officers' wall outlet produced hot coffee and soup. The Germans' official policy was for any such items to be seized by the guards. In fact, searches were occasionally conducted, and one or two of the heating elements would be discovered. Wally made extra ones just for that purpose. The reality of prison life was that the guards desired to own the little soup heaters–coffeemakers themselves. The guards secretly provided Wally with the materials he said he needed, which was always more than he really needed. He made heating elements for them and saved all the extra wiring and parts for his own use.

Once the Germans learned that Wally was a trained electrician, he was called on often to do repair jobs on the camp's shaky wiring system. The weakest storm could plunge the camp into darkness, and Wally was always ready to help restore the lights. He asked nothing in return, but because of his usefulness, he was able to roam around the camp unsupervised. Wally made the most of it. He "liberated" food from the camp kitchen, coal for the barracks stove, blankets and anything else he thought might be useful to his mates.

Wally once confessed to Art that the Germans were really getting a one-sided deal. "Every time the power goes out and they ask me to fix it, I'm sabotaging the electrical system. I get the lights back on, but I'm overloading the circuits. One of these days," the South African smiled, "this whole place is going to burn to the ground."

Art nodded as if he approved, but he really was not sure what such a plan would accomplish for the prisoners. The secret seemed to make Wally happy, so Art kept his doubts to himself. The sergeant was too productive to be discouraged from his activities. One of his proudest accomplishments was accumulating enough parts to build a radio receiver. With their own radio, the Americans and British were able to maintain an up-to-date awareness of what was going on with the war and just how close they were to liberation.

The Germans knew the Yanks and Brits had a radio and staged many surprise raids attempting to seize it, but the device was never discovered. It was hidden well—inside the German commandant's own office. The office doubled as the camp's infirmary, although the Germans had no doctor on staff. There were at least two prisoners in the American and British compound who were doctors. These men treated their fellow prisoners and occasionally even the guards. Because of this, these doctors were allowed access to the commandant's office-infirmary.

Every night at least one of the prisoners would complain of stomach cramps or some other real or imaginary ailment. One of the doctors would request the key to the office to get medicine. Once inside, the doctor would pry loose a floorboard, then retrieve and plug in the prisoners' radio. He would listen to the BBC broadcasts right in the commandant's office. In this manner, the American and British prisoners kept themselves as well informed as their German captors.

Art and his friends did not need the radio to know that the Allies were tightening the noose on Germany. Sometimes they witnessed visible proof. On the morning of his first full day at the stalag, he was awakened by the sound of machine guns firing. From his barracks' window he saw a train with antiaircraft weapons mounted on it; the train sat on the tracks just yards outside the prison's outer fence. Under the international rules of war, the Germans were not supposed to have an armed train so close to a prison camp, but there it was, its guns blazing away at three American P-38 fighters.

The Lightnings made several passes at the train, splintering some boxcars but doing little real damage. Art hoped they realized the compound was a prison camp and not a German army base. Apparently the P-38 pilots were aware their own men were down there, for they soon abandoned the attacks on the train and streaked away. Had they aborted the attacks only because they feared hitting the POW camp, or had the fighter pilots been looking for another target entirely? Art wondered about it and a few days later he got his answer.

The P-38s came back. Again there were three of them, though Art had no way of knowing if these were the same pilots. Once again the heavily armed German train sat on the tracks next to the camp. The antiaircraft gunners fired almost continuously, but the Lightnings were too fast for them. The American pilots, in fact, seemed to pay no attention to the train during this raid. It became obvious to Art and the other prisoners, who all ran into the prison yard to watch the battle, that the P-38s were after something else.

Art looked over at the French compound and noticed the prisoners there had also come out of their barracks to see the show. However, the men were hunkered down on the ground. Beyond them, in the Russian compound, he could see the prisoners there were also curious about the air raid, but they were taking whatever cover they could find. Only the American and British prisoners were standing around watching the battle as if they were spectators at a baseball game.

When the P-38s found their target, Art and his friends were not prepared for the concussion that followed. First there was a soundless fireball explosion less than a mile away. A second or two later came the deafening sound of a large ammunition dump being blown apart. Just as Art and all the Americans and British began to cheer, a strong wind roared across the camp and knocked most of them on their backsides. The prisoners quickly scrambled to their feet and cheered the Lightning pilots' success even louder.

Most days in the stalag were not nearly as exciting. The prisoners' time was mostly occupied by three activities: talking, reading and playing cards. Art was surprised at the number of books in camp. It had been his experience that the German interrogators took most personal items away soon after capture. Perhaps, though they were happy to discover American cigarettes, chocolate bars and watches, the Germans found no use for the English-language paperbacks.

Conversation was by far the most popular pastime. Topics ranged from home life and personal experiences to intellectual and philosophical discussions. Many of the men in the American and British compound were well educated. Two British officers had been Oxford professors before the war. Art not only enjoyed the discussions but realized they were important in keeping his mind sharp and clear.

Appearance was also important. As an officer, Art tried to set an example. Most of the prisoners wore ragged uniforms and there was not much that could be done about that, but a man could wash when there was water, keep his hair trimmed and even shave. For some reason, the Germans allowed the British officers to keep their personal straight razors. These officers were more than happy to share the blades with their American friends.

One day, word spread through the camp that the Red Cross was coming. Art had heard the organization often brought clothing for the prisoners, and he was eager for a fresh uniform.

The Red Cross representative quickly ran out, but Art was able to secure a heavy British greatcoat and a decent pair of shoes. The coat was like a thick horse blanket with sleeves and would keep him warmer at night than the thin German blanket.

Receiving the shoes was even more important to Art. Before he had left the hospital in Merano, he had been given a worn pair of German Army boots. They were at least two sizes too small for him. Art had survived the frostbite with all of his toes intact, but his feet still hurt badly. Walking around the camp in his "new" Red Cross shoes, he discovered that although he was still an invalid, he was in much less pain.

Sometimes the prisoners talked of escaping. For Art personally, such a thought was simply fantasy entertainment. Even after one of the American doctors had removed his leg cast, he was in no condition to walk any great distance, even if he could have somehow managed to get outside of the camp. Everyone realized the odds against escape. If a prisoner even accidentally wandered near the inner fence, a tower guard would point his machine gun and shout a warning. Come near the fence again, and there would be no second warning.

Everyone agreed that if one were going to plan an escape, it could not be through the fences. To make it past the first fence would be an outright miracle, and then you would have accomplished nothing but to become trapped between the inside and outside fences. The tower guards seemed the worst tempered of all the Germans. Art was certain they would not hesitate to use their machine guns.

As March arrived, it was not so much a question of how to escape but *why*. The American and British prisoners knew from the broadcasts they heard on their secret radio that the war would be over in a few short months, if not weeks. Why risk it?

You were more likely to get home sooner by waiting to be liberated than by wandering through the Alps. Of course, there were wounded prisoners who might not hang on until the Allied troops arrived, but those men were in no condition to think of escape.

One British officer saw things differently. Many of the other prisoners knew of his plans and respected his courage and cunning, if not his reasoning. The man dyed a uniform and modified it to look like civilian clothing. Somehow, possibly by trading with a guard, he obtained some German currency. Local civilians often visited the camp on business. In broad daylight, the British officer, dressed in his new clothes, fell in behind one group of civilians and walked right out through the front gate.

If any of the civilians were suspicious, the Brit had a story prepared and he spoke fluent German. When he had been gone for two weeks, the happy speculation among the prisoners was that their comrade had made it. However, a day or so later, the escapee was brought back into camp and thrown into solitary confinement. Although his plan to get out of the stalag had worked perfectly, the British officer had been unable to get out of the Alpine valley. The Germans had simply bottled up both ends of the only road traversing the valley, leaving him only one route of escape—over the impossibly high and rugged mountains.

No one else would attempt escape from Stalag 18, but day by day the prisoners saw signs that indicated they might soon be free. P-47 Thunderbolts were venturing into the valley looking for targets, and then one April morning, Art spotted about thirty airplanes approaching the town of Spittal. A fellow prisoner asked him what they were.

"Those are B-17s," Art replied. His first thought was that the Fortresses were returning home from a mission, but then, noticing the tightness of the formation, Art came to another conclusion: "I think they're on a bomb run!" The words had just left his lips when bombs began to fall on Spittal, causing great excitement among the German guards. Art doubted the prison camp was in very much danger. He guessed the target was Spittal's small train yard. If the P-38s and P-47s had not attacked the camp, there was not much reason to think the B-17s would do so. Apparently the Allied authorities were aware of the camp's location and had placed it out of bounds in their strike plans.

The bombing of Spittal was a good sign, Art concluded. If the American Air Force was hitting targets of such little importance, it had to mean most of the major targets had already been destroyed. The war was nearing its end.

Art was walking along the inner fence of the American and British compound when he first heard of the German surrender. A normally stone-faced guard, who had never spoken to him, said, "Well, the war is over."

"If it is, I haven't heard about it," Art replied.

"Yes, the war is over. We will all be going home soon."

Art had seen the trains rolling past the prison camp, each overloaded with wounded and dispirited German soldiers fleeing the advancing Russian army in the east. They were a beaten-looking bunch, Art thought. And more of the prison guards were disappearing each day. Still Art found it hard to believe he would soon be going home. Later, on the same day that he spoke with the guard, the Americans and British of Stalag 18 received word that the news of the surrender was real.

By monitoring their radio, the prisoners knew the British army was very close, but their first liberator was an American Air Force doctor who parachuted out of a B-24 and landed near camp. There was not a single German guard left to greet him.

The doctor had been sent ahead to treat what prisoners he could and to prepare the worst cases for swift evacuation. He also brought the happy news that plenty of food was on the way.

The following day, Art watched four B-24 bombers approaching the area. The citizens of Spittal were also watching, and as the Liberators' bomb bay doors began to open, most of the villagers scurried for cover. It was not bombs that fell that day, but canisters filled with food and medical supplies. The majority of the canisters landed just outside the stalag and were easily retrieved by the prisoners.

A few of the canisters landed in Spittal; but instead of opening them, the local civilians reported the locations to Allied officers at the prison camp. The villagers wanted the victors to know they were cooperating completely. They were also nervous about the thousands of Russian prisoners who were now unguarded. Their fear was well grounded.

Allied headquarters had sent word that General Eisenhower advised all prisoners to remain in their camps until troops arrived to evacuate them. The Americans, British and French stayed put, but the Russians would not. Many of them invaded the little town of Spittal, hung its gauleiter (the local Nazi leader) from a lamppost, and went on a spree, vandalizing and harassing the local population.

Order was quickly restored when the British Army arrived a few days before May 8, the date set for the official overall surrender of German forces in Europe. Art was given a new British uniform, placed in an ambulance with several other wounded prisoners and driven to an airfield near the Yugoslav border. Allied aircraft were awaiting the POWs' arrival. Art had awakened in a German prison camp that morning, and by the early afternoon he was resting comfortably in an Allied hospital in Italy.

The Army doctors, nurses and staff treated the former prisoners with kindness and understanding. Art received a complete physical examination, and his condition and medical options were carefully documented. The doctors informed him that his feet and legs were healing nicely and that he could expect to regain almost unrestricted mobility. His right elbow joint, however, had been severely damaged and would require an operation. Their opinion did not surprise Art. While the injury to his elbow was not causing him great pain, he had only a few degrees of motion with his right arm.

He was given a choice. The doctors told him they could conduct the operation in Italy or it could be done when he reached the United States. The young navigator wanted to go home. By the third week of May 1945, Art was on board a hospital airplane bound from Naples, Italy, to the United States. He was an alarmingly thin twenty-year-old combat veteran who carried home memories that would remain vivid for the rest of his life.

Many of the memories were painful to recall—awakening in midair, the bone-breaking impact on the mountain, the sense of being dead and the reality of seeing the lifeless body of one of his crewmates beside the smoldering wreckage of his airplane. But there were also good memories—the reunion with four of his buddies at the antiaircraft battery, a German New Year's party, a pretty nurse who brought her enemy a book to read, Hans and Hanslow, and a little Austrian girl with the gift of an apple.

Only days before his departure back home to America, something happened that would become one of Art's most cherished memories. One morning during his stay at the Allied hospital in Italy, Art was escorted along with dozens of other wounded American airmen, sailors, and soldiers to the building's lobby. No one would tell them where they were being taken. When the frail patients arrived in the lobby, they found almost the entire hospital staff there applauding them. Then a team of Army officers moved down the line—stopping, saluting, and placing a medal on the chest of each man. More than a few of the onlookers wiped away tears as each of the battle-wounded veterans stood at attention on his crutch or cane, or sat as erect as possible in his wheelchair. These young Americans, like tens of thousands of others, risked their lives and shed their own blood for their country.

Somehow they had survived in foxholes, on beaches, at sea or in enemy skies. Each would have a story to take home. Some would hold their stories deep inside them for decades after the war. Some would take their untold stories to their graves. Others would share their stories with family and friends and allow them to be handed down to unborn generations. They were remarkable men with remarkable stories.

The presiding officer stepped in front of Sergeant Arthur Frechette Jr., saluted, and then pinned the Purple Heart medal to the airman's shirt. The few spectators who had heard how Art earned his medal knew that his was one of the most amazing stories of survival of the war. He was the man who fell fifteen thousand feet, without a parachute, and lived.

After the War

Arthur Frechette Jr. was admitted to a hospital immediately after his return to the United States. In June 1945 he was pleased to learn the Army was transferring him to another hospital in Massachusetts, not a great distance from his parents in Groton, Connecticut, who had only recently learned their son was alive. Art would remain a patient at the hospital until January 1946, during which time he would undergo two operations on his right arm. Recovery was augmented by daily physical therapy sessions that returned almost normal mobility to his injured arm and knee. Occasional pain in his extremities would be a lifelong reminder of the day he fell in the Alps.

In March 1946, Art was released from military service. He
once again enrolled at the University of Connecticut, changing
his major to business. In the summer of 1947 he decided to attend a semester at the University of Vermont, where he had done
part of his military training. There on the Vermont campus, the
former airman met an attractive and wholesome young coed
named Doris Barnard, who was a teacher taking summer classes.
Art and Doris were married in 1948.

The following year, Art graduated from the University of
Connecticut and soon after went to work for Sears, Roebuck
and Co. In 1959 he joined Doris in the teaching profession. His
first assignment was a fifth-grade class in Haddam, Connecticut.
The early sixties brought a move to the Cheshire school system,
where Art was promoted to supervisor of curriculum. He spent
four rewarding decades in education before retiring in 1986.

Art and Doris Frechette were still living in Cheshire, Connecticut, when the author first met them. They had raised three
sons: Mike, Tom and Bill, and they spoke proudly of their
three grandchildren. Art was active as a guest speaker at area
high schools and libraries, where he related his World War II
experiences to a new generation of young Americans.

In 2003, Art Frechette Jr. passed away, fifty-nine years after
he had cheated death on an Austrian mountain.

Lyle Pearson, Art's wartime pilot, had been forced to march
from Brixen to Bolzano, and from there he was transported to
Frankfurt, Germany. During eight days of interrogation at
Frankfurt, the American pilot was not physically abused by his
captors, but he was repeatedly threatened with death. At one
point, a rifle muzzle was shoved into the back of his head and
the weapon was cocked.

When his interrogators finally determined they could not in-
timidate the American aviator, he was sent by train to a prisoner
of war camp in northern Germany. During a midnight stop in

Berlin, the guards allowed their prisoners out of their boxcars to relieve themselves. Civilians at the train station began to hurl rocks and gravel at the prisoners, and the soldiers hurriedly herded the men back on board the train.

Pearson weighed 190 pounds on the morning of his final bombing mission. Less than five months later, at the time of his liberation from a German stalag, the pilot had lost fifty pounds. Like thousands of other ex-POWs, he was transferred to Camp Lucky Strike in France, in preparation for his return to the United States. It was at Lucky Strike that Pearson enjoyed his first reunion with a crew member. Another thin but cheerful airman walked up to him and asked, "So, Lyle, do you still think you've got it made?" It was his copilot, Sam Wheeler.

After his discharge from the Army in December 1945, Pearson returned to his wife and his home state of Minnesota. For the next five years, he was in and out of various hospitals, seeking relief from continuing knee and back problems. The war injuries would nag Pearson for the rest of his life—and inspire him in a lifelong dedication to help other disabled American veterans.

In 1954, he went to work for the Mankato, Minnesota, Probation Department. Six years later, he became head of the Nicollet County Probation Department. Pearson spent almost thirty years serving Nicollet County, retiring in 1983 as Director of Court Services. Even more fulfilling to Pearson was his membership and leadership in the Disabled American Veterans organization. He rose to the office of Minnesota State Commissioner, and in 1975 he was elected national president of the DAV.

At the age of seventy-seven, he was invited back to the town of Brixen (Italian: Bressanone), Italy. The occasion was the 1998 dedication of two monuments constructed by local citizens to honor the dead airmen of two separate bomber crashes on nearby mountains. Pearson went to pay tribute to four of his crewmen who had perished on December 29, 1944. He was accompanied on the trip by his wife, Katherine, and his lifelong friend and former right waist gunner, Charlie Lyon, and Lyon's wife.

After the dedication ceremony, the former pilot was approached by a man who had been only eleven years old when the fuselage of Pearson's bomber had fallen near his family's farmhouse. The man gave the former aviators and their wives a tour of the site and later took Pearson to the basement of the farmhouse, where the man's father had saved a few pieces of the downed Fortress.

Today, one of the propeller hubs of B-17 number 44-6652 is displayed on a shelf in Lyle Pearson's den. It is a precious reminder and his own little monument to his bomber crew—the survivors and the four boys who never made it back.

Lyle and Katherine Pearson are the parents of seven children (Colleen, Lyle Jr., Rosemary, Lloyd, Ann Marie, Gail, and Kurt) and have ten grandchildren. Pearson continues to serve his country as a member of the National Committee for POW and MIA Affairs and the Disabled American Veterans.

Charles Lyon had a brief reunion with his pilot, Lyle Pearson, in Bolzano before the Germans sent the two men in different directions. Lyon was sent to Stalag 7A near Nuremberg where he spent several hard months. In the last days of the war, many of the Nuremberg POWs were forced to march more than one hundred miles across Germany as their guards sought to avoid Russian troops and surrender to American forces. Lyon's liberation came on April 29, 1945. He was sent home and discharged in November.

In January of the following year, Lyon was in his dress uniform, sitting in the front-row pew of a small church in Anthon, Iowa. Several young women in the congregation found it impossible to keep their eyes off the young air veteran. Lyon, however, focused his gaze on the lovely girl playing the church organ. He especially appreciated the organist's toned, slender legs as they worked the pedals. Her name was Mary Jo Hoskins, and she also had noticed her admirer as well. His stare was distracting but not unwelcome. Charlie and Mary Jo were married the following August.

During his 1998 trip back to Austria, Charlie asked to visit the mountain house where he had enjoyed an Austrian family's warm hospitality on the night of December 29, 1944. The man currently living in the house told Charlie that it was his father, Josef Frener, who had "captured" the young airman, saving him from freezing to death. The senior Frener was by then deceased, but Charlie was reunited with the three daughters who had been so delighted by the visit of the " . . . handsome young American flyer," fifty-four years before.

Charlie was informed that Mrs. Josef Frener was still living in the house, but she was extremely frail and ill. As he was led to her bedside, the old woman began to smile. She took his hand, each of them sensing that a circle of life had been completed.

Beginning in 1945, Charlie Lyon earned his living as a beekeeper, just as his father had before him. From that point, Charlie was the owner of Herrick Honey Farms, which these days produces a million pounds of honey "in a good year" and sells under the Blue Star Honey brand. His son, James, and one grandson have followed the tradition and are beekeepers in the family business, in Anthon. Besides James, the Lyons raised a daughter, Kathy. Five grandchildren and two great-grandchildren were later born into the Lyon family. Charles Lyon died in May 2005.

William "Jack" Ferguson and **Sam Wheeler** were allowed to recover together for a while at a German hospital in Merano. Ferguson ended up in Stalag 7A with Charles Lyon, where he remained until May 1945. During his tour of duty, the bombardier had accomplished something few other airmen could claim: He had survived the crashes and destruction of three B-17s.

Back in the States, Ferguson went to work for his father's Chevrolet dealership in Windsor, Missouri. In the summer of 1945, he met Alice Ebing, the widow of Navy pilot Eugene Webb. Ferguson and Webb had been good friends in high school. Webb had died while attempting to land his torpedo plane on the deck of an escort carrier, leaving a wife, a four-year-old daughter and a baby son he had never seen. In January 1946, Ferguson married Ebing and adopted the two children, Carol and Dennis. Dennis graduated from the United States Air Force Academy in 1966 and served in Vietnam. Two more offspring were born to the Fergusons: a daughter Janice and a son Jerry, as well as two grandchildren and two great-grandchildren.

Ferguson's father retired in 1965, relinquishing control of the auto dealership to his son. Jack headed the company until he too retired in 1988. During their retirement years, Jack and Alice lived on the shore of a beautiful Missouri lake. William "Jack" Ferguson died in 2007.

Samuel Wheeler was sent home to the U.S. soon after his brief reunion with Lyle Pearson at Camp Lucky Strike. Wheeler liked flying, especially when no one was trying to shoot him down, and he decided to reenlist. He spent twenty years as an Air Force officer. A proud highlight of his military service was his participation in the postwar Berlin Airlift. Sam Wheeler is deceased.

Grant Dory also reenlisted and served in the Air Force for twenty years. During his military career, Dory married and the couple had a daughter. After the Air Force years, the Dorys retired to Arizona. Grant Dory died in the late 1990s.

Farrell Haney, Mitchell Vuyanovich, Charles Williams and **Robert Halstein:** All four of these American patriots died in the

explosion and crash of their bomber. Local civilians buried the
bodies of Haney, Vuyanovich, and Williams in a church cemetery
on January 3, 1945. Later that year, the bodies of these three
airmen were transferred to the American Military Cemetery in
Mirandola, Italy, for burial. (It is possible one or more of these
bodies may have eventually been returned for burial in the United
States.)

For days after the B-17 crash, German soldiers searched the
Austrian mountain area trying to locate the bomber's young
radioman, or at the very least, his body. Civilians living near
the crash site would continue looking for years after the war. The
body was never found—only a pair of dog tags bearing the name:
Sergeant Robert J. Halstein.

Today a monument near the town of Brixen stands as a reminder of the terrible cost of war, dedicated by the citizens of
Brixen in the summer of 1998. Inscribed on it are the names
of the four young Americans who died on Rutzenberg Mountain
on December 29, 1944.

Crew Reunion: The six airmen who survived the crash of
their Fortress managed to maintain contact with each other after
the war via telephone and occasionally in person. In 1990, Art
Frechette, Lyle Pearson and Jack Ferguson were reunited at a
301st Bomb Group reunion. Charlie Lyon and Pearson returned
to Brixen together in 1998, taking part in the monument dedication ceremonies. Pearson also visited Grant Dory at Dory's home
in Arizona.

• The Belly Gunner and Big Ben •

GEORGE AHERN
Ball Turret Gunner

351ST BOMB GROUP

509TH BOMB SQUADRON

The gunners who manned the Flying Fortresses always seemed different from any of the other fighting men of World War II. They fought differently. While the B-17 was one of the most effective offensive weapons of the war, the bomber gunner's role was a defensive one—fighting to protect the "Fort."

B-17 gunners even looked different. Dressed in their layers of combat gear consisting of electric suits, flak jackets, parachutes, oxygen masks, goggles and flak helmets, the bomber gunners looked more like invaders from outer space than American soldiers. Their lifestyle was certainly different from that of the infantryman or the sailor. During the day, an Eighth Air Force gunner could be flying through the hellish gauntlet of German antiaircraft fire and fighting off attacks by Luftwaffe wolf packs. In the evening, that same airman could be sharing a draft ale with a young English lovely in a cozy pub.

Like the foot soldier and the sailor, the bomber gunner just wanted to do his duty and survive, but unlike the others, the airman knew exactly how many battles he must fight in order to go home. At least he thought he knew. Twenty-five, thirty, thirty-five combat missions—the numbers kept changing. It was a very large carrot at the end of an increasingly long stick. Thousands would never reach that lucky number, and few ever expected they would. How could they not be different?

If the gunners were different, then one of their subsets was unique. Perhaps no other military specialist of the war emerged with the mystique that surrounded the ball turret gunner. Sometimes even his fellow crew gunners did not understand him, and they knew even less about the strange weapon he operated. If called upon in an emergency, a ball turret gunner could replace a waist gunner, tail gunner or top turret gunner. It was rare that anyone else on board a B-17 could replace the ball turret gunner, nor did they want to.

The ball turret, tucked beneath the belly of the aircraft, was a complicated and forbidding place. The gunner who manned the ball turret was required to have a unique combination of skills and attributes. First, he had to be somewhat small, usually the smallest man on the crew. Naturally, even the slightest tendency toward claustrophobia would disqualify someone from being a ball turret gunner. Another advantage could be youth.

Of course, most B-17 crewmen were young. Many airmen had just turned twenty by the time they flew their first missions. Even some officers, such as navigators and bombardiers, could be as young as nineteen. The pilot/commanding officer was usually the oldest member of the crew. The average age of pilots might have been twenty-four or twenty-five, but twenty-one-year-old pilots were not unheard-of. However, being a mere teenager could give a ball turret gunner a definite edge.

Endurance and flexibility became important qualities when a gunner was required to remain curled up in the ball turret during long missions deep into Germany. Sometimes he would be in the turret almost nonstop for seven to eight hours. During the last hour of a flight over enemy territory, a belly gunner's senses and reaction time had to be as sharp as during the first hour. It also helped if he could control his urinary urges. Ball turret gunners as young as eighteen seemed especially able to meet such demands.

Sergeant George Ahern was still only eighteen years old and stood only five feet, five inches when he earned his gunner's wings and was assigned as the ball turret gunner of Lieutenant Marvin Walker's B-17 crew. Walker quickly demonstrated to his new crew an authoritative command style. Sergeant Philip Duke, a waist gunner, showed up for the first crew meeting without bothering to shave. Walker gave him hell for it. George suppressed a smile. For the first time in his life, he was glad he was too young to need a razor.

Walker's airmen became quick friends. Young George was especially popular, but he was the closest with Duke and the other waist gunner, Sergeant Charles "Buddy" Armstrong. Twenty-three-year-old Duke was from the small town of Wellsville, New York, and had married the girl next door only weeks before. Armstrong, from Blytheville, Arkansas, was a kid with a solid build.

By the first week of June 1944, when the Walker crew took off from Newfoundland, Canada, bound for England, nobody on board had any doubt about their pilot's flying ability. However, there was some concern about his all-business approach to command. That concern was about to turn to appreciation.

As Walker's B-17 approached the coast of England, its fuel tanks were nearly empty. Thankfully, navigator Lieutenant Donald Knuepple's plotting was perfect. Walker could see the airfield in the distance. He could also see several other bombers in the area, and when he radioed the tower for permission to land, he was told: "You'll have to hold." Walker tried to explain that he was flying on fumes and could not afford to hold. The airfield controller was unmoved.

"Hold on. . . . I've got four other planes ahead of you," he replied.

Walker had heard enough. "Well, get them out of the way. I'm coming in!" With that, Walker switched off his radio and brought the Fortress in for a safe landing. From that day on, Lieutenant Marvin Walker had the unwavering respect and confidence of his crew.

Soon after turning nineteen, George was flying his first combat mission with the 351st Bomb Group and the 509th Bomb Squadron out of Polebrook, an air base north of London. The rookie crew's first mission, on July 6, was to hit German V-1 rocket launch sites in France. There was some flak but no enemy fighters to test George's skills.

The following day came the first of many bombing missions into Germany. Now the new ball turret gunner's specialized training came into play. George was shocked at the speed of the German Me-109s. The attacking fighters were within gun range, and seconds later they were gone. On the other hand, George found the smooth operation of the ball turret and its twin .50 caliber machine guns a thing of beauty.

The electric turret could swivel its guns 360 degrees horizontally, or point toward the tail or the front of the aircraft or straight down in a few heartbeats. A good ball turret gunner could cover the entire expansive defensive zone beneath a B-17. To do this required an amazing feat of hand, eye, and foot coordination on the part of the gunner.

Curled in the turret with the gunsight and trigger handles between his knees, the gunner tracked the incoming flights. Looking through the sight, he saw a red horizontal line and two vertical lines. The trick was to put the enemy plane on the horizontal line and then close up the two vertical lines until they reached the attacker's wingtips. The gunner positioned the red horizontal line by using the gun handles to move the turret. At the same time, he used a foot pedal to control the vertical lines of the gunsight. If he could effectively train his crosshairs on the target, the gunsight's mechanical computer would automatically adjust the "lead" needed to hit the rapidly moving enemy fighter. Then the ball turret gunner squeezed the trigger buttons with his thumbs and tried to stay trained on the target as long as possible. Of course, all of this had to be accomplished in a matter of two to five seconds.

The Army Air Corps' *Pilot Training Manual for the Flying Fortress* described the unique nature of the gun turret operation: "The power turret gunners require many mental and physical qualities similar to what we know as inherent flying ability, since the operation of the power turret and gunsight are much like that of airplane flight operation. While the flexible gunners do not require the same delicate touch as the turret gunners, they must have a fine sense of timing and be familiar with the rudiments of exterior ballistics."

The ball turret gunner alone faced the daunting task of trying to hit a streaking target from a fast-moving aircraft (sometimes traveling in the opposite direction), while his body was being moved independently with the guns. Despite these challenges, many of the best Luftwaffe pilots feared and respected the ball turret more than any other gun position on the B-17 bomber.

Many B-17 airmen came to believe the German fighter pilots preferred attacking a B-24 Liberator bomber when given the choice. Indeed, the B-17 was on its way to becoming one of the legendary airplanes in aviation history. Despite the heavy losses over Germany, the Flying Fortress had already gained a reputation as a tough bird to kill. Time and again, battle-damaged B-17s made it back to England when all odds said it was impossible.

They landed with gaping holes in their wings and fuselages, with huge portions of their tails ripped off, with their noses (along with bombardiers and navigators) missing. The B-17 skippers brought the bombers and crews home safely on just three and sometimes only two working engines.

Certainly there were also some miraculous returns by B-24 Liberators, but B-17 airmen were convinced of the superiority of their aircraft. If asked to compare the two airplanes, a B-17 crewman was likely to proclaim, "A B-24 is the crate a new Flying Fortress comes packed in."

On one of his early missions, George witnessed his first fighter attack. It was not on his B-17 group but on an unfortunate group of B-24s flying low and to the front. Later at post-mission interrogation, he would describe how the Luftwaffe "went after the B-24s unmercifully." From his perch in the ball turret, George had an unobstructed view of the lopsided air battle. One after another, the Liberators went down under the relentless guns of the fighters. George felt angry and helpless. The German planes were far out of the reach of his turret guns.

Like all the gunners aboard the bombers in his group, George readied himself for the time when the enemy fighters would turn their attention to the B-17s. It would not happen on this mission. After the German planes had destroyed or damaged many of the bombers in the B-24 group, they were gone as quickly as they had appeared. But it was not the B-17s' reputation that had driven them away. The fighters had simply exhausted their fuel.

Throughout the war, Luftwaffe pilots proved their bravery in aggressive attacks on the heavily fortified B-17s. There was no good way to approach a bomber that boasted thirteen gun positions, especially when it was part of a tight bomber formation.

Yet German pilots destroyed hundreds of the Fortresses by taking great risks and constantly revising their tactics.

The Luftwaffe used captured B-17s to train fighter pilots how to effectively attack the American bombers. Head-on attacks became a favorite early in the war. A frontal attack made the German fighter a much smaller target and protected it from most of the bomber's guns. By attacking the B-17 head on, the fighter and the bomber were flying in opposite directions, and this meant the attack was over in seconds. There was another important benefit for the German aviators. If the fighter pilot scored a hit during a frontal assault, he could very likely kill the bombardier and/or the navigator in the nose section. Frontal attacks remained a mainstay with the Luftwaffe until the Americans introduced the twin .50 caliber chin turret.

By the summer of 1944, the Germans were more desperate than ever to stop the American bombers, and the Luftwaffe pilot corps was by then a mixture of crafty veterans and inexperienced but bold rookies. Even though long-distance fighter escorts were becoming more common, George and the other gunners on Marvin Walker's crew were pitted against German fighters on several missions. The worst attack came on an unescorted mission, and it came not with shocking quickness but with a touch of slow intimidation.

Someone spotted Me-109s and called a warning over the interphone: "Enemy fighters! At nine o'clock!" George swiveled the ball turret to the left. A group of Messerschmitts was cruising outside the range of the American bombers' guns. George picked one out and adjusted his gunsight's horizonal and vertical lines on the target. He was ready, but the German flight commander was not. The 109s stayed there, just out of reach, almost as if they were escorting the American bombers to their target.

The enemy fighters were much too far away to actually see the pilots, but George knew that as he stared at them, they were staring back—young men on both sides, dreading what was about to happen but eager to get it over with.

When the first Me-109 peeled off and headed for the bombers, George quickly moved the turret gunsight to cover the lead fighter. Other fighters rolled out of their formation and came at the B-17s from various approaches. George felt a vibration from overhead. It was the left waist gunner opening fire. Keeping the gunsight on the German fighter was more difficult than George had imagined. In a few more seconds the enemy plane would sail through the bomber group. George squeezed both his thumbs down hard and felt the turret's machine guns respond. His bullets raced through the sky, but the Messerschmitt was gone.

The speed of the German fighters amazed the belly gunner. He swung his weapons first in one direction and then in another, firing quick bursts at anything within range. The noise of the air battle was also surprising. There was the rumble of the four big Fortress engines, mixed with the sound of his machine guns and the constant rattle of the bomber's other gun positions. On top of this was the interphone traffic: "Bandit . . . six o'clock low!" Underneath all the noise, the ball turret motor hummed reassuringly as George moved to meet any threat in the zone below the bomber.

Small puffs of white smoke, like mini flak, popped up in the sky around his turret. George had heard some veteran airmen refer to the small explosions as popcorn: a rather innocent name for the twenty-millimeter German shells that could rip through a B-17's thin metal shell or through the Plexiglas of a ball turret.

George shook off his apprehension about the popcorn explosions and concentrated on eliminating the source. He spotted a German fighter coming up from beneath the bombers.

"Must be a rookie pilot," George said to himself and he rotated the turret guns toward the invader. Most experienced Luftwaffe pilots would avoid attacking a B-17 from underneath. The maneuver forced the attacking fighter to climb up to the bomber. As it climbed, the fighter's rate of approach was slowed significantly, leaving the plane exposed to the bomber's ball turret guns for a few extra seconds.

George used the additional time to line up his gunsight perfectly—horizontal red line across the body of the fighter, vertical lines pulled in tight on the fighter's wingtips. The broad bottoms of the Flying Fortresses must have seemed a fat target to the young German pilot, but he never got the chance to take the killing shot.

George pressed the twin fifty triggers and saw his rounds make violent contact with the Me-109. When the bullets began to hit the fighter, the pilot reacted quickly by turning away from the bomber. The Messerschmitt's turn proved fatal to the aircraft and perhaps to its pilot. George kept his triggers pressed down and watched the bottom of the fighter being torn apart by the turret guns.

Fire erupted from the enemy fighter, and seconds later it began its long fall to earth. George did not see a parachute, but he had little opportunity to look for one. Other Me-109s were pressing the attack and demanded his attention. Lieutenant Walker's gunners protected their bomber well that day and then settled in for their reward—a bomb run through a flak-filled sky.

Later, as George relaxed over a glass of scotch, he relived the Messerschmitt attack for the benefit of an interrogation officer. He told how his turret's bullets had eliminated one German fighter that had attempted an attack from below.

"Do you think you got him?" the interrogator asked.

"I'm sure I did!" George replied.

Afterward, George gave the matter little more thought. He was too busy flying bombing missions to worry about the Eighth Air Force record-keeping procedures. One day he received word that the "official kill" of the Me-109 in question had been credited to an Air Force major. The officer had apparently been flying on the mission as an observer, taking the place of a tail gunner in order to get a good view of the formation. The major had also claimed credit for downing the German fighter and received credit for the kill. The sergeant, of course, did not. George shrugged it off. He was certain he had prevented that particular Luftwaffe fighter from ever shooting down his or any other American bomber, and that was all that mattered.

As the new guys, Walker's crew had been given a patched-up, battle-weary B-17. After the July 13 mission to Munich, she needed even more patches. George knew the bomb run was going to be a tough one long before the bomb group reached Munich. It was his fourth combat mission, and the sky over Munich was darker than it had been at any previous target. A black cloud of flak smoke hovered above the city, the residue of shells fired at earlier bomb groups.

Fresh flak explosions appeared quickly as the 351st began its bomb run. Not only was it the thickest flak George had yet witnessed, it was also the first time he could actually hear shrapnel striking the ball turret. A German antiaircraft shell would explode close by and fragments would cut into the bomber's fuselage, while other pieces would glance off the round metal back of the turret. Sometimes George would not even see an explosion, but still he would hear the stuff thumping against the turret. The air was full of large and small metallic hazards.

Walker's bomber returned from Munich and landed at Polebrook with more than a hundred flak holes adorning it. Miraculously, not one man on board had been hit. Looking at how the flak fragments had sliced through the bomber's metal shell as if it were butter, George began to appreciate the ball turret even more. The outside of the turret was scarred and the metal part showed some denting, but its design had protected him. The back of the turret was armor-plated and thick bulletproof glass (but not twenty-millimeter proof) shielded the front of the gunsight and, as a result, its operator. The rest of the ball turret was Plexiglas, which might not withstand a direct hit but could deflect small fragments off its round form.

While most airmen avoided assignment to the ball turret, George was now convinced it was the best place to be during a bomb run. If he attempted to explain the advantages of his gun position to other crew members, they would just smile and slap young George on the back. After all, ball turret gunners were different.

After a few more missions over Germany, Walker's crew was rewarded with a brand-new airplane. She was a silver B-17G, with the serial number 43-37854. A large "J" painted on her tail signified she was part of the 351st Bomb Group. The letters "RQ" on the bomber's fuselage represented the 509th Bomb Squadron. The letter "V" stood for the aircraft itself.

George and his buddies were proud of her. They all agreed such a beautiful lady deserved a special name. Many monikers were suggested but quickly rejected as not worthy enough. Even as they flew their new B-17 to bomb military and industrial targets in Germany and enemy troops in France, the bomber boys could not come up with an acceptable name. After completing a dozen or so combat missions, Walker's airmen received news that put the name discussion on the back burner.

The crew of the no-name Flying Fortress had been granted a forty-eight-hour pass to London. They all took the train together into the old city and then crammed into a couple of taxis to search for a hotel. The driver of George's cab told his passengers he knew a nice place and assured them they could get all the rooms they needed.

"Let's go!" came the enthusiastic response, and off they went on what was to be a thrilling ride through the streets of London. The boys were waving at young women and pointing at double-decker buses when they heard the air raid siren. Though they had never been to London, the airmen knew the warning meant V-1 bombs were headed toward the city. Here and there they could see the bombed-out buildings. Earlier in the month they had bombed German V-1 launch sites in France. Now they faced being on the receiving end.

Their driver seemed unaware of the loud sirens as he sped by slower traffic. Even the pedestrians were in no particular hurry to reach the bomb shelters. George watched as some of the Londoners calmly ducked into a covered doorway or down the stairs leading to the tube, while others simply ignored the noisy warning and continued on their way.

"Shouldn't we be looking for shelter?" one of the airmen asked.

"No, we will be fine," the driver said confidently. He went on to explain his view that if everyone stopped every time the V-1s dropped, then London would cease to function as a city. One couldn't give the Jerries that satisfaction, he said. He assured the American flyers the rocket bombs would land far away from them, and they did.

George heard the explosions as the V-1s fell in another part of London. Minutes later, the taxi stopped in front of a first-class hotel. The second cab, carrying the rest of the bomber crew, pulled up seconds later. The hotel lobby was crowded with civilians as well as men and women in British and American uniforms. George guessed the taxi driver had been mistaken. *There's not much chance this hotel will have any vacancies.*

"Do you have rooms available?" Lieutenant Walker inquired on behalf of his men.

"We have plenty of rooms available . . . on the top floor, sir."
The desk clerk smiled and waited for a reaction. The top floor
was okay with George and his buddies. They just wanted to
drop off their bags, get out and see the city, and maybe meet
some of its female citizens. Later, an English bartender would
explain why all of London's hotels had rooms available on the
top floor. The regular hotel guests would not stay in a top-floor
room because of the V-1 flying bombs. A V-1 explosion was
powerful enough to destroy the top story of a building and even
do heavy damage to the next. Any of the lower floors were considered safer. Most guests paid a premium for rooms on the
lower floors, leaving many top-floor rooms unoccupied. Hotel
managers slashed the top-floor rates and found American service personnel more than willing to take a little risk in order to
stay at a posh hotel.

George also gained important (although somewhat inaccurate) knowledge about the operation of the V-1s, information
the average Londoner already knew and used almost daily. The
enemy's flying bomb was powered by a jet engine. The engine
was noisy and as it reached the airspace over London, it sput-
tered and then went silent. Hearing this sequence, a pedestrian
had about thirty seconds to find shelter. This design flaw led
many in England to the false conclusion that a flying bomb carried just enough fuel to get it to Britain and, once over its target,
its jet engine simply "ran out of gas."

Actually the German scientists had developed not only a complicated guidance system using a magnetic compass and a gyro-
scope, they had also invented an equally complex system that
shut off the jet engines' fuel supply once it was over the target.
When the power source was starved of fuel, the *flying* bomb was
supposed to fall on its victims, much like a conventional bomb.
In reality, the bombs glided for some time and distance after

the jet engine was heard to shut down. Thus the Germans had unintentionally provided some advance warning of the deadly explosions.

Upon returning to his hotel, George also learned one of the advantages of staying at one of London's better establishments. You never knew whom you might bump into in the lobby—in this case, two American movie stars. Dinah Shore and Danny Kaye were in England on a morale tour; at the same time, they were promoting their new movie, *Up in Arms,* and they were staying at George's hotel. The young ball turret gunner elbowed his way through the crowd surrounding the celebrities and managed to shake hands with the comedian and even get an autograph from the beautiful actress. As she handed him the piece of paper bearing her signature, she flashed that famous Dinah Shore smile in his direction. George was hooked.

Word spread among the lobby crowd that Miss Shore would be performing a song from her movie that very evening during a stage show. George and several of his crewmates were in the audience when the curtain went up. His favorite part of the show was when Dinah Shore sang "Tess's Torch Song." Heading back to Polebrook the following evening, the image of Shore's performance kept running through George's thoughts.

When Walker's crew resumed flying combat missions, someone protested that it was high time they decided on a name for their aircraft. When their popular young ball turret gunner blurted out, "How about Torchy Tess?" to his surprise, no one objected. A vote was taken, and in August 1944 the silver B-17 named *Torchy Tess* (now with a few battle patches) was taking them to Berlin.

George's mission count soon passed any other member of Marvin Walker's crew. As a good ball turret gunner, he was in demand to fly extra missions with other crews. Although the extra missions held the promise of getting him home to the States sooner, he never liked flying with a different crew. The ball turret was a lonely position, and he depended on his buddies above him to keep him up to speed on what was happening in the bomber. Once, when the interphone system was knocked out by flak, George was worried he would not hear the bailout alarm if it sounded. He opened the turret hatch and yelled at Buddy Armstrong, the waist gunner: "Hey, bang on the top of the turret every now and then to let me know you're still up here."

Armstrong smiled and nodded. George ducked back into his turret and closed the hatch, confident that his crewmate would never leave without him. Each time he flew with an unfamiliar crew, he wondered if he could trust them with his life. On his fifth such mission, he decided he had had enough.

With one of the bomber's engines shut down by flak, George sat in his turret and watched the earth gradually coming closer and closer. If he had been flying with his regular crew, they would have been chatting on the interphone all the way back to England. This crew, including the pilot, was strangely silent as their B-17 continued to lose altitude. As soon as they cleared the English coast, the pilot sat the bomber down safely at the first available air base, but George had reached a crucial decision.

He marched into Operations and told the officer in charge that he would gladly fly for Lieutenant Marvin Walker and his crew, "Anywhere, anytime!" But he added, "In the future, I won't fly with another crew!"

The Operations officer was just as direct. "No, if you are assigned to another crew, you will have to fly with them."

George walked out without additional comment, but he was determined to stand his ground. He went straight to Walker's barracks and told his commander of his decision. Walker told his young ball turret gunner to get some rest and then go get a beer. Then the pilot headed in the direction of the Operations building. George would never know what his airplane commander said to the Operations officer, but he was never again assigned to fly with any bomber crew other than Lieutenant Marvin Walker's.

George had come close to insubordination with the Operations officer, but he felt he had a good reason and stood on principle. A separate incident that got him into hot water could only be attributed to foolhardiness. When it was over, he could not explain why he had done it. Perhaps, even after numerous combat missions, there was still much of the teenage boy inside him. Perhaps he did it just to prove once again that ball turret gunners were different.

One night in a local pub he was drinking with a group of airmen when the conversation turned to oddball stunts. One airman happened to mention that he knew of a ball turret gunner who, after returning from a bombing mission, decided he needed just a little more excitement. As the bomber crossed into English airspace, a time when a belly gunner would usually crawl out of the ball turret, the man stayed put. In fact, the storyteller proclaimed, "He rode in that turret all the way down and through the landing."

Most of the airmen at the bar laughed, being of the opinion the tale was far-fetched. However, one veteran ball turret gunner silenced the doubters. "I believe it, because I've done it myself." The man went on to describe in detail the experience of watching the runway rise up at him while he sat beneath the massive aircraft. "When the wheels touch down, your ass is only eighteen inches above the runway."

"What if one of the tires was to blow out, or the landing gear failed?" someone asked.

"Then I wouldn't be here talking about it," the ball turret veteran said, and took a long drink of his ale. George sat quietly as the conversation drifted elsewhere. He was proud of being a ball turret gunner—one of the youngest in the Eighth Air Force. It was sort of a small club. But to be able to say you had ridden in the turret all the way through a landing, that was something George found intriguing.

It took very little investigation to discover that remaining in a ball turret during a landing was a violation of Eighth Air Force regulations. This did not discourage George, but it did require some secrecy. Only one of *Torchy Tess's* waist gunners would need to know of his plan in advance. Eighth Air Force bombers were by then flying missions with nine-man crews. Both waist gunners remained on Walker's crew, but they flew alternating missions. Also, Sergeant Paul A. Schrader, who at over six feet tall was cramped in his tail gunner's compartment, often swapped gun positions with Duke or Armstrong. George would have to let whoever was flying as waist gunner in on his plan, because if he did not emerge from his turret before landing, the waist gunner would surely try to reach him via the interphone and Lieutenant Walker would be listening.

The feat would need to be accomplished following a bombing mission during which *Torchy Tess* was untouched by flak—something of a rarity. George wanted to be beneath a perfectly functioning aircraft when he tried it. Soon such an opportunity arrived.

So George stayed inside the ball turret as Walker piloted the bomber back across the North Sea and past the English coast. During a normal landing, a ball turret gunner would wait until the bomber's wheels were lowered, do a visual check for any flak damage or other potential problems, and then exit through the turret hatch into the main fuselage compartment. In order to use the hatch in this manner, the ball turret's guns had to be pointing straight down. Once inside the bomber, the gunner would use a hand crank to manually rotate the turret so the guns were facing aft. This was the regulation position of the turret during landing.

To escape detection from anyone in the control tower, George would need to turn the turret until his guns faced backward. Once the airplane was on the ground, it would be impossible for him to exit into the B-17. The runway would simply be too close to turn the guns straight down. He would have to make a quick exit out the back of the turret, in the direction of the bomber's nose.

England was lush and green below as *Torchy Tess* began her approach to Polebrook. George saw the bomber's wheels come down from the wings. Everything looked in order. No flak damage anywhere. Up front, all four propellers were spinning smoothly. *No reason it should not be a perfect landing,* he thought, and swung the turret until its guns were pointed at the tail of the bomber.

He would have preferred the forward view of the landing, but his position soon proved thrilling enough. As the surface of the runway raced closer and closer, until it was only a few feet away, the young belly gunner had a second of doubt: *Maybe this wasn't such a great idea.*

The B-17's wheels tweaked the runway. George had a sudden sensation of speed unlike anything he had ever experienced in the air. It was as if he were riding in a fast race car—backward. Then the tail end of the bomber settled down on the small rear wheel, and the ball turret dropped to within inches of the runway.

"What a ride!" George yelled at the top of his voice as Walker slowed the bomber to taxi speed. As soon as *Torchy Tess* came to a stop, George popped open the hatch and lowered himself onto the tarmac. Nobody on board the B-17 was the wiser except his waist gunner friend, and he would never tell. Someone on the ground crew, however, spotted him leaving the turret and reported the incident to the aircraft's commander.

Marvin Walker confronted his young turret gunner, and George immediately confessed the deed. The pilot showed no anger, but he made it clear that such juvenile behavior would not be tolerated on his crew. They were risking their lives on every mission, but unnecessary risks were foolish.

"Don't ever do it again," Walker warned.

"No, sir!" George assured him. Then the two men walked together to the post-mission interrogation room. Almost in a whisper, the pilot asked, "What was it like, George?"

"Great!" the belly gunner replied with a grin.

George Ahern was born on May 10, 1925, in the small town of Branford, Connecticut, which was nestled along the Long Island shoreline just east of New Haven. Most of Branford's male residents worked at the local wire mill. George's father, John, had served as an artillery captain during World War I. His mother, the former Hazel Baisely, raised three daughters and her one son to adulthood, only to suffer the heartache of seeing her firstborn, Patricia, die at twenty-one. Soon afterward, George graduated from Branford High School and joined the Army.

Hazel Ahern wrote to her son often, as did George's sisters, Betty and Joan. Happily, the young airman could usually count on a letter from at least one family member when mail call was announced. Those letters were his lifeline to the world he hoped to return to when all his bombing missions were completed. George tried to think of it as *when* and not *if* he got through all his missions.

As welcome as letters from home were, he regretted not having a girlfriend with whom he could correspond. He had dated several girls during his senior year, but because of his quick departure there had been little time for any serious relationship to blossom. Now, as fellow airmen received letters and packages from girlfriends and wives stateside, George was envious.

A few of his friends had managed to meet English girls but the opportunities were rare, and the competition was fierce. Nineteen-year-old George was experienced beyond his years at warfare, but even he had to admit, he was no smooth operator when it came to women. One day at mail call, his luck changed.

The letter was postmarked Hamden, and the handwriting on the envelope was unfamiliar. George opened it carefully but still had to react quickly to keep a small photo from falling to the ground. The girl in the photo was pretty . . . *very pretty,* George thought. And if it was a recent snapshot, she was just a teenager. He tucked the picture back into the envelope and found a quiet place to read the letter.

Her name was Marie. She was just eighteen but lived on her own at the YWCA in Hamden, Connecticut. That is where she met George's sister Betty during a dance the Y had hosted for cadets from nearby Yale. Betty was certain her brother would enjoy being pen pals with the new friend. Marie hoped it was okay. George tacked her picture on his bunk. It was more than okay.

Once he had replied, Marie's letters came regularly. George read each one over and over. He made sure to answer every letter Marie sent. The text of her letters was light and sometimes funny, and each one revealed a little more of a young woman George was growing anxious to meet.

Marie Spilane had grown into an independent adult quicker than most girls. At the age of eleven, her mother had died and an absentee father allowed little Marie to be taken in by her mother's sister, Aunt Helen, who Marie called Nell. By the age of seventeen, Marie was employed as a bookkeeper at a corset company that had been converted to parachute manufacturing. When she turned eighteen, Marie moved into the YWCA.

One evening at a dance she met Betty Ahern. When Betty proudly produced a picture of her brother "serving with the Eighth Air Force in England," Marie's reaction was, "He's so cute." He seemed much too young to have already seen combat over Germany.

Weeks later, back in England, George returned from every bombing mission hoping there would be a letter from Marie waiting for him. One day an airman passing his bunk asked, "Who's the pretty girl?"

Instead of answering, "My pen pal," George surprised himself by saying, "That's my girl." After a few more letters back and forth across the ocean, the answer to the question became, "That's the girl I'm gonna marry when I get home."

He was careful to make no such declaration in his letters to Marie, and he took considerable good-natured razzing from his crewmates.

"Marry her? George, you haven't even kissed her yet!" one would say.

"Hell, he hasn't even met her!" another would add.

George knew they still thought of him as an impulsive kid. The stunt of riding the ball turret down through a landing had done little to dispel the image. But George was sure about Marie. He could tell from her letters that she was someone special. Since he had begun flying bombing raids in early July, he had only allowed himself to live mission to mission. Now he could not help but think about the day he would fly his last bomb run. He had a long way to go.

By September 1944, George had completed twenty of his required thirty-five combat missions. Fatigued in body and mind, if not in spirit, he welcomed the news that the *Torchy Tess* crew was getting four days of rest, including liberty in London.

Once again the entire crew took the train into the city, each man determined to have some fun and forget about the war. No one could say they had not earned the break. Over Munich, Stuttgart, Schweinfurt, Merseburg and Berlin, the enemy had thrown all the fighters and flak it had at them. They had fought and survived as a crew and were now as close as any blood family.

At the very time George and his crewmates were arriving in London, somewhere behind enemy lines in the Netherlands, German technicians were painstakingly checking every step in the launch procedure of a revolutionary new weapon. It was a fourteen-ton ballistic missile that Adolf Hitler believed would be "the decisive weapon of the war."

Earlier in the war, the German leader had sent waves of Luftwaffe bombers over England in preparation for a planned invasion of the island nation. Only the bravery and sacrifice of its Spitfire and Hurricane pilots allowed the RAF to defeat the German bombers and win the Battle of Britain. The heroism of the English fighter pilots prompted Winston Churchill to pay tribute: "Never in the field of human conflict was so much owed by so many to so few."

With its own offensive bomber forces severely damaged, Germany soon found the table turned. Her major cities suffered devastating nighttime raids by British bombers and later what had once been unimaginable—daylight bombing by the Americans. Hitler looked to German technology to execute his vengeance on England and perhaps turn the tide of the war again in his favor.

The V-1, the jet-propelled flying bomb, was the first of the advanced weapons to strike London in June 1944. Throughout the summer, thousands of V-1s were launched against England. British fighter pilots and antiaircraft gunners managed to shoot down almost half of them. The V-1s that exploded inside London and other English cities caused much death and destruction; however, they only served to strengthen the resolve of the British citizens and did little to slow the Allies' prosecution of the war.

But now Hitler had a larger, faster "vengeance weapon" named the A-4. The Allies would call it the V-2. The A-4 ballistic missile was forty-six feet long and housed a full ton of explosives. After launching, the A-4 would climb to an altitude of sixty miles above the earth and then fall on its target at a speed of thirty-six hundred miles per hour. No Allied fighter or antiaircraft battery was designed to bring down anything as fast as the new German rocket. In fact, it was *so* fast and silent, its victims would never see or hear it coming.

On September 7, Duncan Sandys, the British government's leading authority on the German rocket program, had tried to reassure the public. Mr. Sandys had told the press that while a few more V-1 bombs might straggle into English airspace, the Allies had essentially ended the threat of the German vengeance weapons.

The British and American authorities certainly had reason to brag. V-1 launch sites in France had been pounded again and again by heavy bombers, and after the D-Day invasion, most of the remaining launch sites had fallen into the hands of the Allied ground armies. In truth, the Allied leaders were not telling journalists and British citizens the whole story. They had known since December 1942 that the Germans were working on an advanced missile weapon. By the spring of 1943, Allied intelligence agents had discovered the location of both V-1 and V-2 development sites—Peenemünde, off the German Baltic Coast.

When a test-firing sent one of the German V-2s out of control and smashing into neutral Sweden, secret negotiations resulted in the British obtaining the wreckage of the rocket. Their experts soon concluded the V-2 packed a one-ton warhead, traveled at enormous speed and could be launched at England from more than two hundred miles away.

After receiving this information, Churchill ordered a heavy attack. On the evening of August 17, almost six hundred British bombers took off for Peenemünde. Earlier in the day, sixty American bombers had been shot down during a combined raid on Schweinfurt and Regensburg. The British would lose another forty bombers over Peenemünde. However, the bombing destroyed many of the facilities at Peenemünde, killed several top German scientists, and delayed the German rocket program by several months.

The V-2 ballistic missile program might have collapsed after the Peenemünde raid, except that the most important of Germany's scientists was still alive. His name was Wernher von Braun. Von Braun, who as a boy had dreamed of space travel, cared less about vengeance against the English or wonder weapons than he did about advancing rocket technology. Still, the brilliant scientist designed and developed the first successful version of the ballistic missile of the future, and he put it in the hands of Adolf Hitler.

On September 8, just one day after Mr. Sandy's optimistic prediction, the first V-2 rocket ever fired at England exploded in the Chiswick section of London, killing three and wounding twenty. Every piece of debris that was suspected of being part of the German rocket was removed from the crater and taken away to a reassembly site. The British authorities soon had an amazingly accurate understanding of the workings and capabilities of the new vengeance weapon. A cloak of secrecy was thrown over everything concerning the V-2.

———

A day after the Chiswick explosion, ten American airmen shared a jovial midday meal at the Mayfair Hotel restaurant. Present at the table were pilot Lieutenant Marvin R. Walker; copilot Flight Officer Maurice E. Joncas; bombardier Lieutenant Daniel L. Rader; navigator Second Lieutenant Donald E. Knuepple; flight engineer and top turret gunner Staff Sergeant William R. Schneider; radio operator Staff Sergeant William W. Weaver; waist gunner and backup flight engineer Staff Sergeant Charles S. Armstrong; waist gunner and backup radio operator Sergeant Philip Duke; tail gunner Sergeant Paul A. Schrader; and ball turret gunner Sergeant George E. Ahern.

After lunch, the four officers of *Torchy Tess* said goodbye to the noncoms and went off on their own as officers were inclined to do. The sergeants were in a lively discussion about their afternoon plans when an enterprising cabby approached. His taxi had the room, and for a reasonable sum he promised he would drive them on a tour of London that they would never forget.

At the V-2 launch site in Holland, the German technicians were readying another rocket for firing. Their morale was high. Despite any official English confirmation, spies had informed the German military that their rocket had indeed reached London on the previous evening. Now, assured of the rocket's range and accuracy, they could strike back at the country that was the primary source of bomber raids on German cities.

George and his crewmates were crammed uncomfortably inside their taxi, but none of them complained as the driver swerved along busy London streets while pointing out historic sites and his favorite pubs with equal enthusiasm. The September sky was cloudy, but the weather was otherwise pleasant. It was a great day to be in London and away from the war.

The driver's tour route took them past the majestic landmark Big Ben. Most of them had seen the famous clock tower on their previous visit to London, but as they passed Big Ben an old man caught their attention.

"Hey, pull over," one of the airmen said.

The old man had positioned his camera on a tripod across the street from Big Ben to assure photographs with a striking composition, and he was open for business. One of the *Torchy Tess* airmen was interested.

"Hey, guys, let's get a picture of the crew!" There was some discussion of the matter. The old man adjusted his camera in hopeful anticipation that the decision would go his way. George thought Marie would enjoy getting a photo of him and his pals in London. He voted with the majority to take the time so they could all have a picture with Big Ben.

"It will only take a few minutes," the old photographer said as he motioned for the six airmen to close in shoulder to shoulder. They stood there on a London street—Duke, Armstrong, Schneider and Ahern, all in a relaxed at-ease position and Schrader and Weaver with their hands at their sides. Behind them the Big Ben clock tower loomed protectively.

The camera's shutter clicked, preserving forever the image of six friends and comrades in arms. The old man thought it was a nice shot. He would never know the impact of the photo fate had chosen him to take. The airmen waited as he began the development process.

More than two hundred miles away, a V-2 rocket was climbing straight into the sky, in the first stage of a flight that would take only a few minutes.

The development of the finished photograph took a little longer than the photographer had promised. The seven American flyers were in no particular hurry. They passed a couple of minutes in the type of idle talk that flows so easily between close friends. Nearby, their tour guide and driver leaned impatiently against his taxi.

Sixty miles into space, sunlight reflected off a black-green missile at the very crest of its trajectory. Below, the earth waited like a blue and white marble.

Finally the photo of the *Torchy Tess* gunners and Big Ben was ready. Everyone was pleased. They all agreed it had been worth the wait.

The picture was still being passed around when the explosion shook London. The sound was almost deafening and quite unique—it sounded like two explosions. *Boom. Boom.* Few in London were privy to the knowledge that the double boom was caused by the V-2 traveling many times the speed of sound. First came the sonic boom and then the sound of the explosion itself.

George and his five friends were as startled as everyone else. There had been no air raid sirens and no sound of the jet that propelled the V-1 flying bomb. No enemy bombers could be seen in the sky—nothing, except the birds that had been frightened from the trees.

Pedestrians were running for cover and soon someone pointed out the dark smoke that was beginning to appear above the London skyline. Instinctively the airmen headed in that direction. The sound of ambulance and fire sirens became continuous.

The V-2 rocket had landed only a few blocks away from Big Ben. As they arrived at the scene of the explosion and looked at the great smoking crater and the surrounding area, strewn with street and building debris, the airmen could not imagine what could have caused such destruction.

"We are all lucky to be alive." The voice came from behind them. George and his buddies turned around. It was their taxi driver. His eyes looked empty. His face was pale white. "I always take the same route on my tours. After passing Big Ben, I always head down this very street. If you lads had not stopped me to have that photo made at Big Ben, we would have been here."

The *Torchy Tess* crewmen glanced at one another and then back at the cabby. His expression was familiar to them. They had seen it often on each other's faces after returning from a particularly difficult mission. It was the expression of someone who knew he had just cheated death.

The following morning, George awoke and immediately went to the hotel lobby for an early-edition newspaper. The mystery explosion in London was the subject of much of the front-page coverage. No one claimed knowledge of what had caused the explosion. Newswriters sought information from government and military authorities. Many of them confessed honest bewilderment, while others made themselves unavailable for comment.

Those members of the press who were in a position to know the truth about the terrible new German weapon kept it to themselves in the name of national security. Even as the public began to guess that the new mystery explosions that followed were caused by a rocket of some kind, there was still a general attitude of secrecy about the matter. The English saw little use in publicly complaining about their latest plague, lest they give encouragement to the Germans.

Winston Churchill would not make any public mention of Germany's new ballistic missile until November 10. By that time, the average British citizen was well aware of the silent and deadly V-2s. During the final months of the war, almost twelve hundred V-2 rockets would strike London.

In his postwar book, *Triumph and Tragedy,* Churchill would write: "The total casualties caused by the V-2 in England were 2,724 killed and 6,467 seriously injured. On the average each rocket caused about twice as many casualties as a flying bomb. Although the warheads were of much the same size, the strident engine of the flying bomb warned people to take cover. The rocket approached in silence."

The six gunners of *Torchy Tess* had escaped becoming part of Churchill's cold statistics and not one of them could say why. Why, after surviving so many combat missions, had they almost been killed on a liberty in London? Why had a spur-of-the-moment decision about something so trivial as a photograph proved to be the difference between life and death?

George gave the question considerable thought. He had witnessed the randomness of death on many missions. Why was one bomber struck by flak and destroyed, while another, flying mere seconds behind it, was left untouched? Was it really random, or did fate or even the hand of God intervene? If it was fate, then the fate of each man on *Torchy Tess* seemed to be intertwined. They would all live or die as crewmates, George concluded.

On the day following their close call in London, Marvin Walker's bomber crew was back dodging flak in the sky over Germany. They flew three missions on three straight days. During the second half of September and throughout October, *Torchy Tess* and the other B-17s of the 351st challenged the dangerous air defenses of Germany's major cities—Frankfurt, Cologne, Cologne again, Hanover, Münster and then back to Frankfurt. On November 6, Walker brought his crew back from a raid on Hamburg. For George Ahern it was mission number thirty-four. He had one mission left to fly.

George and Marie had continued their exchange of letters. He wrote about what he saw in England, about the men of *Torchy Tess,* and of the little ways they found to relieve the boredom at Polebrook. One of his favorites was sharing fresh fruit and ice cream with the kids who hung around the air base gates. He never wrote to Marie about his missions. He did not want her to know how bad it really was, and military censorship would have prevented such disclosures anyway.

Now with a single mission remaining, George wanted to let Marie and his family know he would soon be coming home. Once again he enlisted the assistance of his pilot, Marvin Walker, who had been promoted to first lieutenant. As an officer and aircraft commander, Walker was not subjected to the same strict censorship as his crew. On November 8, 1944, Walker penned a thoughtful letter to George's father: "Dear Mr. Ahern, Your son George, is the ball turret gunner on my crew. I told him I'd write you giving you a little information he can't get past the censors, namely: his number of missions. To date, he has completed thirty-four missions and has one to go. We feel we'll finish by the fifteenth of November."

The pilot went on to explain that George might be assigned "further overseas duty not involving combat" for a month or so before he was sent back to the States. The third paragraph of Walker's letter filled John Ahern's heart with pride when he read the lieutenant's words: "George is a fine boy and one we can both be proud of. It has been a pleasure having him on my crew. He has a good record and wears the Distinguished Flying Cross and Air Medal with three Oak Leaf Clusters to testify as to his usefulness."

The day after Walker wrote the letter, the *Torchy Tess* crew got the call to fly again—George's last mission. As the nineteen-year-old veteran ball turret gunner sat in the briefing room with his crewmates, he said a silent prayer that God would let them come home again from whatever German city they were being sent to. When the briefing officer removed the cover, George's eyes followed the red line on the map. It did not extend into Germany. The line ended in France. "Ground support . . ." George vaguely heard. Someone slapped him on the back. He broke into a smile. For his final mission, George had drawn the much-sought-after but seldom seen "milk run."

———

By Christmas, George was back in the United States and home on leave. After a brief reunion with his family, he surprised his mother when he said, "Mom, I'm sorry I have to run, but I gotta get to the New Haven green." Before she could protest, he was out the door, still wearing his dress uniform. In their final overseas letters, George and Marie had made plans to meet.

"Why don't we meet on the New Haven green?" Marie had suggested. "Look for a girl with a red rose." As George walked across the green, its trees barren against a winter sky, his mood was springlike. Because of his uniform, Marie spotted George first.

Oh my God, this guy is so handsome, she thought as she waved to him. George saw the girl with the rose waving to him. *She's even prettier than her picture.*

Though each had been nervous about their first meeting, there was little awkwardness between them. They held hands and laughed when they both tried to speak at the same time. Within minutes the young couple was embraced in a kiss, oblivious to smiling passersby on the New Haven green. George and Marie knew from that moment, they were destined to be together.

The war in Europe and the Pacific was still unfinished business, and the Eighth Air Force needed veteran specialists to teach new recruits. George's and Marie's future would have to wait. He received orders to report to Gunnery Instructor's School in Texas. His separation from military service did not happen until after the surrender of Japan in August 1945.

George returned home that fall and promptly asked Marie to marry him. She said, "Yes." A year later, on October 19, 1946, the former wartime pen pals were wed.

After the War

George Ahern: After their wedding, George and Marie settled in Branford, Connecticut. They bought a home there and raised three daughters, Kathleen, Sharon and Suzanne, and one son, John. Twelve grandchildren were born into the Ahern family.

George's first civilian job was in the shipping and receiving warehouse of a wholesale distributor of major kitchen appliances. Soon he was offered a promotion as a sales representative, servicing the accounts of retail stores. He practiced this occupation successfully for twenty-five years. Finally, a desire to "get off the road" pushed him to go back to school. Completing college courses in municipal waste treatment technology enabled him to secure employment with the public works department of his hometown. In 1990, George retired after serving ten years as the superintendent of Branford's waste treatment plant.

In 2002, George was elected commander of American Legion Post 83 in Branford. He is also a founding member of the Connecticut chapter of the Eighth Air Force Historical Society and served nine years as its secretary.

During the spring of 2000, George and Marie traveled to England to attend a 351st Bomb Group reunion. After being welcomed by the mayor of Peterborough, the former airmen and their wives (two hundred in all) were taken to the site of the old Polebrook air base. The base property is now under private control, but the 351st veterans group retains ownership of a small section of runway where a monument to its members has been erected.

The owner of the air base has also created a living monument to the brave men who died while serving with the 351st Bomb Group. In a field near the runway, the landowner has planted a small forest of trees—one tree for every 351st bomber that was lost during World War II.

As George and Marie stood with the others paying silent tribute to fallen comrades, they heard a familiar sound coming from far away. It was a sound most of the former bomber boys had not heard in more than five decades—the unmistakable sound of four mighty B-17 engines. The same man who had planted the tribute trees had also arranged for a restored Fortress to do a fly-over. The bomber made several passes over the former Polebrook runway. Finally, as George watched the B-17 disappear into distant clouds, Marie watched her husband, knowing his thoughts were taking him back to a time when he was a young ball turret gunner and she was his pen pal.

George and Marie had been happily married for fifty-nine years when she passed away on November 3, 2005. George still lives in his Branford home with his little friend Mitzy, a dog he rescued from the local animal shelter.

Marvin R. Walker, Maurice E. Joncas, Daniel L. Rader, Donald F. Knuepple, William R. Schneider, William W. Weaver, Charles "Buddy" S. Armstrong, Philip H. Duke and Paul A. Schrader: These nine other members of the original *Torchy Tess* crew completed their tours of duty soon after George had completed his. All but two of the airmen received the Distinguished Flying Cross for having flown thirty-five combat missions. (Duke and Armstrong flew thirty-five combat missions like the others, but by the time they completed their tours of duty, Eighth Air Force rules had changed and the two waist gunners were denied this medal.) Although they had returned from some of their missions with their aircraft riddled with flak holes, all the members of Marvin Walker's regular crew returned without serious injuries to their families in the United States.

Philip H. Duke and Buddy Armstrong were the last of the crew to finish their combat rotation as a result of flying alternating missions as waist gunner on Walker's crew. Duke did not go on his thirty-fifth mission until January 3, 1945.

Despite his longer combat tour, Philip Duke returned to Wellsville, New York, and his wife, Virginia, in time for the couple's first wedding anniversary on February 3. When he was transferred to an air base in Florida, Ginnie went with him. It was comforting to have her there, but the air combat veteran found the daily base routine boring. Over his wife's objections, Duke volunteered for gunner duty on a B-29 bomber. He flew one practice mission aboard a Superfortress before the war in the Pacific ended.

Duke worked ten years in the family oil well–drilling business in Pennsylvania and twenty years back in New York with the Wellsville Lumber Company, most of them as manager. From 1971 until 1981, he was tax assessor and building inspector for the town of Wellsville, a position he left to become project manager for a federal housing program. Duke retired in 1986.

Philip and Virginia Duke raised a son, Philip Jr., who became a major in the U.S. Air Force, the third generation of Duke military aviators (Philip's father had received his pilot's wings near the end of WWI). The couple also had a daughter, Reita. The children grew up in the home Philip had built himself in 1960. Three grandchildren and two great-grandchildren followed. The Dukes celebrated their fifty-first wedding anniversary in February 1995. Virginia Duke passed away the following July.

Philip still lives in his Wellsville home. He has donated countless hours to delivering Meals on Wheels over the past two decades. He enjoys his weekly game of golf for both fun and exercise, although recently he has given up his lifelong practice of walking the course to the comfort of a golf cart.

Charles S. "Buddy" Armstrong was finally assigned to duty as a flight engineer during his last few combat missions. He completed his thirty-fifth mission in February 1945, and returned to the United States three months later. By early May, he was on his way home to Blytheville, Arkansas, for a thirty-day leave and to await reassignment. When his train stopped in St. Louis, the airman got off to buy a newspaper. The headline announced that Germany had surrendered. The war in Europe was over, and Armstrong was discharged in July.

It was easy for the former airman to fall back into the farm life he had grown up with, the life he loved. In 1946 he married Louise Brownlee, and the following year a son was born. The couple named him Charles, after his father. Two daughters completed the Armstrong family. Linda was born in 1949 and Diane in 1950.

The former aviator was good at farming. Starting with two hundred acres under cultivation just after the war, Charles expanded the operation every year, producing cotton, soybeans, cattle and hogs. By the time he retired at age seventy-five, Armstrong was managing a farm of over fifteen hundred acres.

Louise Armstrong passed away in 1988. Charles Jr. runs the family farm now, while his dad enjoys his retirement and his nine grandchildren.

Torchy Tess: The aircraft that George Ahern had named after a Dinah Shore song continued to fly combat missions during the winter of 1944–1945. By late February 1945, *Torchy Tess* had brought her various crews back to Polebrook fifty-seven times. On February 25, she headed to Munich with Lieutenant Charles R. Ablanalp as her pilot. It was only the second combat mission Ablanalp's crew had flown.

Over Munich that day, *Torchy Tess* was hit by flak and heavily damaged. An explosion to the left and near the nose of the bomber wounded its navigator and bombardier, and knocked out the number one and two engines. Soon the two remaining right-wing engines were leaking oil. Ablanalp knew the only hope was to try to reach Switzerland, which is what the valiant pilot managed to do. But with only two weakened engines, the B-17 could not reach a landing strip.

With two Swiss Air Force fighters escorting him down, Ablanalp brought *Torchy Tess* in for a crash landing. The landing area was mostly open land that was dotted with a few trees. Most of the crew, huddled in the radio room, could not see what was happening, but they could feel the bomber sliding across the field, and they could hear parts of their aircraft begin to break away. The bomber had almost come to a stop when it hit a tree.

Several members of the crew were injured, including Ablanalp and his copilot, Second Lieutenant Harold V. Gividen. Soon after being removed from the wrecked Fortress, Ablanalp, who had saved all of his men, was dead. The crew buried their pilot with full military honors in Münsingen, Switzerland.

Torchy Tess was a total loss at the end of her fifty-eighth mission, but she would never be forgotten by the numerous 351st airmen who had flown her and loved her.

Crew Reunion: In the early 1990s, George Ahern began to attend 351st Bomb Group reunions, where he has been reunited with former crewmate Charles "Buddy" Armstrong on several occasions and once with Philip Duke. The three old friends stay in touch today via telephone and e-mail.

• Manna from Heaven •

BOB VALLIERE
Navigator

385TH BOMB GROUP

550TH BOMB SQUADRON

The play at first base was extremely close. The runner's foot touched the bag at the very instant the ball slammed into the first baseman's mitt. The umpire hesitated only a second or two before making his call, but even that minuscule delay did not go unnoticed by the hometown crowd. When the official jerked his right thumb into the air, the fans at Ebbets Field showered him with boos.

With the game close and his team struggling through a .500 season, Brooklyn manager Leo Durocher had been poised on the top step of the dugout. When the umpire called his runner out, Durocher stormed toward first base. Even with the protesting runner screaming at him, the ump kept his eyes on the Dodgers' flamboyant leader. Durocher, in his fifth season as a major league manager, had already earned a reputation for being both combative and brilliant.

In a choice seat behind the Dodger dugout, nineteen-year-old Bob Valliere watched the argument escalate as Durocher placed himself between his player and the umpire. Bob smiled, knowing that in the press box a radio announcer was probably describing Durocher's language as "colorful." Bob was close enough to the fray to hear some of the manager's harsher comments, but even he could not always tell when Durocher had truly lost his temper or when he was just acting.

Bob knew the Dodger manager well—well enough to call him by his first name and, in fact, Durocher had provided his ticket to the game that day. Leo was family; he and Bob were second cousins. Throughout his teenage years, Bob had been allowed access to the Dodger dressing room and dugout, where he had met many of Brooklyn's beloved Bums.

On the field, the umpire had grown tired of Durocher's verbal assault, and he turned to walk away from the manager. Durocher was having none of it. When his language failed to achieve the desired result, the hot-tempered manager resorted to one of his favorite tactics. Baseball rules prohibited anyone from touching an umpire, but the rules said nothing about a player or manager taking his anger out on the ground. Durocher was determined to exercise this right of expression, and soon he was kicking his cleats into the dirt with such gusto that a small dust storm seemed to be brewing around first base.

If some of the dirt and a few small pebbles kicked up by the Dodger manager happened to strike the umpire's trousers, Durocher did not feel responsible. The umpire saw things differently. "You're out of here!" the ump screamed, loud enough for Bob and everyone else in the box seats to hear. For those out of earshot, the umpire emphasized his action with a dramatic gesture, pointing a finger toward the Dodger dugout. Durocher had been thrown out of the game.

Bob watched with complete enjoyment as cousin Leo kicked a little more dirt in the umpire's direction. The manager then strolled to the home dugout under the appreciative cheers of the

Dodger fans. Bob knew Leo had gotten just what he wanted. There had never been any doubt that the umpire's controversial call would stand. Leo had taken the heat away from the runner, one of his starting players. He had fired up the rest of his team and at the same time he had entertained the hometown crowd. He had done what needed to be done at the time.

Bob Valliere was in a similar situation as he left the ballpark that afternoon. It was the summer of 1943 and after having completed two years of studies at Michigan State University, Bob was prepared to put his personal plans on hold to go to war. He had been accepted into the United States Army Air Corps and was looking forward to the challenges of navigation school in San Marcos, Texas. With some luck, Bob estimated he could become a navigator, complete his bomber training, fly his twenty-five combat missions and still be back in the States in time to see the Dodgers play in next season's World Series—if cousin Leo could work a miracle and get his team there. It never crossed Bob's mind that the Dodgers' chances were better than those of a combat bomber navigator.

Bob Valliere was born in Brooklyn, New York, on August 23, 1924. His parents were first-generation Americans. Bob's father, Armand, was of French heritage, and his mother, the former Marie Signaigo, was Italian. The Vallieres shared a two-story brick home with Marie's mother and father—Bob and his parents lived on the second floor and the Signaigo grandparents occupied the downstairs.

It was a warm and fertile atmosphere for an only child who grew up indulged but who showed continuing signs of above-average intelligence. A straight-A student, Bob graduated from high school at age sixteen and then breezed through two years of college courses. Army Air Force testing officers were surprised when Private Bob Valliere achieved a perfect score on his navigation school entrance exam.

For Bob, a young man blessed with a natural ability for mathematics, the Air Corps' tough navigation school proved to be no more an obstacle than Michigan State had been. Bob graduated near the top of his class and, commissioned as a second lieutenant/navigation officer, headed to MacDill Field in Florida. At MacDill, the young navigator met his new bomber crew and began flying training missions, eagerly applying the skills he had acquired in navigation school.

The weeks flew by. Combat training was completed, and Bob and his crewmates awaited assignment with nervous anticipation. But before they could take off for overseas, there was another in a seemingly endless string of physical examinations. Bob did not give it a second thought. He had already passed half a dozen physicals since his initial enlistment. He was sure there had been some kind of mistake when the examining doctor told him, "Son, you have a hernia."

"I can't have a hernia," Bob responded and explained how he had passed all the previous Army physical exams.

"Well, they missed it, because you have had it since birth. Don't worry, we will admit you into the base hospital and schedule an operation. You'll be as good as new."

"How long will it take? I'll be leaving with my crew in just a few days," Bob said.

"No, you can't fly for at least two months after the operation." The doctor informed him it was Army regulations. A day or two later, Bob watched his bomber crew take off in a new B-17, headed for the war in Europe without him.

Bob resigned himself to the delay and decided to enjoy his hospital stay. After a successful operation, the navigator was free to roam the hospital, flirt with the nurses and even go carousing in town during the evenings. If the Army was forcing a two-month liberty on him, *Why not enjoy it?* he thought. The newspaper headlines made it clear the war would still be there after his hospital stay ended.

When he was finally discharged from the hospital, Bob moved into the transient barracks and dutifully checked the bulletin board every day to see when he would be assigned to a new bomber crew. Day after day and then week after week, the name Bob Valliere failed to appear on any of the crew lists. After a month had passed, he approached an assignment officer, only to be told, "Be patient." Still, nothing happened, and Bob realized his records were lost somewhere in the vast Army bureaucracy.

One day, seven full months after leaving the MacDill field hospital, Bob bumped into another officer, whom he had known at San Marcos Navigation School. The ribbons on his friend's uniform indicated he was a combat veteran who had completed his tour.

"Hey, Bob, when did you get back?"

"I'm still here!" Bob said. "I've never been assigned."

As the two friends caught up, Bob found his book from navigation school and opened it to a photograph of their graduation class. The veteran officer pointed to one of their classmates in the photo. "He was killed in action." Pointing to another, he added, "He was also killed in action." Again and again, he placed his finger on a different face in the photo and repeated the phrase, "Killed in action."

A few days later, Bob checked the new-assignments board and was surprised to see his name listed as the replacement navigator for a rookie crew that was headed to the Eighth Air Force in England.

Bob and his bomber crewmates made their Atlantic crossing on the *Queen Elizabeth* along with thirteen thousand other military personnel. After disembarking in Scotland, the airmen spent a few days waiting for their bomb group assignment. The rookies found there was no shortage of war rumors floating around. One of the most prevalent rumors concerned the 100th Bomb Group.

The 100th had earned a reputation as a hard-fighting and hard-luck bomb group. In truth, their losses did seem to come in bunches. Of twenty-four B-17s shot down during the August 17, 1943, raid over Regensburg, nine were from the 100th Bomb Group. On October 10, 1943, the 100th sent thirteen of its bombers to Münster as part of a larger formation. Only one plane returned.

In March 1944, the 100th along with the 95th Bomb Group comprised the first Eighth Air Force formation to bomb Berlin; the 100th lost one of its Fortresses in the process. Eight more 100th bombers went down in July over Merseburg. Then during a mission to Ruhland in September, the Luftwaffe came "out of the sun" to devastate the 100th Bomb Group again—shooting down eleven bombers. Finally, on the last day of the year and only days before Bob Valliere's arrival in Scotland, the 100th Bomb Group lost twelve B-17s while flying a raid on Hamburg.

So when Bob and the others on his new crew heard, "If you get assigned to the 100th Bomb Group, you might as well make out your will," it was as much fact as it was rumor. Every veteran airman of the Eighth Air Force had heard of the "bloody 100th." When their assignment came, everyone on Bob's crew was relieved to hear that they would be heading to Great Ashfield air base to become members of the 351st Bomb Group and the 550th Bomb Squadron.

Bob reached Great Ashfield airfield with his eight new crewmates. (By January 1945, the Eighth Air Force had decided one waist gunner could handle both midship gun positions.) The crew commander was Lieutenant Michael Swana, who was comfortable with his men calling him "Mike." Born in Dudley, Massachusetts, Swana was the son of Czechoslovakian immigrants. Only twenty years old, he was also one of the youngest bomber pilots in the Eighth Air Force.

Copilot Lieutenant Wallace MacCafferty had trained as a fighter pilot before being assigned to bombers. The bombardier was Flight Officer Marvin Hydecker. Nineteen-year-old Leonard Weinstein, who had been a running back on the New York University football teams of 1942 and 1943 and now held the rank of Tech Sergeant, would be the crew's radio operator and gunner. The rest of the crew members were: flight engineer, Staff Sergeant Al Hareda; waist gunner, Tech Sergeant William Wells; tail gunner (and sometimes ball turret gunner), Staff Sergeant Charles DuShane. The crew's regular ball turret gunner was a staff sergeant named Shinberg. After one or two missions, a new ball turret gunner was assigned to Swana's crew. The replacement gunner was a staff sergeant by the name of Goldstein.

Swana and his crew were given a B-17 that had been named *The Stork Club* by its previous crew. Although *The Stork Club* had plenty of combat mission miles on her, the bomber appeared to be in good condition, and she sported some creative nose art. The airplane's name was proudly displayed in bold letters, and beneath it was a painting of a stork carrying a bundle that contained not a baby, but a large bomb. Swana's bomber boys liked the nose art, and they liked the Flying Fortress. *The Stork Club* had a history, but now she was all theirs.

The rookies were eager to get their first combat mission behind them, especially Bob, who had waited so long. When the day finally arrived, he nervously climbed into the nose compartment. He carried with him a small gift from his mother—a string of rosary beads. As he hung the beads near his navigation table, he noticed the bombardier, Marvin Hydecker, watching him. Bob felt a little self-conscious, until Hydecker smiled and nodded to indicate his approval.

When *The Stork Club* taxied onto the runway, every man on board tried to calm his *first-mission jitters*. Bob touched the rosary beads and said a silent prayer: *Don't let me screw up. Don't let anything go wrong.* Lieutenant Mike Swana piloted his aircraft into the air. During the next half an hour, something *was* going to go terribly wrong for the crew of *The Stork Club*.

The flying techniques for joining a bomber formation had changed very little throughout the war. *The Stork Club* was flying about thirty seconds behind one B-17 and thirty seconds ahead of another. As the bombers disappeared into the cloud cover, they began their circling ascent. Bob and Hydecker sat silently, peering out the Plexiglas nose. They could see nothing. Formation assembly was mostly a matter of trust—trusting that the other squadron pilots were flying the correct pattern and trusting your own airplane's radio compass.

The B-17 pilot used the radio compass readings to guide his turns until his aircraft lifted above the clouds, where he could once again visually locate the other bombers in his squadron or group. At that point, it became the navigator's responsibility to guide his pilot to the target.

Bob checked his watch—more than twenty-five minutes since takeoff. *We should be breaking into blue sky any minute now,* he thought. Bob had heard the veteran airmen talk about the thrilling feeling of rising above the clouds and seeing sunlight reflect off the wings of dozens of other bombers. Everyone on board *The Stork Club* was anticipating the glorious moment that would signal an end to blind flying.

As the final wisp of cloud vapor disappeared across the bomber's nose, Bob gazed on the scene in amazement. Before them was endless, empty blue sky, as beautiful as any he had ever seen. With the exception of *The Stork Club*, there was not an airplane to be seen.

Bob and Hydecker looked at each other, and then without speaking they scrambled to the nose compartment's side windows. Bob could see nothing beyond the bomber's right wing but sky. Hydecker shook his head. Nothing to the left either.

The interphone was strangely silent as the other members of the crew searched their sections of sky in disbelief. Finally the silence was broken by Mike Swana's voice: "Charlie, can you see anybody back there?"

The tail gunner quickly reported back, "Not a thing, Mike."

"Anybody else? Anybody see any planes?" Swana asked in a calm that belied his mounting concern. The interphone jumped alive with chatter as everyone reported all at once that they had nothing to report.

"Okay. Quiet down now," Swana said firmly. Then to his navigator: "Bob, do you have any idea where we are?" Bob thought he just might; at least he felt he knew where they weren't. Swana's bomber should have been over the eastern English coastline of the North Sea, but moments before, the clouds below *The Stork Club* had opened. Looking at the terrain thousands of feet below, Bob sensed they were flying in the wrong direction.

The navigator checked the airplane's G-Box radar unit and his map before he keyed onto the interphone and informed Swana they were indeed headed the wrong way.

There was a short period of silence. Bob knew the pilot was considering his options. There were only two courses of action. He could turn *The Stork Club* around and try to catch the lost bomber formation before it reached enemy territory. If they could not locate the other bombers or if they could not catch up in time, it would mean flying into German airspace alone.

The second option was not really much of an option at all, not for Swana. Aborting the mission and returning to their base was a humiliation the pilot was not about to put his crew or himself through. Even if the investigation proved, as he suspected, a faulty radio compass had led them drastically off course, the rookie crew would never live it down.

"Bob, we need to find the group. Can you give me a direction?"

"Mike, just turn around 180 degrees, and barrel-ass as fast as you can. I'll get back to you with a course adjustment."

"All right," the pilot acknowledged. Almost immediately, Bob felt *The Stork Club's* left wing dip as the bomber began a long turn back to the east.

Loaded with bombs, ammunition and a full crew, a B-17G model could still reach an impressive top speed of just over three hundred miles per hour. Swana pushed his Fortress to her limits. He estimated the rest of the bombers in the 385th Bomb Group would be cruising to the target at a speed somewhere below two hundred miles per hour. *The Stork Club* had a chance of closing the gap in time, if her young navigator could find the missing formation.

Like most rookie navigators, Bob had taken comfort in the knowledge that the navigator on board the group's lead bomber would be guiding the rest of the B-17s to the target. Now, on his very first mission, Bob was being asked to recalculate his own bomber's position and then plot an intercept course for a moving target—a challenging task for even a more experienced navigator.

His mom's rosary beads swayed above his head as Bob worked over his charts. Once he was confident that he had the right coordinates, he gave Swana the course correction. Bob was not so confident that he neglected to say a silent prayer that he *was* right. After that, there was nothing to do but watch and wait. He and Hydecker sat together in the nose compartment, peering into the sky ahead, searching for any speck in the distance that might be a B-17.

Somewhere short of German airspace, someone on Swana's bomber spotted a flight of aircraft. The gunners test-fired their weapons and prepared for the possibility that the mystery airplanes could possibly be Luftwaffe.

Swana soon reassured his crew: "That's an American bomber group ahead of us," he said. Hydecker slapped Bob on the back as they listened to the cheers of their crewmates over the interphone.

Swana knew that somewhere ahead, lost in the distant sky, was their own 550th Bomb Squadron and the rest of the 385th Bomb Group. He was also aware that he was burning precious fuel and straining *The Stork Club*'s engines by continuing to fly at pursuit speed. Under their present circumstances, one bomb group was as good as another—at least they would not have to fly over the target alone.

"We're going to join up with this group in front of us," the pilot announced to his men. The words had barely left Swana's lips when Bob identified the group by the tail markings of its bombers.

"Mike, that's the 100th Bomb Group!"

"Are you sure?" Swana asked.

"The Bloody 100th?" another crewmate wanted to know.

"Yeah, I'm sure," Bob said.

"Keep going, Mike!" urged another member of the crew. Quickly, everyone else chimed in. It was unanimous. Their first mission had started off on the wrong foot. Nobody wanted to compound their problems by joining the bomb group that had the worst reputation for bad luck in the entire Eighth Air Force. Swana was the aircraft commander and it was his decision to make. He was not superstitious by nature and did not intend to allow his crew to believe that his bomber command operated as some kind of democracy. Still, his gut told him to keep going. *The Stork Club* flew on past the 100th Bomb Group.

When his bomber finally caught up with the 385th Bomb Group, Swana cheerfully commended his navigator.

"That's pretty good navigation, Bob."

"Well, I figured we'd better find them," Bob replied as if it were no big deal, and then he reached out and rubbed the rosary beads.

The jubilant atmosphere on board *The Stork Club* lasted until the bomb group began its run on the day's target. There was flak, but the rookie airmen all knew their pilot could not take evasive action until the bombs were dropped. Time dragged by until everyone heard the words, "Bombs away!"

Swana began evasive flying immediately, and soon his Fortress had cleared the flak area. Her gunners scanned the sky for enemy fighters and were encouraged that the depleted Luftwaffe had remained invisible thus far. But their first combat mission, which had begun in such an unusual and dangerous way, was about to get even weirder.

It was the tail gunner Charles DuShane who made the incredible report. "Mike, there's a B-17 firing at us!"

"What are you talking about, Charlie?" asked Swana.

"There's a B-17 right behind us and they are firing at us." DuShane sounded perfectly sane to Bob as he listened to the tail gunner's seemingly illogical statement. If *The Stork Club*'s pilot had any doubts about his tail gunner's report, they remained unspoken.

"Well, fire back at them," Swana ordered, and DuShane did so.

Crewmen on other 385th bombers watched in bewilderment as the two B-17s engaged in a short gun battle. DuShane could not be certain if any of his bullets actually hit the other Fortress, but he made it hot enough that the mystery bomber soon backed off and then disappeared.

Bob and his crewmates swapped speculations about the aggressive B-17 all the way back to Great Ashfield, where Swana landed his bomber safely. The pilot's suspicion of an equipment failure was quickly confirmed by his ground crew mechanics—a faulty radio compass had led Swana off course at the beginning of the mission. The crew was also informed that Charles Du-Shane had not imagined the attack by another B-17 (something he knew all along). The mysterious Fortress had been captured by the Germans, repaired and then flown into the American bomber formation by Luftwaffe airmen. Bob felt this was an extremely underhanded tactic, but he also saw it as an indication of just how desperate the enemy had become. The end of the war was on the horizon.

The working relationship between a bomber's navigator and bombardier was as intimate as the relationship between pilot and copilot. The navigator and bombardier spent hours together in the cramped nose compartment. During bomb runs, when flak bursts were shoving their B-17 around and shrapnel fragments were noisily glancing off the Plexiglas, the two airmen could see the fear on each other's faces. They shared an understanding of the demands and pressures their combat assignments placed on them—one was responsible for getting his crew to the target and back to their home base; the other, with actually hitting the target. Their important and dangerous work was a little more tolerable if the two men became friends.

It was on his second mission that Bob realized what an inventive and entertaining crewmate Marvin Hydecker could be. There was an immediate bond due to common backgrounds. Hydecker had grown up in New York City, just across the East River from Bob's Brooklyn home. Off duty, *The Stork Club*'s bombardier was a cutup who enjoyed making his friends laugh. In fact, when Hydecker began some extensive redecorating just before takeoff, Bob at first thought his pal was just fooling around.

Bob arrived at his navigation station to find that Hydecker had smuggled five extra flak jackets on board, in addition to the two jackets already in the nose compartment. The bombardier said, "Hi, Bob," but never looked up from his work, which seemed to be an attempt to carpet the floor with unauthorized flak jackets.

"Hi, Marv . . ." Bob stopped himself from asking the bombardier what he was up to. A gut feeling told Bob that it might prove convenient later if he could plead no involvement in Hydecker's scheme. The five extra flak jackets would add from two hundred fifty to three hundred pounds of weight in the nose of the aircraft, the equivalent of carrying two additional crewmen.

It should be an interesting takeoff, Bob thought. *On the other hand, if we're able to get into the air with all the extra weight, it will be nice to have some flak protection under our butts.*

As Mike Swana taxied *The Stork Club* onto the runway to begin his second mission as an aircraft commander, he was confident he could handle whatever the day might bring. His crew's maiden flight had proven that strange things could happen on any mission—things that were not covered by the pilot training manual. A good pilot had to be prepared for the unexpected.

He pushed the throttle forward. The bomber seemed a little sluggish in reaching takeoff speed. Swana had to use most of the runway to get the Fortress airborne. He could not understand why he had to struggle with the flight controls. When he finally got the aircraft into a steady ascent, the pilot had a question for his bombardier and navigator: "What the hell is in the nose?"

Hydecker confessed immediately. Swana ordered the offending flak jackets moved to the radio room, midship. Nothing else was said about the matter, at least until the mission was over, when Swana called Hydecker over for a private conversation.

Bob imagined that the pilot threatened the bombardier with dismissal from the crew if he ever pulled another risky stunt. Hydecker would not say what the pilot had actually told him, but from then on he went by the book on bombing missions. That did not mean he gave up his quest for something to increase the odds of survival. At the beginning of their third mission, Hydecker asked: "Bob, do you think your mother could send me a string of those rosary beads?"

By the third week of April 1945, Marshal Georgy Zhukov's Russian army was hammering its way through the suburbs of Berlin. With the German capital and its military command structure doomed, the American and British air forces ended offensive combat operations in Europe. The airmen who had flown the Fortresses, Liberators, Lancasters, Mustangs, Thunderbolts, Lightnings, Spitfires and all the other Allied aircraft had destroyed Germany's fuel supply, her once mighty Luftwaffe and many of her cities. There was simply nothing of importance left to bomb.

During these climactic days, one nation still suffered under German occupation. The Netherlands had been under the Germans' harsh control since May 1940. In western Holland, an isolated German command now held on stubbornly, waiting for word from Berlin. Although posing no immediate military threat to the Allies, these German ground forces were a deadly curse on the Dutch people.

After nearly five years of occupation, the Dutch had not lost their will to resist the invaders. Holland's underground forces blew up bridges and railroads. The Germans retaliated by destroying dams and flooding much of the lowland country's farmland. Dutch workers went on strike. Railroad and seaport activity came to a halt. Food and fuel shortages and rationing soon followed. Then came the cruel winter of 1944.

With no fuel to heat their homes, the Dutch used what they could. Once beautiful trees lining streets were cut bare. Fences disappeared and bombed-out homes were dismantled. Thin children spent hours scouring railroad beds for tiny bits of coal. Across Holland money was worthless. There was nothing to buy anyway. Stores were long closed for lack of stock. Warehouses were empty.

By the time spring arrived, people were starving to death. Word of the dire situation in the Netherlands made its way to England. General Dwight D. Eisenhower was informed of the tragedy but could do nothing to address it until active combat campaigning stopped. By that time, an estimated one thousand Dutch men, women and children were dying every day.

In late April, Eisenhower's representatives approached the German commanders in Holland with a unique proposal. The Allied plan was to deliver food to the Netherlands using the very American and British bombers that had brought destruction to much of Germany. The mercy mission would require a truce between the two opposing forces, which were officially still at war. The Germans were assured the Allied airplanes would carry no bombs. The German antiaircraft batteries, which had shot down many Allied bombers on their way to the fatherland, would be required to stand down. While the Allies sought the German commander's cooperation, they also made it clear that the food flights would happen one way or another.

The Germans' reply was prompt. They agreed with the plan, in principle. Operational details were soon worked out, including drop zones where the bombers would be allowed to fly at extremely low altitude without the threat of fire from enemy antiaircraft guns.

The mercy missions to save the people of Holland would be a massive undertaking, involving a large force of RAF bombers and ten American bomb groups. The British dubbed the project Manna. The Americans called it Chowhound. The Eighth Air Force bomb groups assigned to Chowhound were: the 34th, 95th, 96th, 100th, 385th, 388th, 390th, 452nd, 490th and 493rd. As part of the 385th, Bob Valliere and the airmen of *The Stork Club* would be flying over enemy-occupied Holland at an altitude of just over four hundred feet and hoping that the truce would hold.

After *The Stork Club* completed combat mission number twelve and landed at Great Ashfield airfield, Mike Swana's crew was informed it would be their last bombing raid. Bob experienced the same feelings his crewmates were experiencing—relief, joy and satisfaction. Nobody would miss taking the risks that came with each mission. Euphoria swept over them—they were going to live, and they would soon be going home to the country they had helped protect. They had arrived late in the war, but they had made a difference by helping drive the last nails in the Nazis' coffin.

That evening they celebrated the way Eighth Air Force airmen across England were celebrating: with laughter, reminiscences and large amounts of alcohol. A few days later, rumors of a mercy mission to the Netherlands began to circulate. There was some concern about whether the Germans in Holland could be trusted, but mostly Bob and his pals looked forward to the food flights. It was a chance to help save people, a welcome change from their previous occupations.

The RAF flew the first Manna mission on April 29, dropping tons of packaged raw food at racetracks and airfields near Dutch population centers. The German antiaircraft batteries in Holland were manned but remained silent. Every British aircraft returned unharmed. On the first day of May, it was the Americans' turn.

Once on board *The Stork Club,* Bob checked out the new payload in the bomb bay. He marveled at how quickly the bomber ground crews had adapted the Fortresses to drop boxes and sacks stuffed with meat, cheese, flour, coffee, sugar, powdered milk and eggs, and even chocolate. Everyone on the crew was in a jovial mood. Their war was over and they were looking forward to heading back to the United States, but in the meantime they had been given an opportunity to be part of a great humanitarian effort.

Bob made his way to the nose section. It seemed odd not to have his friend Marvin Hydecker along on this mission. Bombardiers had been exempted from the mercy missions. The bombers would be flying over Holland at four hundred feet, so there would be no need to use the sophisticated Norden bombsights. It would be the responsibility of the navigator to release the food payload as the aircraft passed over the authorized drop zone.

Since the RAF mission had gone off without a hitch, Bob had little concern about the Germans, but as *The Stork Club* left the North Sea and crossed over the coast of the Netherlands, a tingling little chill ran up the navigator's spine. Bob knew it was a conditioned response, left over from his combat missions.

Nobody on board *The Stork Club* was prepared for the reception they would receive in Holland that day. As they passed over the rooftops of a Dutch village, Bob saw crowds of people in the streets waving to the American airmen. Had it not been for the noisy B-17 engines, the airmen would have also heard the wild cheers of the Hollanders. Up ahead, Bob spotted something written in large white letters on a rooftop. The message was simple but inspiring: "THANKS, YANKS!"

It was the same all the way to the drop zone—thousands of grateful Dutch filling the streets to greet their Eighth Air Force angels. Pots of Holland's famous tulips had been arranged to spell out THANK YOU. It was a tribute that the airmen of Operation Chowhound would never forget.

The Stork Club made its run over the drop zone. Bob released the bomber's precious cargo. The boxes and sacks fell within the boundaries the Germans had designated. Mike Swana pulled his aircraft into a slow turn to head back to Great Ashfield. Below, Bob and his crewmates could see hungry Dutch citizens surrounding the field, waiting for the signal that it was safe to retrieve the food. The airmen could also see the German antiaircraft guns tracking their bomber and the other Fortresses of the 550th Bomb Squadron. It was not a comfortable feeling to be in the enemy's crosshairs at an altitude of only four hundred feet, but the real threat to *The Stork Club* was a sack of food that had become entangled in the bomb bay.

Flight engineer Al Hareda discovered the maverick sack on a visual inspection of the bay. It was too far down to reach. Swana tried closing the bomb bay doors, hoping the bag would simply tear away, but the doors would not close. Someone was going to have to climb down and get rid of the sack. Copilot Wallace MacCafferty volunteered.

The bomb bay housing was much too confining to allow MacCafferty to wear a parachute. He climbed down to the bottom of the bomber to loosen the errant sack of food. One slip of his foot would send him tumbling to his death. Swana's hands tightened on the controls of *The Stork Club* as he held the aircraft as steady as possible. MacCafferty's uniform flapped wildly in the wind. The copilot cut the bag loose and its contents fell away, enriching the dinner table of some poor Dutch family and ending the threat to the bomber crew.

When *The Stork Club* arrived back at Great Ashfield, her crew members not only had a new admiration for the bravery of their copilot but also a new appreciation for the importance of the Chowhound missions. The Eighth Air Force bombers had delivered nearly eight hundred tons of food to the starving people of Holland. Bob and the rest of Swana's crew were looking forward to the next day's food mission to Hilversum. It would be a mission that would endanger all of them and earn the 550th Bomb Squadron and more specifically, *The Stork Club*, a unique place in Eighth Air Force history.

On May 2, most of the citizens of Hilversum, the Netherlands, went to the racetrack. The track's grassy infield had been designated as a drop zone for the Eighth Air Force food mission that day. The malnourished people watched the western horizon with joyful anticipation. They heard the Fortress engines well before the bombers came into view.

Tears ran down hollow smiling faces when the B-17s began to swoop down even lower to begin their runs over the racetrack. Dutch fathers, mothers and children vowed never to forget these American airmen. As the first boxes of food fell to the infield, a cheer that no horse race had ever inspired rose from the crowd at the Hilversum track.

On board *The Stork Club*, Lieutenant Michael Swana spotted the racetrack ahead and began to bring his bomber down as the aircraft of the 550th Squadron prepared for their runs. Bob had a good view of the entire operation. Down there was the racetrack with its grassy target in the center, the enthusiastic Dutch waving their welcome and thanks. One thing went unnoticed by the navigator. On the outskirts of the racetrack, a German antiaircraft gunner was tracking the American bomber with the painting of a stork on its nose.

In the cockpit, Swana was focused on the job at hand. "Let it go, Bob," he ordered his navigator. Bob hit the switch and confirmed the release of the food. The antiaircraft gunner watched the B-17 drop its lifesaving cargo and then begin a slow banking climb to head for home. Then, for a reason known only to himself, the German squeezed the trigger.

"They're firing at us!" someone screamed over the interphone, but Swana knew it was even worse than that. From the corner of his eye, the pilot saw two red flashes and he felt the immediate effect on his aircraft's flight controls. *The Stork Club*'s left wing, at first pushed up by the twenty-millimeter flak explosions, quickly dipped drastically. Swana fought to control the bomber as it began to bank sharply to the left. He could see the cause of the problem—two flak holes adorned the left wing between the engines. The larger of the holes, near the front of the wing, was a ragged puncture more than two feet across. The smaller breach was about five feet to the rear. The flak explosions had ripped into the bottom of the wing and exited through the top.

The immediate challenge for Swana was to keep *The Stork Club* flying straight. The ragged holes in the left wing were creating such a drag that the Fortress continued to pull in that direction. To compensate, the pilot banked his airplane to the right, raising the left wing by about thirty degrees. With the left wing elevated at this angle, Swana was able to manhandle the bomber into straight flight. He had found the solution in a matter of seconds, because at an altitude of four hundred feet, seconds was all the time he could afford.

Meanwhile, Charlie DuShane had the offending German flak battery in his tail position gunsight. He checked with his aircraft commander before returning fire: "Mike, I've got that German battery covered. Should I shoot?"

Swana's decision and his order came instantly. "No, Charlie! Don't shoot! Everyone hold your fire!" It was a decision that almost certainly saved the lives of his crew and also the lives of numerous airmen aboard other B-17s flying close by—in addition to sparing the lives of many Dutch spectators and German soldiers in Holland. Once fired upon, the flak batteries around Hilversum would have had a field day shooting at American bombers that were flying so low over the racetrack. The Allied retaliation would likely have been swift and severe, with hundreds of P-51 Mustangs sweeping in from England to attack the Germans. But a dangerous incident did not erupt into a bloody battle at Hilversum, because Lieutenant Michael Swana and all the other B-17 pilots kept cool heads. Tempted as they were, the American bomber gunners held their fire.

As Swana managed to gain valuable altitude, he warned his crew, "Keep your eyes open for fuel and oil leaks." He knew the flak holes were in the vicinity of the left-wing fuel tank. If the tank had been penetrated, fire or even an explosion was a likely possibility. Not retaining enough fuel to reach England was another. Everyone focused on the wounded wing while their pilot began a slow and laborious turn to the west.

No leaking fuel or oil appeared, and Swana began to feel encouraged about their chances of making it back to Great Ashfield. The return flight proved to be a tiring effort for *The Stork Club*'s pilot and copilot. Each of them took turns at the flight controls, struggling to keep the bomber's left wing elevated enough to sustain a relatively straight flight path.

In the B-17's nose, Bob watched as little Dutch villages and farms flashed by below. The same countryside that had been so welcoming on the flight to Hilversum now seemed endless. By the time she reached the North Sea coast, *The Stork Club* had managed to climb to about one thousand feet. Bob could see the rest of the 385th Bomb Group Fortresses far ahead.

The flight from Hilversum to Great Ashfield took more than two hours, but with MacCafferty's assistance, Swana was not exhausted as he brought *The Stork Club* into a landing approach. He realized his technique of keeping the bomber's left wing elevated at a thirty-degree angle would not work for the landing. The left and right wheels would need to touch the runway simultaneously. At fifty feet, he brought the left wing down to a level position—the Fortress instantly pulled to the left.

Swana was prepared. He pulled at his controls and felt his aircraft float back to the right. The tricky correction proved to be a little too much. The left wheel made contact with the runway ahead of the right wheel.

The Stork Club swerved to the right and headed off the runway. Swana's quick reaction was perfect. He juiced the power to the right wing's outside engine. The B-17 straightened itself. By nursing first the left brake and then the right brake, Swana was able to complete an awkward but safe landing.

The news of the Germans' violation of the truce had spread like wildfire. By the time Swan brought his Fortress to a stop, newspaper photographers and reporters were on the scene. Bob and his crewmates laughed and downplayed the danger of their flight. It was easy to do once they were standing safely on the familiar tarmac.

A close inspection of the flak damage proved just how lucky the crew of *The Stork Club* had been. The twenty-millimeter explosions had missed the internal fuel tank by a mere six inches. A direct hit on the fuel tank could have blown away the wing. At four hundred feet, there would have been no time for any of the crew to bail out.

Fate had spared the men of *The Stork Club,* but questions remained: Why had the Germans fired on them? Would the incident affect the truce or even stop the mercy missions to Holland? The latter question was answered quickly by the Eighth Air Force headquarters. The Chowhound relief missions would continue. In fact, Mike Swana's crew would participate in three more flights aboard a new bomber.

There would be no further incidents with the Germans, who claimed the 550th Bomb Squadron had ventured out of the designated flight area on May 2. Bob and everyone else in the 550th knew this was a lie, because *The Stork Club* had just finished dropping food on the racetrack infield when it had been hit. The truth of why the German gunner had fired on their bomber would never be known.

On May 7, 1945, the incident at the Hilversum racetrack, along with other events of World War II, became a part of history. The war in Europe, half of the greatest armed conflict the world has ever known, officially came to an end at 2:41 a.m. that day (the Japanese would surrender in August). The men who had taken part in operations Manna and Chowhound were told they should be proud of what they had accomplished. In a single week, British bombers had dropped 7,029 tons of food and the American Fortresses had contributed another 4,155 tons. Tens of thousands of Dutch citizens had been saved from starvation.

Before they packed to head back to the States, Swana's crew paid a visit to an old friend. Bob walked underneath the nose of the bomber with the familiar painting of a stork. He climbed through the hatch as he had done so often before. Inside, he retrieved a string of rosary beads that hung over his navigator's table.

Maybe I should leave them here in the old girl, Bob thought. *No, the war is over for her, too.* The war *was* over for them all— the airmen in Europe who had given their lives, the airmen who had survived the long odds, the ground crews who had kept them flying and the families and loved ones who had waged a war of waiting at home. And yes, the war was also over for *The Stork Club*—the last Eighth Air Force bomber to be hit by German antiaircraft fire during World War II.

After the War

Bob Valliere returned to Michigan State University and graduated with a degree in mechanical engineering in 1948. After graduation, he maintained a long-distance relationship with Nancy Dalzell, a fetching coed he had met during his junior year. Bob and Nancy were married on June 24, 1950. Later that summer, he took his new bride to her first major league baseball game. She was quite impressed with her new husband when he introduced her to Leo Durocher, who was by then the manager of the New York Giants. Bob assured Nancy that his cousin Leo would someday lead the Giants to a World Series championship. Four years later, Durocher did.

The newlyweds made their home in Brooklyn, and Bob joined his grandfather's importing business in New York City. Bob would spend the next forty-five years building and improving the company. He traveled the world searching for new and unique products, and Nancy happily went along with him. In 1952, Nancy gave birth to Patricia Valliere. A second daughter, Roberta, was born two years later.

The year 1985 was a busy one for the Vallieres. Bob moved the import company that he now headed to New Haven, Connecticut, where he had built a new headquarters. The family celebrated Bob's sixtieth birthday in August. However, a phone call shortly afterward began the most monumental event of that year and one of the most memorable events of Bob's life.

The man on the other end of the line identified himself as the secretary of the Dutch Freedom Committee. Twenty-eight American and British bomber veterans were being invited to come to the Netherlands for the fortieth anniversary of the Chowhound and Manna relief missions. Bob was both surprised and pleased that there were people in Holland who still remembered. He accepted the invitation, unprepared for the reception he and the rest of the former airmen were about to experience from people they had once helped but had never met.

Serving as representatives of all the airmen of Chowhound and Manna, the twenty-eight visitors were honored by the Dutch in ceremonies and with medals. There were dinners, parties and tours of the small towns and villages that had benefited from the food drops. As rewarding as the official events were, for Bob, nothing compared to actually meeting the people who had waved to the Allied bombers as they had dropped food forty years before.

Many who came to shake his hand remarked that though they had been mere children in May 1945, the memory of the friendly bombers was still vivid. Smiling strangers pressed pictures and small items into the hands of the American and British veterans. As Bob and Nancy returned to their hotel one evening, he discovered his jacket pockets were filled with these little gifts. A decorative tile caught his eye. Hand-painted on one side of the tile was a Dutch windmill. Bob turned the tile over and he could not stop the tears that came to his eyes. When Nancy noticed his reaction, he showed her the words that were written on the back of the tile: "Thanks for saving my life."

Ten years later, the Dutch government invited all living air veterans of the Chowhound and Manna missions to Holland for a second celebration. What had begun in 1985 as a heartfelt but contained anniversary commemoration had become a national holiday of appreciation by 1995. Bob and the other visiting airmen rode in vintage WWII Jeeps through the streets of Rotterdam, while ticker tape rained down and an estimated five hundred thousand spectators cheered them as heroes.

Bob closed his import company in 1993 and retired to spend more time with Nancy. For the next ten years, the Vallieres lived happily in Branford, Connecticut, enjoying their five grandchildren. Bob was active as the treasurer of the Connecticut Chapter of the Eighth Air Force Historical Society. In 1985, he became director of the Chowhound organization, a position he held for more than ten years, and from 1995 to 1997 he served as president of the 385th Bomb Group Association. Nancy Valliere passed away in 2003. Bob Valliere continued to live in Connecticut near his two daughters until his death on January 7, 2006.

Michael Swana earned a degree in physics from Clark University in Worcester, Massachusetts. After college, he found work with the General Telephone & Electronics Corporation, where he remained for more than thirty years. Swana became a valuable member of GT&E's equipment design department, often working on classified radar and communications systems for the U.S. government.

In 1952, Swana married Phyliss Bukowski. The couple raised three sons (Michael, David and Steven) and three daughters (Linda, Susan and Mary Ellen). The Swanas were rewarded with seven grandchildren. Phyliss Swana passed away in 1978, and Linda (Swana) Allard passed away in 2008.

Mike Swana retired in 1987. He currently lives in Stow, Massachusetts, and in recent years has enjoyed travel to the Grand Canyon, Yellowstone National Park, Israel and Italy.

Leonard Weinstein resumed his college studies after the war, earning a BA in business from New York University. He found employment as an insurance broker and soon opened his own insurance agency in New York City.

In 1961 Leonard married Sheila Finkel. The couple's first child, Rita, was born in 1961. Their first boy, Bruce, was born in 1964 and another daughter, Amy, in 1965. The Weinsteins raised their children in the Dix Hills community of Long Island, where Leonard had relocated his insurance business. Leonard and Sheila Weinstein separated in 1998.

Leonard now lives with his son, Bruce (and Bruce's wife, Celeste, and their two children), in Fairfax, Virginia. He enjoys playing Ping-Pong and pool at the local senior center and spending time with his grandchildren.

Crew Reunion: During the mid-1950s, Bob Valliere and Michael Swana met again at a 385th Bomb Group Association gathering in New York City. Over the years, Bob visited his former pilot in Massachusetts, and Swana maintained a correspondence and telephone contact with Charlie DuShane.

Bob and Marvin Hydecker became even closer friends in the postwar years. Decades following the war and after Hydecker had retired to Florida, Bob paid a visit. Displayed prominently in his friend's home was a string of rosary beads that Bob's mother had sent to Hydecker back when he was a young bombardier.

In 2008, a twelve-year-old boy named Kalman Weinstein was passing time doing an Internet search of his grandfather's name. The search took Kalman to TheBomberBoys.com, where he discovered a photo of three World War II airmen—his grandfather, Bob Valliere and Michael Swana. The Weinstein family contacted the author of *The Bomber Boys* to inform him that Leonard Weinstein, of the *The Stork Club* aircrew in the picture, was alive and well. As a result of young Kalman's interest in his family's history, former B-17 pilot Mike Swana and former B-17 radio operator and gunner Leonard Weinstein were reunited via telephone.

In memory of Bomber Boy John Conners,
and in memory of Thomas Ayres

• Author's Research Note •

The primary research sources used in writing *The Bomber Boys* were individual in-person interviews conducted by the author with the five main subjects. Ahern, Frechette, Seniawsky (Scott), Teta and Valliere were each interviewed (and recorded) for a minimum of five hours, beginning in 2001. In addition, follow-up interviews, both in-person and via telephone, were conducted as needed until the book's completion in 2004. The author estimates that the total interview time for these five men exceeds forty hours.

Also contacted and interviewed were the living former crewmates of the five main subjects. Armstrong, Chart, Cuffman, Duke, Lyon, Pearson, Pogorzelski, Swana and Weinstein each participated in numerous telephone interviews. Spodar was interviewed in person. Sons and daughters of former airmen, now deceased, provided additional details of their fathers' postwar lives (and occasionally their wartime memories).

Due to the volume and lengthy time span of the interviews, the author has chosen not to list individual interviews as part of the bibliography and hopes his explanation of his interview process will be sufficient to the reader.

It is the author's intention to eventually offer the actual audio recordings of *The Bomber Boys* interviews to the U.S. National Archives in Washington, D.C., or to the Mighty Eighth Air Force Museum in Savannah, Georgia.

Ahern, Frechette, Seniawsky, Teta and Valliere, as well as Cuffman, provided official wartime documents, letters or diaries that were used in research. These items are listed in the bibliography under the name of the person who provided them. Pearson and Pogorzelski contributed memoirs that have previously appeared in veterans organizations' newsletters. These are listed under Articles in the bibliography.

• Selected Bibliography •

BOOKS

Angelillo, Barbara Walsh and Sullivan, George / Andrews, Robert / Davenport, Giuliana / Davenport, Fionn. *Italy '97: The Complete Guide with the Great Cities, Tuscan Hill Towns and Renaissance Treasures.* New York: Fodor's. 1996.

Angelucci, Enzo and Matricardi, Paolo / Pinto, Pierluigi. *Complete Book of World War II Combat Aircraft.* New York: Barnes & Noble. 2001.

Baily, Ronald H. and the editors of Time-Life Books. *The Air War in Europe (WWII).* Chicago: Time-Life Books. 1981.

Baily, Rosemary (Project Editor). *France (Eyewitness Travel Guides).* New York: Dorling Kindersley. 1994.

Bishop, Cliff T. and Stanley D. Bishop. *Fortresses of the Big Triangle First.* East Anglia Books. 1986.

Breeden, Robert L. (Editor). *The Alps.* Washington, D.C.: National Geographic Society. 1973.

Caidin, Martin. *Flying Forts: The B-17 in World War II.* New York: Ballantine Books. 1968.

Castiglioni, Dr. Manlio (Chief Editor). *The International Atlas.* Chicago: Rand McNally & Company. 1969.

Cooksley, Peter G. *Flying Bomb: The Story of Hitler's V-Weapons in World War II.* New York: Scribner, 1979.

Craven, John V. *The 305th Bomb Group in Action: An Anthology.* Burleson, TX: 305th Bombardment Group (H) Memorial Association. 1990.

Daniel, Clifton (Editor in Chief). *Chronicle of the 20th Century.* Paris: Jacques Legrand International and Mount Kisco, NY: Chronicle. 1987.

Editors of Fodor Travel Publications. *Fodor's France 2002.* New York: Fodor's Travel. 2001.

Hess, William N. and Johnsen, Frederick A. / Marshall, Chester. *Great American Bombers of WWII.* Osceola, WI: MBI Publishing Company. 1998.

Jablonski, Edward. *Flying Fortress: The Illustrated Biography of the B-17s and the Men Who Flew Them.* Garden City, NY: Doubleday & Company. 1965.

Keegan, John. *The Second World War.* New York: Viking Penguin. 1990.

Matthews, Georgina (Managing Editor). *Italy (Eyewitness Travel Guides).* New York: Dorling Kindersley. 1996.

Miller, Russell (and the editors of Time-Life Books). *The Resistance.* Chicago: Time-Life Books. 1997.

Morrison, Wilbur H. *Fortress Without a Roof: The Allied Bombing of the Third Reich.* New York: St. Martin's Press. 1982.

Overy, Richard. *Why the Allies Won.* New York: W.W. Norton & Company. 1995.

Read, Anthony and Fisher, David. *The Fall of Berlin.* New York: W.W. Norton & Company. 1992.

Sharpe, Mike. *Aircraft of World War II: A Visual Encyclopedia.* Osceola, WI: MBI. 2000.

Speer, Albert. *Inside the Third Reich.* New York: The Macmillan Company. 1970.

U.S. Army Air Force. *TARGET: GERMANY The Army Air Forces' Official Story of the VIII Bomber Command's First Year Over Europe.* New York: Simon & Schuster. 1943.

ARTICLES

[Author unknown]. "Employee's Brother Asks for Flying Fortress." *Production for Victory* (Vol. II, No. 9): 1944.

[Author unknown]. "Mercy Mission." *Third Air Division Strikes*: 1945.

Bullock, Keith M. and Piok, Andreas. "Inauguration of War Memorial on the Penderalm Above St. Leonhard Near Brixen, Italy." Internet article: 1998.

Houghton, Jerry, Pvt. "Chute Fails, Airman Falls 4 Miles, Lives." *Stars and Stripes*: (date unknown).

Laxact, Robert. "The Enduring Pyrenees." *National Geographic*: 1974.

Pearson, Lyle, Sr. "Nazi Germany 1945." *Reveille*, Official Publication of Walter H. Strand Post No. 950, Veterans of Foreign Wars: Mankato, MN. 1995.

Pogorzelski, Frank. "War Me." (publication and date unknown).

Shepherd, Dik. "Saga of Torchy Tess." *Air Classics Magazine* (Vol. 34, No. 2): 1998.

Stursberg, Peter. "Holland Was Saved Just in Time." *Daily Herald*. 1945.

DOCUMENTS, LETTERS AND DIARIES

AHERN, GEORGE

Letter to George Ahern's father from Pilot/Aircraft Commander First Lieutenant Marvin R. Walker. 1944.

Official Combat Missions List for Staff Sergeant George Ahern. Lieutenant Maurice Joncas, Assistant Operations Officer, 509th Bombardment Squadron. 1944.

CUFFMAN, JOHN

Personal Combat Missions List and Missions Diary of Sergeant John Cuffman. 1943/1944.

FRECHETTE, ARTHUR

German Medical Records for POW "Artur" Frechette. 1945.

Letter to Mrs. Katherine E. Pearson confirming her husband, Lyle, as "missing in action." General C.F. Born, Acting Commander, Fifteenth Air Force. 1945.

Letter to the Quartermaster General from Arthur Frechette, regarding his dead crewmates. 1946.

Official Certificate/Combat Missions List for Arthur J. Frechette. First Lieutenant Lawrence D. Snyder, Operations Officer. (undated).

Official Crew List of Lieutenant Lyle C. Pearson's B-17 aircraft, shot down December 29, 1943. U.S. Army Air Forces. (undated).

Official Medical Records of First Lieutenant Arthur Frechette Jr., Army Service Forces, First Service Command. 1945.

Recommendation for the Distinguished Flying Cross Award to First Lieutenant Lyle C. Pearson. (undated).

SENIAWSKY/SCOTT, PETER

"Confidential" Document verifying the identity of Staff Sergeant Peter Seniawsky (after his escape from behind enemy lines). Special Agent, CIC. 1943.

Letter of Commendation for Peter Seniawsky. Colonel J.K. Lacey, U.S. Army Air Forces. 1943.

Letter to Mrs. Margie Bile informing her that Peter Seniawsky was "safe and interned in a neutral country." Major General J.A. Ulio, The Adjutant General, U.S. War Department. 1943.

Letter of Recommendation for Peter Seniawsky's promotion to Master Sergeant. Captain H. E. Frink Jr., U.S. Army Air Forces. (date unknown).

Official Missing Air Crew Report (date Oct. 15, 1943) for First Lieutenant Giles Kauffman Jr.'s B-17 aircraft. Captain C.H. Crowy Jr., Air Corps Adjutant, U.S. War Department. 1943.

Official Notice of Award of the Silver Star to Staff Sergeant Peter Seniawsky. Brigadier General C.C. Chauncey, Chief of Staff, on behalf of Lieutenant General Eaker. 1944.

Postal Telegraph Message reporting Peter Seniawsky "missing in action." Secretary of War. 1943.

TETA, ANTHONY

Official Movement Orders (overseas) for Lieutenant Jerome J. Chart and his B-17 crew. Headquarters, 273rd AAF Base Unit (SB), Lincoln Army Air Field, Lincoln, Nebraska. 1944.

United States Army Military Records and Report of Separation/ Certificate of Service—Anthony Teta. 1947.

VALLIERE, ROBERT

Letter to Walter E. Brown (Editor of the Magazine of the Eighth Air Force Historical Society) from Robert A. Valliere. 1999.

INTERNET SOURCES

Leo Durocher's Hall of Fame Biography. National Baseball Hall of Fame. Cooperstown, NY: 2003. www.baseballhalloffame.org.

385th Bomb Group History. Mighty Eighth Air Force Museum. Savannah, GA: 2003. www.mightyeighth.org.

• About the Author •

Travis L. Ayres is a former broadcast professional who spent fifteen years on the air in New York City, as well as during extended stays in New Orleans and Hartford, Connecticut. A U.S. Navy and Vietnam War veteran, he now lives and writes in the foothills of the Ozark Mountains in Northwest Arkansas.